What Is Democracy?

WHAT IS DEMOCRACY?

Alain Touraine

translated by
David Macey

Westview Press
A Member of Perseus Books, L.L.C.

A translation subsidy from the French Ministry of Culture and Communication is gratefully acknowl-
edged.

French edition, *Qu'est-ce que la démocratie?* © Librairie Arthème Fayard, 1994

Published in 1997 in the United States of America by Westview Press, 5500 Central Avenue, Boulder,
Colorado 80301-2877, and in the United Kingdom by Westview Press, 12 Hid's Copse Road, Cumnor
Hill, Oxford OX2 9JJ

Library of Congress Cataloging-in-Publication Data
Touraine, Alain.
    [Qu'est-ce que la démocratie? English]
    What is democracy? / Alain Touraine ; translated by David Macey.
        p.   cm.
    Includes bibliographical references and index.
    ISBN 01-8133-2706-7 (hard).—ISBN 0-8133-2707-5 (pbk.)
    1. Democracy.   I. Title.
JC421.T7313   1997
321.8—dc21   96-51212
                                                                                        CIP

10   9   8   7   6   5   4   3

Contents

Part 2
A History of the Modern Democratic Spirit

Part 3
Democratic Culture

Part 4
Democracy and Development

Preface and Acknowledgments

This book is an extension of the reflections with which I ended my previous work, *Critique of Modernity* (Touraine 1995). I felt the need to take up once more the themes of its final chapter, which deals with democracy, and to expand on them. Just as there is in contemporary thought a close connection between moral philosophy and political philosophy, I wanted to demonstrate that there is a necessary link between democratic culture and the idea of the subject.

In 1989, UNESCO Director General Federico Mayor Zaragoza asked me to take intellectual responsibility for an international colloquium on democracy to be held in Prague in 1991 under his chairmanship and that of President Vaclav Havel. The introductory and concluding reports that I presented in Prague provided the starting point for this book. I wish to thank Federico Mayor Zaragoza for the great interest he has taken in my work and for encouraging me to write this book.

François Dubet and Michel Wieviorka kindly agreed to read the text before publication, but I owe even more to the constant exchanges I have had with them for so many years. They know how important those exchanges have been to me. Simonetta Tabboni also helped in the preparation of this book. Jacqueline Blayac's remarkable organizational and communications skills made it possible to prepare this work. I owe her much more than she knows.

Alain Touraine

What Is Democracy?

Introduction

For several centuries we have associated democracy with human liberation, thanks to a combination of reason, economic growth, and popular sovereignty, from the prisons of ignorance, dependency, tradition, and divine right. We undertook to give society an economic, political, and cultural impetus by freeing it from all absolutes, religions, and state ideologies, so that it would be subject only to truth and to the criteria of knowledge. We placed our trust in the apparent links between technical efficiency, political freedom, cultural tolerance, and personal happiness.

But we also have long been beset by worries and fears: Although freed from its weaknesses, is not society now a slave to its own strength, its technologies, and above all its tools of political, economic, and military power? How could the workers who were subjected to Taylorist methods see the rationalization of industry as the triumph of reason, when they were being crushed by a social power in the guise of technology? How could bureaucracy be defined purely as a rational and legal authority, when public and private administrations were controlling and manipulating our personal lives and at the same time promoting their own interests rather than their managerial role? Popular revolutions throughout the world have degenerated into dictatorships over the proletariat or the nation, and the red flag more often flies over the tanks that crush popular uprisings than it does over workers in revolt.

Great revolutionary hopes have been transformed into totalitarian nightmares or state bureaucracies. Revolution and democracy have proved to be enemies, and one does not lead to the other. The world, exhausted by calls for mobilization, would readily settle for peace, tolerance, and well-being, with liberty reduced to meaning protection from authoritarianism and arbitrary rule.

On the European continent, where modern democracy was born, the greatest misfortune of the twentieth century has been not poverty but totalitarianism, and we have therefore fallen back on a modest conception of democracy as a set of guarantees that can prevent a leader from coming to power or holding power in defiance of the will of the majority. Our disappointments have been so profound and so prolonged that, for a long time to come, many of us will agree that the limitation of power is the primary definition of democracy. The appeal to human rights, which was first heard in the United States and France at the end of the eighteenth century and was thereafter silenced so quickly in all countries, is heard

1

once again in protests against all states that claim to represent a truth higher than the sovereignty of the people.

We must, however, define more clearly this necessary limitation of the state, as it can ultimately lead to the omnipotence of the masters of money and information. Limitations on political power can even lead to the decomposition of political society and political debate, which in turn leads to a direct and unmediated confrontation between an internationalized market and introverted identities. The nation-state that was created in Great Britain, the United States, and France was primarily a set of mediations between the unity of the law or science and a diversity of cultures. This nation-state today is being dissolved into the market or, at the opposite extreme, transformed into an intolerant and identitarian nationalism that results in the scandal of ethnic cleansing and condemns minorities to death, deportation, rape, or exile. Squeezed between a globalized economy and aggressively introverted cultures that proclaim an absolute multiculturalism implying a rejection of the other, the political space is fragmenting and democracy is being debased—reduced, at best, to a relatively open political marketplace, which no one troubles to defend because it is not the object of any intellectual or affective investment.

This book offers an answer to the question that arises when we reject both the excessively arrogant mobilizing state and the highly dangerous confrontation between markets and tribes: What positive content can we give to an idea of democracy that is not reducible to a set of guarantees against authoritarian power?

Such an inquiry impinges equally on political philosophy and on the most concrete of acts aimed at reconciling majority rule and respect for minorities, insuring the integration of immigrants and the participation of women in political decisionmaking, and bridging the divide between North and South.

The answer we seek must, first and foremost, protect us from a most immediate threat—the growing dissociation between the instrumentality of the market and the technological world on the one hand and the closed world of cultural identities on the other. How are we to combine the unity of the former with the fragmentation of the latter, the motion with the direction, the objective world with the subjective? How are we to recompose a world that is fragmenting socially, politically, geographically, and economically?

It is primarily at the level of the concrete social actor—whether group or individual—that this reconstruction must take place. Only at this level can we reconcile the instrumental reason that is indispensable in a world of technology and trade with the memory and creative imagination without which there can be no actors producing history but merely agents reproducing a self-contained order. I have defined the subject as the effort to integrate these two facets of social action.

The assertion of the subject does not, however, occur in a social void. It is grounded in the struggle against the logic of dominant apparatuses; it presupposes institutional conditions that are the very definition of democracy, and it results in the combination of cultural diversity with universal reference to the standards of law, science, and human rights.

We must learn to live together with our differences, to build an increasingly open world that is also as diverse as possible: Without unity, communication becomes impossible; without diversity, death prevails over life. We cannot sacrifice one for the sake of the other. Democracy should no longer be defined as the triumph of the universal over the particularized, but as a set of institutional guarantees that makes it possible to reconcile the unity of instrumental reason with the diversity of practical experience, and to bring together social exchange and political freedom. As Charles Taylor put it, democracy is based on a politics of mutual recognition (Taylor 1992).

Democracy must do battle on two fronts: On the one, it risks reappearing as an ideology in the service of the most powerful; on the other, its name is threatened with exploitation by an arbitrary and repressive regime. My goal in writing this book was to aid in reconstructing the political space and to promote the rebirth of democratic convictions by combating both these threats.

To the Reader

After reading Chapter 1 the reader may move directly to Part 3, which contains this book's central ideas, before going back to Part 1. Part 2 is a continuation of Part 1, but adopts a historical rather than an analytic approach. Part 4 outlines an answer to the difficult question of the relationship between democracy and development.

PART 1

The Three Dimensions of Democracy

A New Idea

Democracy is a new idea. Now that authoritarian regimes have collapsed in the East and the South and the United States has won the cold war against the Soviet Union—which, after having lost its empire, its all-powerful party, and its technological pride, has finally ceased to exist—many people believe that democracy has won. Many now believe that democracy is of necessity the normal form of political organization, the political face of modernity, whose economic form is the market economy and whose cultural expression is secularization. Reassuring as this belief may be for those living in the West, it is so flimsy that we should find it worrisome. An open and competitive political market is no more identifiable with democracy than a market economy is in itself constitutive of an industrial society. In both cases, we can say that an open system—whether political or economic—is a necessary but not a sufficient precondition for democracy or economic development. There is indeed no democracy unless the ruled are free to choose their rulers, or without political pluralism, but we cannot speak of democracy if the voters' only choice is between two fractions of the oligarchy, the army, or the state apparatus. In the same way, the market economy ensures that the economy is independent of state, church, or caste; but if we are to be able to speak of an industrial society or self-sustaining growth, there must also be a legal system, a public administration, an inviolate territory, entrepreneurs, and agents who redistribute the national product.

There are now many indications that the regimes we describe as democratic are, like authoritarian regimes, being weakened, and that they are dominated by the demands of a world market that is protected and regulated mainly by the United States and by agreements between three main centers of economic power. This world market tolerates the participation of countries with strong authoritarian governments, countries with decaying authoritarian regimes, or even oligarchic regimes. It also tolerates the participation of what might be called democratic regimes, or, in other words, regimes in which the ruled are free to choose the rulers who represent them.

As states, democratic or otherwise, decline in importance, involvement in politics also declines, and we have what has rightly been called a crisis of political representation. Voters no longer feel that they are represented. They voice that feeling by denouncing a political class that appears to be interested only in its own power or in the accumulation of personal wealth by its members. The awareness of citizenship fades, either because many individuals feel that they are consumers rather than citizens, and cosmopolitans rather than nationals, or because a certain number of individuals feel that they have been marginalized by or excluded from society for economic, political, ethnic, or cultural reasons.

Once democracy has been weakened in this way, it can be destroyed either from above, by an authoritarian power, or from below, by chaos, violence, and civil war. Alternatively, it may be destroyed from within as power comes under the control of oligarchies or parties that accumulate economic or political resources so as to impose their choices on citizens, who have been reduced to the role of voters. The twentieth century has been so strongly marked by authoritarian regimes that their destruction seemed to many to be adequate proof of the triumph of democracy. Yet if we content ourselves with purely indirect or negative definitions of democracy, we restrict the analysis to an unacceptable extent. Giovanni Sartori was right in both his first (Sartori 1957) and his most recent book (Sartori 1993) to reject absolutely the distinction some have made between two forms of democracy, described respectively as political and social, formal and real, or bourgeois and socialist, depending on which vocabulary these ideologues preferred. Sartori correctly reminded us that there is only one form of democracy—firstly, because we could not use the same word to designate two different realities if they did not have a great deal in common, and secondly, because a discourse that culminates in the claim that an authoritarian or even totalitarian regime is democratic cancels itself.

Have we no choice but to follow the pendulum as it swings back to constitutional liberties after having attempted, throughout the long century that began in 1848 in France, to extend political liberty to economic and social life? Adopting that stance does not help us to answer the question of how to reconcile or combine government by law with the representation of interests. It merely underlines the incompatibility of the two goals and, therefore, the impossibility of constructing or even defining democracy. We thus come back to our starting point.

We therefore have to agree with Norberto Bobbio, who defined democracy in terms of three institutional principles. According to Bobbio, democracy is primarily "a set of rules (primary or basic) which establish *who* is authorized to take collective decisions and which *procedures* are to be used" (Bobbio 1988: 24). To this one might add that the greater the number of people who participate either directly or indirectly in decisionmaking, the more democratic the regime; and, finally, that the choices to be made must be real choices. One might also agree with Bobbio that democracy is based on the replacement of an organic conception of society by an individualistic vision, the main elements of which are the idea of a contract, the replacement of Aristotle's political animal by *homo œconomicus,* and by utilitarianism and its pursuit of the greatest happiness for the greatest number.

But having established these "liberal" principles, Bobbio showed us that political reality is very different from the model he outlined. Large organizations such as parties and labor unions exert an increasing influence on political life. The supposed sovereignty of the people therefore often has no basis in reality. Individual interests do not disappear in the face of the general will, and oligarchies perpetuate themselves. Finally, the democratic process has not penetrated most domains of social life, and secrecy, which is antithetical to democracy, continues to play an important role; thus behind democratic structures, a government by technocrats and apparatuses frequently forms. In addition to these worries, there is a more basic cause for concern: If democracy is no more than a set of rules and procedures, why should citizens actively defend it? A few parliamentarians may be willing to die for an electoral law, but no one else is.

In sum, we must go beyond procedural rules, although these are indispensable if democracy is to exist. We must investigate how the will that represents the majority's interests is formed, expressed, and applied at the same time as is the awareness that all are citizens, responsible for the social order. Procedural rules are nothing more than a means toward ends that, while never achieved, nonetheless lend their meaning to political activities—preventing arbitrary rule and secrecy, responding to the demands of the majority, and ensuring the participation of as many as possible in public life. Now that authoritarian regimes are in retreat and "people's democracies," which were merely one-party dictatorships over peoples, are a thing of the past, we can no longer content ourselves with constitutional and juridical guarantees, abandoning economic and social life to the domination of increasingly remote oligarchies.

Distrusting participatory democracy, disquieted by all forms of the central powers' ascendancy over individuals and public opinion, and hostile to appeals to the people, the nation, or history—which invariably attribute to the state a legitimacy that it no longer obtains from free elections—I embarked on this study of the social and cultural content of democracy today.

As the nineteenth century came to an end, limited democracies were outflanked in the West by industrial democracies and newly emergent social-democratic governments supported by labor unions, and in the East by Leninist-inspired revolutionary parties and others who prioritized the overthrow of the old regime rather than the establishment of democracy. That era of debates about "social" democracy is over, and in the absence of any new content, democracy is degenerating into the freedom to consume, into a political supermarket. Public opinion was satisfied with that impoverished definition at the time when the Soviet regime and empire were collapsing, but we cannot in the long term surrender to the facile attractions of a purely negative definition of democracy. In "liberal" countries and around the globe, this impoverishment of the democratic idea can only result in the extraparliamentary, or even extrapolitical, expression of social demands, protests, and hopes—here, in the privatization of social problems, and there, in a "fundamentalist" mobilization. Is it not obvious that democratic institutions are becoming quite ineffective, being seen as either a more or less rigged game or an agency for the penetration of foreign interests?

Faced with this loss of meaning, one can only turn to a conception of democratic action as the liberation of individuals and groups who are dominated by the logic of a power, or, in other words, subject to control by the masters and managers of systems, who view them as mere resources.

In the struggle against absolute monarchies, some called on the people to seize power; but that revolutionary call led either to new oligarchies or to populist dictatorships. In a period dominated by every form of political, cultural, and economic mass mobilization, we must move in the opposite direction. That is why we are witnessing the return of the idea of human rights. That idea is stronger than ever because it has been sustained by resistance fighters, dissidents, and critical thinkers who fought totalitarian powers in the darkest hours of our century. From the workers and intellectuals of Gdansk to those of Tiananmen Square, from U.S. civil rights activists to the European students of May 1968, from those who fought South African apartheid to those who are still fighting dictatorship in Burma, from Chile's Vicaría de la Solidaridad to the Serbian opposition, from Salman Rushdie to embattled Algerian intellectuals, the democratic spirit has been brought to life by all who have opposed increasingly absolute powers in the name of their right to live in freedom.

Democracy would be a poor word indeed if it were not defined by the battlefields where so many men and women have fought for it. And if we do need a strong definition of democracy, it is partly because we must wield it against those who, in the name of old democratic struggles, have become or are becoming the servants of absolutism and intolerance. We no longer want participatory democracy, and we cannot be content with deliberative democracy; we need a liberating democracy.

We must of course begin by making a distinction between individual conceptions of "the good society" and the definition of a democratic system. We can no longer conceive of a democracy that is not pluralist and, in the broadest sense of the term, secular. When a society sees its institutions as the incarnation of a conception of "the good," it is liable to impose its beliefs and values on a highly diversified population. Just as public schools make a distinction between the educational realm and the family or personal realm, so a government cannot force everyone to accept the same conception of good and evil. It must ensure that all may assert their demands and opinions, freely and without risk, so that the decisions made by legislators might reflect as broadly and accurately as possible the people's opinions and interests. The idea of a state religion is particularly incompatible with democracy, if it signifies the imposition of moral and intellectual dogmas. Freedom of opinion and freedom of assembly and organization are essential to democracy in part because they imply that the state may make no judgment about moral or religious beliefs.

This procedural conception of liberty alone, however, cannot serve as a basis for organizing social life. The law takes us further in what it permits or forbids, which imposes a conception of life, property, and education. Yet, a social right is hardly reducible to a legal code.

How, then, are we to respond to two apparently contradictory demands—on the one hand, for the greatest possible respect of personal liberties (that is, negative liberty), and on the other, for a social system that is regarded as fair by the majority (in other words, positive liberty)? That question will run through this book to its very end; but as a sociologist I cannot wait that long to offer a sociological answer, one that explains the behavior of social actors in terms of their social relations: The link between negative and positive liberty is the democratic will to enable those who are subordinate and dependent to act freely and to discuss rights and guarantees on equal terms with those who possess economic, political, and cultural resources. That is why the introduction of collective bargaining and, more generally, industrial democracy, was one of democracy's great victories: The action of the labor unions allowed wage-earners to negotiate with their employers in the least unequal situation possible. Similarly, freedom of the press not only protects an individual liberty; it gives the weakest the opportunity to make themselves heard even though the powerful are moving behind the scenes to defend their interests, secretly mobilizing networks based on kinship, friendship, and mutual benefit. Procedural democracy lacks passion, and participatory democracy lacks wisdom. The alternative is democratic action aimed at freeing individuals and groups from the constraints that weigh on them.

The founding fathers of the republic wanted to create a citizen-man, and they admired above all else individuals who sacrificed themselves to the higher interest of the city-state. Republican virtues today arouse our suspicion rather than our admiration. We no longer appeal to the state to rescue us from tradition and privilege: We who live at the close of a century dominated even more by totalitarianisms and their instruments of repression than by the growth of production and consumption in some parts of the world are afraid of the state and of all forms of power. The appeal to the masses and even to the people has so often been the language of despots that it cannot but inspire horror in us. We no longer accept even the impersonal disciplines that have been imposed on us in the name of technology, efficiency, and security. Perhaps we now understand that democracy is vigorous only when it is sustained by a desire for liberation that constantly looks to new frontiers both distant and close at hand, running counter to all forms of authority and repression that affect our most personal experiences.

In this way, the democratic spirit can respond to what seemed at first two contradictory exigencies—limiting power and meeting the demands of the majority. But under what conditions and to what extent can it do so? This book has been written to answer these questions.

The Liberty of the Subject

All these themes converge in the central theme of the liberty of the subject. I use the term "subject" to describe the construction of the individual (or group) as actor through his efforts to transform events and experiences into a life-project. The subject is an attempt to transform a lived situation into free action; it introduces liberty into what initially seem to be social determinants and a cultural heritage.

Is this liberating action exercised in disengagement or in withdrawal into self-consciousness or by existential meditation? On the contrary, in modern society the assertion of liberty is characteristically expressed by active resistance to social power's increasing hold over the personality and over culture. Industrial power imposed normalization, the so-called scientific organization of labor, requiring that workers submit to a regular schedule and tempo. Subsequently, the consumer society demanded that they consume as many signs of participation as possible. The mobilizing political power likewise exacted displays of belonging and loyalty. The subject resists all such powers, which, as Tocqueville was already aware, place even greater constraints on minds than on bodies, imposing a self-image and worldview rather than respect for law and order. The subject asserts itself through both its particularity and its desire for liberty, or in other words, by its self-creation as an actor capable of transforming its environment.

Democracy is not simply a set of institutional guarantees or a negative liberty. Democracy is the battle waged by subjects, in the context of their culture and their liberty, against the domineering logic of systems. Democracy is, to use the expression coined by Robert Fraisse, the politics of the subject. At the beginning of the modern era, when most human beings were confined to restricted collectivities and crushed by the weight of systems of reproduction rather than the ascendant forces of production, the subject asserted itself by identifying itself with reason and labor. However, in societies that have been invaded by technologies of mass production, consumption, and communication, a great change occurs: Liberty is so alienated from instrumental reason that it may completely reject it in order to defend or recreate a space that accommodates both memory and invention, thus facilitating the emergence of a subject that is, at one and the same time, existence and metamorphosis, tradition and progress, body and mind. Democracy's great task is to produce and defend diversity within a mass culture.

French political culture has taken the republican idea to extremes, identifying personal liberty with legal principles, human beings with citizens, and the nation with the social contract. It has succeeded in seeing itself as the agent of universal values and has almost completely erased its particularities, its very memory, in legislating a society based on principles of rational thought and action. One can best understand how the democratic idea, thus defined, has been transformed by examining the difference between French-style republican culture and democratic culture. Republican culture seeks unity, whereas democratic culture protects diversity. Republican culture identifies liberty with citizenship; democratic culture contrasts human rights with the duties of the citizen or the demands of the consumer. For democrats, as Claude Lefort put it, people's power does not mean that the people sit on the prince's throne; it means that there is no longer a throne (Lefort 1986). People's power means the ability of the greatest number to live freely or, in other words, to construct their individual lives by relating what they are to what they want to be, and by resisting power, in the name of liberty and of loyalty to a cultural heritage. The democratic regime is the form of political life that gives the greatest liberty to the greatest number, that protects and recognizes the greatest possible diversity.

As I write, the most violent attack on democracy is that being waged by the Serbian army and regime in the name of ethnic purity and the cultural homogenization of the nation. Bosnia, where people with different national or religious allegiances have been living together for centuries, is being dismembered. Hundreds of thousands of individuals have been driven out of their territory by force of arms and by rape, looting, and famine, so that ethnically homogeneous states can be constructed. Because democracy in any given period is best defined by the attacks that are being made on it, in Europe today, democrats can be recognized by their opposition to ethnic cleansing. The adoption of such a policy by Serbia required an antidemocratic dictatorship; the fact that Milošević and even more extreme nationalists speak for the vast majority of Serbs is of little relevance in defining the nature of this regime. What has happened in Bosnia proves that a democracy is not defined by participation or consensus but by respect for liberties and diversity. For the same reason, we greeted the end of apartheid in South Africa as a victory for democracy. Direct elections and universal suffrage could have allowed the black majority to eliminate the white minority; but, on the contrary, the de Klerk–Mandela agreements and the recognition of the diversity of a country that is inhabited by black Africans, Afrikaners, people of British descent, Indians, and others mark a great step toward a real democratization.

Our European nation-states, which were for the most part monarchies, became democracies because in most cases they recognized—willingly or under duress—social and cultural diversity, rejecting the religious territorialism (*cujus regio, ejus religio*) that was so widespread in the sixteenth and seventeenth centuries. States in which the central power was penetrating ever deeper into the daily lives of both individuals and collectivities learned to reconcile centralization with the recognition of diversities. The United States, and especially Canada, built societies that recognized a pluralism of cultures and reconciled it with respect for the law, the independence of the state, and reliance on science and technology. Democracy cannot exist without a recognition of the diversity of beliefs, origins, opinions, and values.

The defining characteristic of democracy is therefore not simply a set of institutional guarantees or majority rule but above all a respect for individual or collective projects that can reconcile the assertion of personal liberty with the right to identify with a particular social, national, or religious collectivity. Democracy is not based solely on laws but above all on a political culture. *Democratic culture* has often been defined in terms of equality. That definition is adequate, if we adopt Tocqueville's interpretation of the notion, for democracy presupposes the destruction of a hierarchical system and a holistic vision of society. To adopt Louis Dumont's terminology, *homo æqualis* takes the place of *homo hierarchicus* (Dumont 1977). But once that victory has been won, individualism can lead to a mass society or even to authoritarian totalitarianism, as Edmund Burke was already pointing out at the time of the French Revolution (Burke 1955 [original ed. 1790]). If it is to be democratic, equality must mean that everyone has the right to choose and govern their own existence. It must mean the right to individuation in the face of all moralizing and normalizing pressures. In that sense the defenders of negative liberty are correct and the defenders of positive liberty err. One may find the former's position unsatisfactory, but the principle is correct because, attractive as it may be, the principle of positive liberty is so fraught with danger.

This conclusion shows the limitations of the distinction I made earlier between the liberty of the ancients and that of the moderns. We must abandon the most heroic images of the democratic tradition, namely the images of popular revolutions that mobilize nations against enemies without and within. Revolutions, often intended to save democracy from its enemies, have instead given birth to antirevolutionary regimes due to their concentration of power, evocation of national unity and unanimity, and denunciation of adversaries, who are deemed traitors with whom it is impossible to coexist, rather than spokesmen for different ideas or interests.

Liberty, Memory, and Reason

Threatened by a form of popular rule that uses rationalism to forcibly destroy all social and cultural loyalties and obliterate all checks on its own power, and reduced to a political marketplace, democracy is also under attack on a third front by a culturalism that takes respect for minorities to such lengths as to eradicate the very idea of a majority and to drastically reduce the purview of the law. The danger here is that culturalism, in the name of respect for differences, will encourage the formation of localized powers that will impose an antidemocratic authority within particular communities. Should that happen, political society will be no more than a marketplace where communities locked into an obsession with their identities and internal homogeneity enter into loosely regulated transactions.

The only defense against such closed communities, which pose a direct threat to democracy, is rational action—or in other words, an appeal to scientific reason, a recourse to critical judgment, and an acceptance of the universal rules that protect the liberty of individuals. This takes us back to the oldest democratic tradition of all: the simultaneous appeal to knowledge and liberty as a defense against all powers. That appeal is all the more necessary in that authoritarian states tend increasingly to lay claim to a narrowly communitarian legitimacy rather than the more "progressivist" legitimacy of the communist regimes and their allies.

These three struggles define the political culture on which democracy is based. This culture is not reducible to the power of reason, the freedom of interest groups, or communitarian nationalism. Democracy reconciles elements that tend constantly to diverge and that, when they do become isolated from one another, degenerate into principles of authoritarian government. The liberated nation degenerates into a closed and aggressive community. The very logic that attacked inherited inequalities degenerates into "scientific socialism," and the individualism that was once associated with liberty may reduce the citizen to little more than a political consumer.

Given that modernity is based on the difficult management of the relationship between reason and subject, rationalization and subjectivization, and that the subject itself is an attempt to combine instrumental reason with a personal and collective identity, democracy is best defined as a will to reconcile rational thought, personal liberty, and cultural identity.

An individual is a subject to the extent that his or her behavior combines a desire for *liberty*, membership in a *culture*, and reliance on *reason,* or in other words, a principle of individuality, a principle of particularism, and a principle of universality. In the same way and for the same reasons, a democratic society combines the liberty of individuals and respect for differences with the rational organization of collective life by means of the techniques and laws of private and public administration. Individualism is not a sufficient principle for the construction of a democracy. Individuals who are guided by self-interest, the satisfaction of needs, or even the rejection of central behavioral models do not always promote a democratic culture—even if it is easier for such individuals to prosper in a democratic society than in any other—because democracy is not reducible to an open political market. Those who are guided by their own interests do not always defend the democratic society in which they live; they often prefer to save their lives by running away or simply by adopting the most effective strategies with no regard for the defense of principles and institutions. Democratic culture cannot come into being unless society is seen as an institutional construct whose primary goal is to reconcile the liberty of individuals and collectivities with the unity of economic activity and legal standards.

No debate divides the contemporary world more profoundly than that between the supporters of multiculturalism and the defenders of an integrating universalism, or what is often called the republican or Jacobin conception. Democratic culture cannot, however, be identified with either. It rejects with equal force both the obsession with identity that confines everyone within a community, reduces social life to a space of tolerance, and thus paves the way to segregation, sectarianism, and holy wars; and the Jacobin spirit, which, in the name of its universalism, condemns and rejects the diversity of private beliefs, loyalties, and memories.

Democratic culture can be defined as an attempt to reconcile unity and diversity, liberty and integration. That is why democratic culture has, from the opening pages of this book, been defined as a combination of common institutional rules and diverse interests and cultures. We must abandon the rhetorical dichotomy between the power of the majority and the rights of minorities. Democracy is the regime in which the majority recognizes the rights of minorities because it recognizes that today's majority may be tomorrow's minority and may have to obey laws that, while they might not represent its interests, will not prevent it from exercising its basic rights. The democratic spirit is based on this awareness of the interdependence of unity and diversity and sustained by never-ending disputes over the ever-shifting border between the two and about the best ways to strengthen their association.

Democracy does not reduce human beings to the status of mere citizens. It recognizes them as free individuals who also belong to economic or cultural collectivities.

Development and Democracy

This defense of pluralism takes different forms in countries enjoying endogenous development and in those that are not. It is easier to make individuals, groups, or minorities autonomous from the constraints of the economic and administrative system in the most developed countries. In dependent societies where modernization is inevitably the result of outside intervention by the nation-state or another agency rather than the work of social actors, the rights that are being demanded are more often those of the community than of the individual and more likely to be used to resist a policy of enforced modernization than to defend individual freedoms. Does it, then, go without saying that this tension always has antidemocratic effects and there is no room for democracy in a society that is torn between authoritarian state intervention and communitarian defenses or in which there is always the possibility that the state will speak the language of community and thus become authoritarian? A positive answer would imply the harsh conclusion that democracy can exist only in the richest countries, those that dominate the planet and world markets. Such an assertion, which has often been made in both scholarly and popular forms, openly contradicts the analysis I have just put forward. I have defended the idea that democracy is an attempt to reconcile private liberty and social integration or, in the case of modern societies, subject and reason. To regard democracy as an attribute of economic modernization and therefore as a stage in the progress of history toward instrumental reason, is a very different matter. According to the first view, democracy is a choice, and in every situation the opposite, antidemocratic choice is always possible and often adopted. In the second view, democracy emerges naturally at a certain stage of development, and the market economy, political democracy, and secularization are three aspects of a general process of modernization. The objection to this theory of modernization must be that democracy is as threatened in developed countries as in other countries, either by totalitarian dictatorships or by a laissez-faire attitude that leads to greater inequalities and concentrates power in the hands of restricted groups. More important still, the presence of democratizing action—and the forces opposing it—can be detected in societies undergoing modernization of both exogenous and endogenous origin.

The appeal to community destroys democracy whenever it strengthens political power in the name of a culture, whenever it destroys the autonomy of the political system and imposes a direct relationship between a power and a culture, and particularly between a state and a religion. In many countries in the Third World, the only real choice appears to be that between a nationalist dictatorship and a communitarian dictatorship. In such cases, democratic thought must fight against both authoritarian solutions. It must defend the victims of both fundamentalism and militarism—and especially intellectuals—and it must aid the social forces that are resisting both.

Defending a community against an authoritarian power can, however, be a catalyst of democratization if the community collaborates in the task of modernization rather than regarding it as a threat. This is possible even in endogenously modernizing countries where there have been, or are, calls for rationalization that would eliminate or repress cultural orientations and impose the utilitarian vision denounced by Nietzsche. The only difference is that in the first case, the community is liable to reject rationalization and, in the second, rationalization is liable to destroy the actor's freedom.

Describing authoritarian regimes as democratic because they have appropriated the heritage of national liberation movements is clearly unacceptable. It is as unacceptable as calling Stalin a democrat because he was once a revolutionary or as describing Hitler as a democrat because he won an election. There are, however, no grounds for saying that poverty, dependency or internal struggles make democracy impossible in less developed countries. Democracy, defined as the creation of a political system that respects basic liberties, is under threat in all countries, no matter how wealthy, although the threat to democracy obviously takes very different forms in different parts of the world. Still, it is in the heart of Europe that we are witnessing the triumph of violently antidemocratic regimes, which are committing enormous crimes against the most basic human rights; and although the former Yugoslavia is not as rich as the Netherlands or Canada, it is much wealthier than Algeria or Guatemala.

Modernized countries do not automatically evolve toward democracy any more than countries undergoing exogenous development are destined to become authoritarian, as is perfectly evident from history. In modernized countries, however, positive democratic action does tend to limit the state's power over individuals, whereas in dependent societies the collective appropriation of the instruments of modernization begins with the defensive assertion of a community. In one case, individual liberties produce democracy but may also make it the prisoner of private interests; in the other, the defense of the community leads to democracy but may also destroy it in the name of national, ethnic, or religious homogeneity. These two aspects of historical reality correspond to the two faces of the subject. The subject entails both personal liberty and membership in a society or culture, both project and memory, disengagement and commitment.

In endogenously developing countries, the democratic spirit can take on the positive tasks of organizing social life. In other countries, in contrast, its action is primarily negative and critical: It calls for liberation and independence, the destruction of oligarchic power, the independence of the judiciary, or the organization of free elections. In these countries, the transition from liberation to the organization of liberties is difficult and often interrupted. In a dependent society, liberation implies a militaristic mobilization, and there is therefore a strong possibility that the liberation struggle will result in authoritarianism. We have just lived through a long half-century that was to a very large extent dominated by authoritarian regimes born of national or social liberation movements. We are no longer tempted to call these regimes "democratic," but neither should we forget the hopes of liberation that they exploited in order to seize power. Because Algeria's Front de Libération Nationale has been transformed into a military dictatorship, should we no longer recognize that it inspired a national liberation movement? Because communist dictatorships masqueraded as the vanguard of the proletariat, does that mean the labor movement was not inspired by democratic demands? The developing world can hardly avoid making the leap from demolishing enemies and external obstacles to creating democratic institutions and mores, and the totalitarian monster stalks the space that lies between liberation and liberties. The only effective weapon against it are social actors who can act rationally at the economic level and manage their power relations. Only strong, autonomous social movements, involving both rulers and ruled, can resist the ascendancy of an authoritarian state that is both modernizing and nationalistic, for they represent a civil society that can negotiate with the state and thus give political society true autonomy.

If we recognize the artificiality of the distinction between North and South, then we can no longer characterize developed countries as democracy's homelands and underdeveloped countries as destined to have authoritarian regimes. We no longer live on a planet that is divided in half but in a dualistic global society. The North is penetrating the South, just as the South is present in the North. There are North American, English, and French enclaves in the South, just as there are Latin American, African, Arab, and Asian enclaves in the cities and industrial centers of the North. *One world* is not merely a call for solidarity; it is above all a statement of fact. Democracy therefore cannot exist anywhere in the world if it can only exist in certain countries or a certain type of country. The historical reality is that although the dominant countries developed liberal democracy, they also imposed colonialism or imperialism on many less-dominant polities, and they despoiled the environment on a planetary scale. At the same time, national and social liberation movements emerged in the dominated countries, calling for democracy. Neocommunitarian powers also emerged to mobilize ethnic, national, or religious identities in defense of dictatorships or modernizing despotisms.

The *subject* is both freedom and tradition, and democracy is the political precondition for its existence. In dependent societies, the subject is in danger of being crushed by tradition; in modernized societies, it is in danger of being dissolved into a liberty whose meaning has been reduced to the freedom to consume in the political marketplace. Reason and technological modernization, which lead to the functional differentiation of political, economic, religious, and familial subsystems, are essential weapons in the struggle against the ascendancy of community. However, it is impossible to resist the seduction of the marketplace without support from social and cultural roots. In both cases, the central axis of democracy is the idea of the sovereignty of the people and the assertion that the political order is the product of human action.

Democracy is threatened on all sides, but it has made inroads in many parts of the world since its emergence in seventeenth-century England and eighteenth-century France and America—particularly in today's Latin American national-popular regimes and in the postcommunist countries. The democratic spirit is everywhere at work—and everywhere at risk.

The Limits of the Political

For a long time, modern philosophy regarded the interests of society as the principle of the Good: What was useful to society was good, and what was harmful to society was bad. As a result, human rights were confused with the duties of citizens. This rationalist, progressive faith in the correspondence between personal interests and the collective interest is no longer acceptable today. To their credit, the defenders of negative liberty have replaced that dangerous faith with a cautious mistrust and the demand for participation with a quest for guarantees, rather than means, of participation. This defensive policy is, however, incomplete without the more positive principle that defines democracy as the recognition of the right of individuals and collectivities to be the actors of their own history and not simply to be set free from their chains.

Democracy serves neither society nor individuals. Democracy serves human beings insofar as they are subjects, or in other words, their own creators and the creators of their individual and collective lives. The theory of democracy is nothing but the theory of the political conditions of existence of a subject, which must never be confounded with the ego, as the ego is illusory. Social organization penetrates the ego so completely that the quest for self-consciousness or a purely personal experience of liberty is only an illusion. Such illusions are most common in individuals who rank so high or so low on the social scale that they believe they have not been placed there but belong to a purely individual and nonsocial world or, at the opposite extreme, to a world defined by a permanent and general human condition.

Political sociology can do no more than circulate restlessly between these inseparable assertions: Democracy is based on the recognition by social institutions of individual and collective liberty; there can be no individual or collective liberty unless the ruled are free to choose their rulers and the greatest possible number are able to participate in the creation and transformation of social institutions.

All those who believed that true liberty lay only in the individual's identification with a people, a power, or a god, or that individual and society both became free only by submitting to reason, paved the way for authoritarian regimes. Democratic philosophy survives today only insofar as it rejects such one-sided answers. If human beings are nothing more than citizens and if citizens are the agents of a universal principle, there is no room left for liberty, and it is destroyed in the name of reason or history. It is because they have resisted these dangerous illusions that the defenders of negative liberty and the open society—that is, liberals—have done more to defend democracy than those who sought the fusion of individual and society in a "people's democracy":—a term that one can no longer bring oneself to utter.

Human Rights, Representation, and Citizenship

A distinction must be made between two aspects of political modernity. On the one hand, we have the concept of a juridical foundation limiting the arbitrary power of the state and, moreover, helping the state to constitute itself and to establish a framework for social life by proclaiming the unity and coherence of the legal system. There is no necessary connection between this rational-legal authority and democracy; it may be an obstacle to democracy, or it may encourage it. On the other hand, we have the idea of the sovereignty of the people, which makes a much more direct contribution to the advent of democracy. There is an almost inevitable transition from the general will to the will of the majority, and unanimity is quickly replaced by debate, conflict, and the emergence of a majority and a minority. The existence of the legal state (Rachtsstaat) therefore leads to all kinds of separation between the political or juridical realm and social life, whereas the idea of the sovereignty of the people tends to make political life subordinate to relations between social actors. The idea of the sovereignty of the people leads to democracy, provided that it does not become triumphant and remains a principle of opposition to the established power, whatever that power's nature.

The sovereignty of the people paves the way to democracy if, instead of giving popular power an unlimited legitimacy, it introduces it into political life on ethical principle. If they are to defend their interests and sustain their hopes, those who do not exercise power in social life need such a principle. Without this social and moral pressure, democracy is quickly transformed into oligarchy as political power becomes associated with every other form of social domination. Democracy is not born of the legal state but of the appeal that is made to ethical principles—liberty and justice—in the name of a powerless majority and against dominant interests. Ruling groups try to conceal social relations behind instrumental categories, as Marx explained in his account of interests and commodities. They isolate purely economic categories and refer to rational choices. Dominated groups, in contrast, replace the economic definition of their situation, which implies their subordination, with an ethical definition. They speak in the name of justice, liberty, equality, or solidarity. Political life is based on the contrast between political and juridical decisions that favor dominant groups and the appeal to a social ethics that defends the interest of the dominated or of minorities. That appeal is heeded because it also promotes social integration. Democracy is therefore never reducible to procedures or even institutions; it is a social and political force that strives to transform the legal state in such a way that it corresponds to the interests of the dominated. In contrast, juridical and political formalism uses the legal state in a different, oligarchic way, to reject social demands that threaten the power of ruling groups. The difference, even today, between an authoritarian and a democratic way of thinking is that the former stresses the formality of juridical rules, whereas the latter attempts to go beyond the formality of the law and the language of power to reveal social choices and social conflicts.

The Principle of Recourse

At a deeper level still, political equality, without which democracy cannot exist, not only accords all citizens the same rights, but also compensates for social inequalities among citizens in the name of moral rights. The democratic state must therefore grant its most disadvantaged citizens the right to act, within the framework of the law, against an unequal order, the state itself being part of that order. The state places limitations on its own power because it recognizes that the function of the political realm is to correct social inequalities. Ronald Dworkin, who is one of the best representatives of the contemporary liberal school, expressed this well: "Political equality . . . supposes that the weaker members of a political community are entitled to the same concern and respect of their government as the more powerful members have secured for themselves, so that if some men have freedom of decision whatever the effect on the general good, then all men must have the same freedom" (Dworkin 1977: 199).

Arguing against the theses of utilitarianism and legal positivism, Dworkin contrasts basic rights with legally defined rights because the former, which are defined by constitutions, conjoin legal rights with moral principles. This means that although basic rights are recognized by the state itself, they can still be used against the state. Theorists of democracy from Locke to Rousseau and Tocqueville were aware that democracy is not content to invoke an abstract equality of right but that it also appeals to that equality in order to combat actual inequalities—notably in the access to the decision-making process. If democratic principles did not serve as a recourse against inequalities, they would be hypocritical and ineffective. And if the law is to play the role that Dworkin has suggested, "the weakest members" must make active use of that recourse. The majority must also recognize the rights of minorities and, above all, must not force a minority to defend its interests or to express its point of view solely by using methods appropriate to the majority or the most powerful groups.

The idea of democracy cannot be divorced from the idea of rights, and it is therefore irreducible to the theme of majority government. This conception, which Dworkin expresses so forcefully and which is an extension of the theme of resistance to oppression, differs from the conception that, like Rawls's in *A Theory of Justice* (Rawls 1971), defines the principle of justice by referring to an idea of the common good. As Rawls understood it, the common good is the provision of compensating benefits for the least advantaged members of society. This idea also can be expressed in utilitarian terms as the pursuit of the greatest possible advantage for the whole of the community. The idea of basic or moral rights, in contrast, is not based on the enlightened interest of society but on a principle that is external to the organization of collective life. Democracy, therefore, cannot be reduced to public institutions, to a definition of powers, or even to the principle of the election of leaders at regular intervals; democracy is inseparable from a theory and practice of rights.

Ancients and Moderns

The legal state and democratic recourse, or even the republic of citizens and the protection of personal rights, are as different as the liberty of the ancients and the liberty of the moderns, as defined by Benjamin Constant (Constant 1980 [original ed. 1819]). Appeals to the general will, the civic or republican spirit, and popular power, from Jean-Jacques Rousseau to the revolutions of the twentieth century, are but distant echoes of the liberty of the ancients.

Before we compare these very different conceptions, however, we must recognize that they do have something in common: Whether we appeal to the civic spirit or to basic rights, we are saying that the good regime is not defined in terms of distributive justice. When we demand that all be paid in accordance with their labor, talent, utility, or needs, we introduce the economic image of a desirable correspondence between contribution and reward; but although this equilibrium can explain the satisfaction or the demands of actors, it cannot define any political regime, particularly democracy. Democracy must be defined in terms of a conception of equality that has nothing to do with distributive justice. Aristotle was a most forceful opponent of the reduction of politics to the satisfaction of interests and demands, and the defenders of natural law were just as hostile to the economic conception of politics. For all of them, the key to understanding the nature of politics lay in studying power and the organization of collective life.

Although they agree as to the specific nature of the political, ancients and moderns, Aristotelians and liberals disagree completely in other respects. Aristotle specifically argued that the nature of the sovereign could not define a regime. He contrasted three regimes: monarchy, where power is held by one; aristocracy, where it is held by the few; and what we spontaneously call democracy, described by Aristotle's contemporaries as *isonomia*, where power is held by many. All of these regimes were designed to defend the interests of those who wield power, be it a tyrant, an oligarchy, or the *demos*. Aristotle then described three other regimes with similar configurations of power but based on the common good and, in other words, truly political. That is the meaning of chapter seven of book three of *The Politics*, which offers a classification of political regimes: Aristotle made no distinction between rulers and ruled, but defined citizens in terms of the political relations that were established among them, for all had some degree of power either juridical or deliberative. "The citizen in this strict sense is best defined by the one criterion that he shares in the administration of justice and in the holding of power" (Aristotle: 85). That is why a concern for others and friendship with others are an essential part of the good regime, which Aristotle called the *politeia*. This is the political regime par excellence, and it corresponds to the sovereignty of the people when the latter is not exercised to defend the interests of the poor masses but rather to build a political society.

Such is the liberty of the ancients. It is, to borrow an image from Aristotle, like the liberty of the heavenly bodies, for it consists in integration into a totality. The goal of the city is to make everyone happy: It is not "a social association that comes into existence for the sake of mere life; it exists for the sake of a good life," as Aristotle wrote in book one of *The Politics*, where he introduced his definition of man as "a political animal." For what was happiness but civic integration, when it resulted not in fusion into a collective being but in the highest possible degree of interaction? A collective decision, according to Aristotle, was better than a decision taken by even the best of individuals, because politics was a matter of opinion and experience rather than knowledge. A great deal of experience and practical wisdom or *phronesis* (see Pierre Aubenque [1993] for an analysis of the central importance of this notion for Aristotle) was required if relative integration was to be achieved and if individual perceptions and opinions were to be reconciled. Aristotle can be regarded as the main inspiration behind the liberty of the ancients, even though he condemned what he called democracy because he saw it as the triumph of the selfish interests of majorities and feared that the city would be destroyed by democracy, which was as different from the constitutional regime as monarchy was from tyranny. The citizen and the private individual were not the same in his view: "It is thus clear that it is possible to be a good citizen without possessing the excellence by which one is a good man" (Aristotle: 91). This divorce between public life and private life, which worked to the advantage of the former, was to become the most salient feature of the civic conception of liberty and of the republican or revolutionary ideologies that would evoke it in the modern world.

In what sense does the liberty of the moderns differ from this civic or republican conception of democracy? The difference is that in the modern world, politics is no longer defined as the expression of the needs of an association or city, but as action on society. The distinction between state and society, with the first acting on the second, emerged with the formation of absolute monarchies at the end of the Middle Ages and marks a definitive break with the theme of the city; even city-states like Venice, in the fourteenth and fifteenth centuries, became modern states just like France and England.

Once the state has been constituted, sociopolitical actors can use it against their social adversaries or fight it in order to ensure that all social actors enjoy the greatest possible autonomy. Irrespective of whether we take the revolutionary path or the liberal path, politics is now a matter of collective action on society rather than the creation of a political community.

That is why those who transposed the liberty of the ancients, the civic conception of democracy, into the modern world paved the way for the destruction of liberty, whereas the defenders of social liberties protected and strengthened democracy even as they were pursuing their own interests. If we make liberalism synonymous with the liberty of the moderns, with defending social actors against the state, then those who are not liberals are responsible either directly or indirectly for the destruction of democratic regimes. Whether they act in the name of the liberation of a nation, the interests of a people, or loyalty to a charismatic leader is largely irrelevant: In the world of states, the only possible definition of democracy is the control that social actors have over political power.

It was the emergence of the category of the social that indirectly permitted the formation of the state in the modern world. Society was no longer an order, hierarchy, or organism; it was made up of social relations, of actors defined by their cultural orientations, their values, and their relations—conflict, cooperation, or compromise—with other social actors. Democracy was no longer defined as the political creation of the city, but as the entry of the greatest possible number of social actors, both individual and collective, into decisionmaking. As a result, "the locus of power becomes *an empty place,*" as Claude Lefort (Lefort 1986: 17) put it. If that is so, then it is difficult to understand why the same author insisted on defining politics as "the constitution of social space, the *framework* of society, the essence of what was once termed 'the city'" (Lefort 1986: 11). It also becomes difficult to explain the idea of the sovereignty of the people; to imagine that the people is sovereign in place of the king does not take us very far toward democracy. We enter modern democracy only when there is no longer a sovereign and when power changes hands as a result of regular elections.

In the modern world, there are no ideal societies. At best, there may be an open society founded on historical memory. In contrast, the defining characteristic of an antidemocratic society, especially a totalitarian society, is that it is immobile and antihistorical. It is no longer possible to elevate the political above the social (as Hannah Arendt did in the extreme when she contrasted the economic and social world that is dominated by needs with a political world that is the world of freedom), for it is the idea of social rights that gives the idea of human rights its full force in the modern world. Any attempt to introduce a dichotomy between a universalistic politics and particularistic social actors results either in the demand by a wise elite, far removed from the concerns of ordinary workers, for privilege and the right to rule or in the reduction of politics to a clash of private interests.

Three Dimensions of Democracy

If we define democracy as the freedom of the ruled to choose their rulers at regular intervals, we have a clear definition of the institutional mechanism without which democracy cannot exist. Our analysis must remain within the boundaries of this definition. No popular power can be described as democratic if it has not been achieved and renewed by an act of free choice; nor can there be any democracy if a significant proportion of the ruled do not have the right to vote, as has usually been the case. Until recently, restrictions of this kind applied to all women, and they still apply to those who have not reached the age of legal majority. This creates an imbalance in favor of older and retired people that is detrimental to those who have yet to begin work. Democracy is also hampered or destroyed when voters' freedom of choice is restricted by parties that mobilize political resources and force voters to choose between two or more candidates for power even though it is not clear that the differences between them correspond to what the voters see as the most important choices. Likewise, it is impossible to speak of democracy when legitimate power cannot be exercised, or when violence and chaos reign in the greater part of society.

The criteria that allow us to identify nondemocratic situations cannot, however, provide an adequate analysis of democracy. Democracy exists when there is a political space that can protect citizens' rights from the omnipotence of the state. This definition contradicts the idea that there can be a direct correlation between people and power: the people do not govern directly; the rulers merely speak in the name of the people. Similarly, the state cannot be merely an expression of popular feeling, as it must ensure the unity of political association, represent it, and defend it against the outside world. Democracy exists when the distance between state and private life is recognized and preserved by political institutions and the law. Democracy is not reducible to procedures because it represents a set of mediations between a unitary state and a multiplicity of social actors. The basic rights of individuals must be guaranteed. What is more, individuals must feel that they are citizens and must participate in the construction of collective life. The two worlds of state and civil society must therefore remain separate, but they must also be bound together by the representativity of political leadership. The three dimensions of democracy—respect for basic rights, citizenship, and the representativity of leaders—are complementary. It is their *interdependence* that constitutes democracy.

The first requirement of democracy is that rulers be *representative;* democracy implies the existence of social actors and of political agents who are their instruments or representatives. Moreover, given that civil society is made up of a plurality of social actors, democracy cannot be representative unless it is pluralistic. Some believe in the multiplicity of conflicts of interest, others in the existence of a central axis of social relations of domination and dependence; but all democrats reject the image of a unanimous or homogeneous society and agree that the nation is a political figure rather than a social actor. Indeed, they argue that a nation—not to be confused with a people—without a state is inconceivable, even though some nations have suffered the loss of their states. The plurality of social actors is inseparable from the autonomy and dominant role of social relations. A political society that does not recognize this plurality of social actors and relations cannot be democratic, even if the government or party in power insists that it has the support of the majority and, therefore, that it understands the general interest.

The second characteristic of a democratic society is implicit in its definition: voters are, and regard themselves as, citizens. The freedom to choose rulers is meaningless if the ruled are not interested in the government, if they feel no sense of belonging to a political society but merely to a family, a village, a professional category, an ethnic group, or a religious confession. This awareness of belonging is not universally present and not everyone demands the right to be a citizen. Some may be content to have a place in society without attempting to modify the decisions and laws that govern its workings; others might wish to avoid responsibilities that could involve great sacrifices. The government is often seen as belonging to a world that is divorced from the world of ordinary people: as the saying goes, *they* do not live in the same world as *we*. Democracy was originally associated with the formation of nation-states, and it is doubtful that it can, in the contemporary world, exist outside them, even though we can all readily accept that democracy cannot exist solely at the national level. It must percolate downward to townships or regions and upward to federal states, such as the united Europe that is struggling to come into being or the United Nations organization. The idea of citizenship is not reducible to the democratic idea; the two can come into conflict when citizens become nationals rather than voters, and especially when they are called to arms and accept that there are restrictions on their liberty. It is, however, impossible to imagine a democracy that is not based on the definition of a polity, and therefore a territory.

Thirdly, freedom of choice cannot exist if there are no *limitations* on the power of rulers. Their power must be limited both by the very existence of elections and, more concretely, by respect for the laws that define the limits within which power can be exercised. A recognition of the basic rights that restrict the power not only of the state but also of churches, families, or companies is essential to the existence of democracy. In sum, the representation of interests combined with the limitation of power within a political society provides the most accurate definition of democracy.

Can these three components of democracy be viewed as three aspects of a more general principle? It seems almost natural to identify democracy with liberty or, more accurately, with liberties; but what might seem a refinement of our analysis would in fact be a step backward, toward too narrow a definition. The idea of liberty does not imply representation and citizenship; it merely guarantees the absence of constraints. Thus, talk of liberty is too vague; we should instead speak of the freedom to choose rulers, or in other words to choose those who will hold political power or who will have the monopoly on legitimate violence.

The autonomy of the components of democracy is in fact so great that it would be more accurate to speak of democracy's dimensions or preconditions rather than its constituent elements; for even as the dimensions exist in combination with one another, they also tend to conflict.

To begin with, citizenship results in social integration and in an awareness of belonging not only to a city, a nation-state, or a federal state but also to a community that is united by culture and history. Such a community exists within specific borders, and those outside may be enemies, competitors, or allies; thus, the sense of belonging can contradict the universalism of human rights. Secondly, representativity is bound up with a conception of political power as an instrument for promoting private interests. Thirdly, the recognition of basic rights need not go hand in hand with democracy. The concept of natural law is Christian in origin and is based on a premise that is not necessarily democratic: that respect is due to all the elements of creation—living or inanimate beings as well as human beings—that were created by God and that fulfill a function within the divinely ordained system.

The juxtaposition of representation, citizenship, and the limitation of power by basic rights is not enough to constitute democracy in all cases. Furthermore, as no single general principle can be distilled from these three elements, we can only conclude that the bond that unites and reconciles them is purely negative; it is, precisely, the absence of any central principle of power and legitimation. The rejection of all essentialist theories of power is an indispensable aspect of democracy and finds its concrete expression in majority rule. Majority rule is an instrument of democracy only if we recognize that the majority represents nothing more than fifty-one percent of the electorate, that it therefore changes constantly, and that even majority views may change as the problems requiring resolution change. Majority rule is the antithesis of popular power and of recourse to the will of the people, which have spawned authoritarian regimes and destroyed democracies rather than creating them.

Three Types of Democracy

There is no ideal balance among the three dimensions of democracy, nor is there an ideal democracy that we can contrast with the exceptionality of particular democratic experiments. There are, however, three main types of democracy, depending on which element predominates. The first type gives central importance to the limitation of state power by the law and by the recognition of basic rights. I am tempted to say that in historical terms this type is the most important, even though it is not superior to the others. This liberal conception of democracy easily accommodates a limited representativity of rule, as witnessed by the triumph of liberal regimes in the nineteenth century. It does, however, afford social or economic rights the best protection against the attacks of absolute power, as we can see from the centuries-old example of Great Britain.

The second type of democracy accords primary importance to citizenship and to the constitution and the ethical or religious ideas that ensure the integration of society and give the laws a solid foundation. In this case, the driving force behind democracy is the will to achieve equality rather than the desire for liberty. The experience of the United States, in the view of several interpreters, corresponds most closely to this type. As Tocqueville put it, this type of democracy has a social rather than a political content. Tocqueville saw in the United States the triumph of equality, or in other words, the disappearance of the *homo hierarchicus* characteristic of holistic societies.

The third type of democracy, finally, places more emphasis on the social representativity of rulers and contrasts democracy, which defends the interests of popular categories, with oligarchy, which can be associated either with a monarchy defined by the enjoyment of privilege or with the ownership of capital. This type can be seen in the political history of twentieth-century France—although not the France of the Revolution—where public liberties and social struggles have been more closely associated than in the United States or even in Great Britain.

It is impossible, however, to identify a type of democracy completely with one or more national experiences. At the time of the French Revolution the idea of citizenship was dominant, and Marx criticized the French for always having prioritized political categories over social ones. That judgment was ratified by historian François Furet (Furet 1981 [orig. ed. 1978]), who demonstrated that France's Revolution could be explained only in political terms and not as a social revolution—pace Albert Mathiez, who saw the events that took place in France in the late eighteenth century as the first stage in a victory for the popular classes that would culminate in the Soviet Revolution. Great Britain, in contrast, has always attached great importance to the representation of interests, to utilitarian theory, and to the role of intermediary bodies.

However, political debate in the second half of the twentieth century has contrasted English-style democracy with French political life. The theory of English democracy was expounded by influential liberal thinkers, and it was all the stronger in that communist ideology had little influence in Great Britain. In France, the experience of the Popular Front and the long-standing and dominant influence of the Communist party, especially over the labor movement, meant that French political life was dominated on the left by the idea of class struggle and on the right by the need to resist the threat of a communist dictatorship. The United States, which has always attached exceptional importance to ensuring that its laws are constitutional and to defending liberties, also has instilled in its predominantly immigrant population the awareness of belonging to a society governed by ethical and legal standards and designed to promote certain values and a certain way of life. We can therefore speak of English, American, and French models, but only as elements in the postwar political debate and not as historical types.

These three models of democracy (English, French, and American) are of equal importance in philosophical terms, although the French example has been vastly more influential in Europe and Latin America than have the other two, which have not often been closely imitated.

We could investigate the strengths and weaknesses of these three models in various historical situations, but it is more important to recognize that the democratic model has no central form. We can only juxtapose our three models—which may also be described as *liberal* democracy, *constitutional* democracy, and *conflictual* democracy—and note that they define the space within which all historical examples of democracy have been constructed. The differences among the three are due to variations in the balance they establish among human rights, the representation of social interests, and citizenship—or in other words, among a universal principle, particular interests, and a political association. The ethical, social, and civic dimensions are closely related; democracy is the antithesis of pure politics, of a political system with autonomous internal mechanisms.

The Separation of Powers

The conception of democracy introduced here departs from the conception that concentrates solely on the political and institutional system. The latter finds its classic expression in the definition of democracy given by Robert Dahl: an elective polyarchy (Dahl 1956). I have no quarrel with the second word, even though most regimes that recognize the separation of powers do not elect those who exercise juridical power and agree that the executive should be chosen by the legislative power, as in parliamentary regimes. On the other hand, it would seem to me an exaggeration to make the *separation of powers* an essential element of democracy. To do so is to confuse a formal organization of powers with the limitation of power by basic rights, which must in fact be protected by constitutional laws applied and defended by an independent judiciary. The separation of juridical and executive powers is as crucial as the separation of legislative and executive powers is limited in virtue, ambiguous in effect, and open to challenge by parliamentarians. The former has given American democracy its particular strength and has had a telling effect also in France, a country whose political and ideological history did not prepare it to accept that a constitutional court should verify the conformity of its laws to the general principles enshrined in its constitution. Those principles are organized around the defense of basic human rights; therefore, it is inadequate to speak of the separation of powers when the problem is not in fact one of relations between different decision-making centers within political soci-

ety but of a direct clash between the state and basic rights, and thus of the limitation, rather than the separation, of powers.

In the early history of democracy, the separation of powers served primarily to
restrict democracy and the power of the majority and to protect the interests either
of an aristocracy, as described by Montesquieu (Montesquieu 1989 [orig. ed.
1748]), or of an enlightened elite, as in the early American republic. Conversely, in
countries that have undergone dependent development and that are marked by the
dualization of the economy and by pronounced social and regional inequalities, we
find what I have described, with reference to Latin America, as a world of participation and a world of exclusion—the two being widely separated (Touraine 1988).
National-popular regimes have attempted to narrow the distance between the two
worlds (even though their adversaries can easily show that they have also helped to
perpetuate it); parliaments defended oligarchic interests until such time as populist
movements expanded the political system to include the majority of the urban population and a smaller proportion of the rural population. The revolutionary political movements were expressions of democratic aspirations, at first co-opted and
later repressed by the postrevolutionary regimes: The revolutionary movements
have created powers that then destroyed them. As Farhad Khosrowkhavar has
demonstrated in the case of the Iranian revolution of 1979, a social movement designed to liberate the people was transformed into a clerical dictatorship as quickly
as the regime born of the October revolution in Russia was transformed into a one-
party dictatorship (Khosrowkhavar 1993). Revolutions transform democratic
movements into antidemocratic regimes. Living in a world that was almost dominated by totalitarian postrevolutionary regimes, we were so relieved by their fall that
we forgot that the revolutionary movements were an expression not only of the interests of the popular majority but also of the will to destroy an absolute monarchy.
They expressed the hope of those who were subject to arbitrary decisions of being
liberated and becoming citizens. Conversely, the separation of powers and the triumph of a purely institutional conception of democracy can mask the rule of the
market and increased inequalities if political institutions and juridical rules are used
to segment and weaken a challenge to oligarchic power.

If the separation of powers were complete, democracy would disappear. The
political system would become self-contained and would lose its influence on
both civil society and the state. Democracy was initially defined as the expression
of the sovereignty of the people; but what would become of the sovereignty of the
people if every power were independent of every other power? The law would
rapidly become an instrument for defending the interests of the powerful, if it
were not being constantly transformed and if jurisprudence did not set great store
by public opinion. Similarly, the legislative power must have an influence on the
executive power: It is the role of political parties to ensure that it does.

Liberal thought, in contrast, tends to increase the separation of powers.
Michael Walzer (1983) regarded as essential the autonomy of various domains of

social life, with each domain corresponding to a dominant good and constituting a "sphere of justice." The freedom of individuals was based on this separation or differentiation of subsystems. In practice, however, this extreme separation of powers rarely exists, especially when the state mobilizes society in order to transform it, irrespective of whether the goal is development, revolution, or national integration. Democracy is not defined by the separation of powers but by the nature of the links between civil society, political society, and the state. If influence is exerted in a downward direction, there is no democracy; but we can describe as democratic a society in which social actors control their political representatives, who in turn control the state. How can we not recognize that the principle of the sovereignty of the people takes precedence over that of the separation of powers? The level of political institutions must not be separated from the level of social actors. The corollary of this general idea is that there must exist, at the level of both state and political system, a nonpolitical element that is autonomous with respect to the will of the people. At the level of the state, this means that civil servants must be independent professionals; at the level of the political system, it means that the law and control-mechanisms must ensure that the decisions taken are both legal and constitutional. This combination of a principle of unity—the majority social demand—and principles of autonomy is preferable to the politicization of the administration and of social actors whereby they merge in neocorporatist fashion with political power and the *partitocrazia*.

The above assertions go hand in hand. The limitation of state power is indeed the basis for democracy, and the defenders of negative liberty are right; those who allow the struggle for positive liberty to destroy democracy's institutional foundations are wrong. The liberal position must not, however, lead us to describe as "democratic" regimes in which state power is limited by the power of the oligarchy or by local customs. The recognition of basic rights would be devoid of substance if it did not lead to the security of all and to the constant expansion of legal guarantees and state intervention in behalf of the weakest. In the poorest and most dependent countries, this means first of all guaranteeing everyone the right to life—a right that cannot be taken for granted in many parts of the world. "Democratic action" is now based on an ever closer association between the negative democracy that protects the population from the ravages of arbitrary power and the positive democracy that allows the greatest possible number to take greater control of their own existence.

For a long time, people described as "democratic" state interventions into economic and social life that were intended to reduce inequalities and to guarantee everyone a certain level of educational, medical, and economic aid. Most of us no longer do so because we now believe that state intervention should be no more than a means to the primary end of increasing everyone's ability to intervene in their own lives. That ability is not the automatic result of the collective accumulation of wealth: it is won by force or through negotiation, through revolution or through reforms. None of the reasons for which we condemn the postrevolutionary state should make us forget that the vital thing is to give everyone greater liberty and to make politics increasingly representative of social demands.

The democratic idea was initially associated with the republican conception of the state and with the creation of a rationally governed nation-state. The republican conception itself had been a protest against absolute monarchy, which it defeated in England and Holland first, and later in the United States and France. A liberal elite of enlightened citizens then identified themselves with that republican power and held itself aloof from the popular masses, who were deemed ignorant and unstable; but the people drove that elite out of power, first in the United States, then in France, and much later in England, where the elite had enjoyed a golden age between the electoral reforms of 1832 and 1867.

The political elite then began to be replaced by parties and class movements. The defense of private interests finally spilled over from the world of labor into all aspects of social life, which had been transformed by mass production and mass consumption. The distance between the domain of the state and that of its citizens, who are now consumers and private persons, has steadily increased. As a result, democracy leads increasingly to the autonomous organization of a political life that can be identified with neither the state nor the demands of consumers. Indeed, its autonomy has often become so great that political life seems to have nothing to do with either the problems of the state or the demands of civil society. In other countries, the republican idea took on new forms during this period. Political rationalism became more militant or even revolutionary with the emergence of left-wing socialists who were dissatisfied with industrial democracy, and particularly with the emergence of the Bolshevik and revolutionary wing of German and Russian social democracy. This revolutionary republicanism turned its back on democracy so violently that it is impossible to describe as democratic the regimes that were born of the communist revolutions or their Third World equivalents, and that it is no longer possible to define democracy other than in terms of a combination of the three elements we have just identified.

A Note on John Rawls

The absence of any central principle that can define democracy or justice is the logical result of the divorce between politics and religion that defines modernity in the political domain. Secularization forces us to look for principles of social organization that do not depend on a philosophical or ethical conception, even if they are consonant with it. John Rawls reminded us that this was the necessary starting point for any thinking about rights. He concluded that a theory of rights must have political rather than philosophical foundations, and he therefore defines justice as fairness. Moreover, justice is conceivable only as a combination of principles which are not simply independent, but centrifugal: liberty and equality.

Rawls's answer was that the principle of liberty must take priority over the others but that it must be combined with a principle of equality in two respects: Equality of opportunity must exist, and liberty must reduce inequalities.

Most thinkers agree that a conception of democracy must indeed reconcile liberty and equality. I am attempting to reconcile the two by identifying three dimensions of democracy: respect for basic rights, which is inseparable from liberty; citizenship, and representativity. But these ideas do not refer to the same representation of social life as Rawls's idea. For Rawls, the combination of liberty and equality means a combination of an individualist vision of actors and a truly political vision of society. Individuals in pursuit of rational advantages, or what is good for them, begin to cooperate and constitute society. This conception is quite in keeping with the idea of a social contract, which Rawls in fact referred to at the beginning of *A Theory of Justice* (Rawls 1971: 11). A person is thus defined as both an economic and a political being whose moral character is grounded in "a conception of their good and 'a sense of justice'" (Rawls 1971: 19), and therefore in an awareness of the needs of collective life. That conception departs from the idea I am expounding here: I am defending a social rather than a political idea, and it replaces the individual who is free and equal to others with an individual or group involved in social relations that are always relations of inequality or control. The goal of collective action is not to give everyone their due but either to strengthen the position of the dominant or to appeal, in the name of the dominated, to the idea of equality as an instrument in the struggle against inequality. Given that any form of social organization is hierarchical, justice struggles against an established hierarchy in the name of an ethical principle of equality that might be described as "natural." Like the idea of democracy, the idea of justice implies what I term "recourse," and therefore a reference to a conflict. Thus, justice is not based on consensus, but on a compromise that is constantly being challenged by social or political actors who modify the law.

There is an ethical dimension to Rawls's vision, which—as we have known since Tocqueville—is an essential part of American society, where it coexists with an individualism that finds its economic expression in free enterprise. Interest and justice are complementary, as are the economy and religion. The history of democracy, which has always been a history of mobilizations and reforms, means that the theme of equality of opportunities—a vague combination of individualism and social integration—must give way to the theme of representativity, or in other words, of the plurality of interests. In modern society, the principle of the plurality of values, of which Rawls rightly reminded us, must be taken to its logical conclusion, which will eliminate any ultimate reference to justice as a state of equilibrium and consensus in society. That is why it seems to me impossible to start out from Rawls's original position, bracketing out the interests, values, and objectives of individuals, who are not only or primarily citizens but also social actors. The sound and the fury present in the history of all societies cannot be seen as alien to an order defined independently of inequalities, social conflicts, or cultural movements. As François Terré has reminded us, we cannot divorce the political order from social relations (Terré 1988).

A theory of democracy and justice must, as Rawls demanded, be political; but a theory of politics cannot be divorced from an analysis of social relations or of the collective action that pursues cultural values through social conflicts. Democracy establishes mediations between a power, which is always disputed and inegalitarian, however it is distributed, and the recourse to natural law, which is the source of the will to attain both liberty and equality.

Limitations on Power

No principle is more centrally important to the democratic idea than the limitation of the state by the demand that it respect basic human rights. It is impossible to forget that in our century, democracy's principal adversary has not been the monarch ruling by "divine right" nor the oligarchy of landowners and feudal lords but totalitarianism; and that in order to combat totalitarianism, nothing is more important than the recognition of limits to state power. This feeling is so strong that we are now tempted to accord much less importance than did the thinkers of the seventeenth and eighteenth centuries to the idea of the sovereignty of the people or to the idea of equality as Tocqueville defined it. This is so because the structured, hierarchical communities that were once protected by powerful mechanisms of social control have been completely destroyed by the blows of rapid change under modernization and in the decomposition of the established order. The traditional order was destroyed by no founding act or oath of social contract but by modernity, with or without democracy. Traditional monarchies and ruling classes are things of the past the world over, and so are the forms of family- or school-based authority that instilled a respect for supposedly natural hierarchies. Throughout the world, "orders" have been replaced by classes, and classes may in turn be replaced by a multiplicity of interest groups. As a result, the state's power can be limited only by political decision or moral conviction. History, however, tends to give the state increasing power in mobile societies where it is more than an agent of reproduction of the social order, a central actor in the processes of change and of accumulation and redistribution. The assertion of the democratic idea is therefore much more clearly present in such voluntary self-limitation, which runs counter to modern society's tendencies, than in the rupture of traditional authority by states that have been more often authoritarian than democratic.

Our political culture facilitated the birth of modern democracy because it was based on the separation of temporal power and spiritual power, whereas in other civilizations the two were intermingled, making the state sacred. Europeans and

Americans alike find in their heritage both the idea of the *sacred* and that of *transcendence*. The idea of the sacred fuses the human with the divine and gives a symbolic meaning to objects and modes of behavior; it mingles the spiritual and the temporal, acknowledging no difference between the two. Transcendence, in contrast, sunders what the sacred has brought together because it is manifested only as an event, the disruption of the social order or the appearance of a prophet or of the son of God himself. Without that intervention, God is present throughout the order of things and even in the human mind. The personal presence in the world of the son of God, in contrast, visibly divorces the realm of the spiritual from the realm of the temporal. It brings about the disenchantment of the world recommended by the Gospel—or at least the broadest interpretation thereof: "Render unto Caesar the things that are Caesar's; and unto God the things that are God's."

Our modern history has been influenced by these two religious heritages, which Max Weber describes, respectively, as ascetic and hierocratic. On the one hand, secularization transformed the sacred worldview and hierocratic power into an absolutism that acquired a religious legitimacy. State religions existed in Christian countries just as they existed in Islamic countries, and our kings were thaumaturges. At the time of the great dispute between the pope and the emperor, the church stressed the indirectly religious origins of temporal power and the role played by the people in its legitimation. On the other hand, the transcendent God was transformed into the consciousness, the soul, to use Descartes's word, into worldly asceticism, and then into natural law. In our society, it now takes the form of social justice and the ethics that must govern the way we behave toward living beings. Religion cannot be regarded as liberty's enemy; nor, for that matter, can reason. Churches have, however—to restrict the argument to the Christian world—very often attempted to create or defend a Christian society, or what Jean Delumeau calls Christendom, as opposed to Christianity; and the same tendency can be seen in politico-religious movements with a high eschatological content, such as liberation theology. On the other hand, religious faith has fought against the arbitrary nature of political power and has defended the most disadvantaged and the persecuted, from Suarez and Las Casas at the time of Spain's colonization of the New World to Chile's *Vicaría de la Solidaridad*. The democratic spirit owes a great deal to the religious experience, althouth it also has often had to fight churches that have lent their support to established powers.

Human Rights Versus the Sovereignty of the People

The limitation of political power was born of the alliance between the idea of natural law and the idea of civil society. The latter was initially seen as an economic society whose actors demanded the freedom to do business, to trade, and to express their ideas. Without this "bourgeois" freedom, the idea of basic rights would have remained purely a critique intermingled with the resistance to oppression defended by most political philosophers from Hobbes to Rousseau. If these basic rights had not been defended, the spirit of free trade would not have been transformed into the democratic spirit, which was born of the alliance between the spirit of liberty and the spirit of equality.

The appeal to human rights and the political philosophy that dominated the century between England's revolution and France's have very different implications. According to political philosophers like Rousseau and Hobbes, politics is self-creating and the political realm is the realm of liberty, as contrasted with the natural order, which is dominated by the boundless desires of individuals, and with a social realm dominated by inequality and corruption. In this domain, as in others, the task of modernity is to allow reason, or in other words order, to triumph over chaos, violence, and egotism. It is by becoming citizens that individuals gain access to civilization. This "classic" liberal thought did not, however, invent democracy. It invented the nation-state, which was born in England and reached its full maturity in the France of the ancien régime and then the Revolution. The democratic idea took shape in opposition to this political rationalism, this modernism of the social realm, rather than in alliance with it. The reason why England is the mother of democracy and why France has so often betrayed democracy is that, in England, democratic thought asserted the autonomy of the individual and civil society, whereas France was dominated by the very different quest for a rational order and a complete identification of man with citizen and, therefore, of society with state. Democracy developed in opposition to the modern state and even the legal state, which usually served the interests of the absolute monarchy rather than those of human rights. The Declaration of the Rights of Man and Citizen of 1789 does not mark the beginning of the revolutionary period in France; it is the culmination of the long tradition of Augustinian dualism that infused the thought of Luther, Descartes, and, later still, Locke. In France, 1789 was a break in the almost continuous history of the triumph of the state, as traced by Tocqueville in an essay that explains the French revolution by studying the ancien régime (Tocqueville 1964 [orig. ed. 1856]). In the France of 1789, the heritage of Locke was more important than that of Rousseau because Locke's legacy is present in the idea of human rights, which was more important than that of the sovereignty of the people. However, this democratic tradition was rapidly forgotten when the French nation mobilized in order to defend liberty and the republic against the princes. That mobilization brought Napoleon to power and justified the nationalistic and voluntaristic modernizing regimes that dominated the history of the world until the end of the nineteenth century—though they never conquered Great Britain. Despite the pressures of war and danger, Great Britain never deviated from the democratic spirit and institutions it inherited from 1688.

The democratic idea has, then, undergone such a profound transformation that it has been inverted. It once asserted that there was a correspondence between the individual will and the general will, or in other words the state. It now defends the opposite position in order to protect the liberties of individuals and groups from the omnipotence of the state. Rousseau was hostile to the English parliamentary system and advocated "a form of association which will defend and protect with the whole common force the person and goods of each associate, and in which each, while uniting himself with all, may still obey himself alone, and remain as free as before" (Rousseau 1973: 191 [orig. ed. 1762]). Yet in his study of democracy, Hans Kelsen (1988 [orig. ed. 1920]) criticized the contradiction that weakens this argument: The idea of a social contract is based on a subjective will; but the general will is not the will of all, and still less is it the will of the majority. In addition, it is as objective as the collective consciousness described by Durkheim. Because there is never any correspondence between individuals and the state, Kelsen passionately denounced the notion of the people, which uses social terms to mask the state. Marxism's contribution to this debate was decisive. Rousseau's argument postulated as its unit of reference an isolated, universal individual just like all other individuals. If, however, we observe social reality, we find that it is made up of interest groups, social categories, and social classes; political life is therefore dominated not by a unitary state but by a plurality of social groups. Kelsen, who was very close to the Austrian social democrats after World War I, deduced from this observation that parties were indispensable to democracy; but more important still was his refusal to identify the state with the people, for such an identification would have given the state unlimited authority over individual wills.

Republicans Versus Democrats

For a long time, English democracy retained an aristocratic dimension that French democracy constantly fought. English history was dominated by the alliance of common people and aristocracy against the king, whereas the history of France was dominated by the alliance of the people and the king—or in other words the state—against the aristocracy. The social realm has always been the weak element in English democracy, the political realm in French democracy.

The weakness of the French democratic tradition—which is characteristic also of Spain, Latin America, and to a lesser degree Italy, where the nation-state was a late development—stems from the struggle it had to wage against a State that was bound up with the forces perpetuating and reproducing the social order, above all the Catholic church. Hence the importance of the republic's antireligious and anticlerical action; and hence too the predominance in France, and many other countries, of truly political and ideological struggles rather than social reforms, especially during the Third Republic. As a result, French thought identified the republic with democracy and, what is more important, preferred the alliance of republic and revolution to one of democracy and social reforms. Workers in France received extensive civic rights at a very early stage but limited social rights at a very late stage: Not until fifty years after the birth of industrial democracy in

Great Britain and of labor legislation in Germany did the Popular Front give French workers social rights, and the economic and international conjuncture soon rendered those rights null and void.

These two very different types of political society might be described, respectively, as republican and democratic, to adopt the dichotomy used by Régis Debray, who recognized that because it gives central importance to the transformation of the state and to state intervention, the republican spirit differs from the democratic one, which gives social actors the central role (Debray 1989). Living as we do in an age that no longer believes in revolutions, it is sometimes useful to recall the greatness of the revolutionary states and their armies; but it is still more necessary, no matter where we live, to recall the most important thing of all—that the mobilizing state was and is democracy's greatest enemy. Thus, while one might contrast the mediocrity of democracy's political mores with the heroism of calls for popular and national mobilization, the defenders of democracy must assert that it cannot exist unless society and its social actors are free and unless the state recognizes that its role is to serve them. Democracy cannot exist unless the state is servant not only to the country and the nation but also to social actors and their will to achieve liberty and responsibility.

The democratic idea—even in its simplest formulation, defending the freedom of the ruled to choose their rulers—therefore does not simply mean that social actors existed prior to political power. It also implies that, as Dworkin put it, "men have moral rights against the state" (Dworkin 1977: 147). One must choose between two paths, both of which purportedly lead to democracy. On the one hand, there is the path we have just described, which subordinates politics and the law to the principles that constitute a natural law; on the other, we find the regime that allows the whole population to participate as much as possible and that abolishes the power of ruling minorities. However, would it not be more accurate to describe the latter form of popular rule as revolutionary? It might well be an expression of democratic aspirations, but respect for the general will is an inadequate definition of democracy. One of democracy's essential principles is that it defends us from arbitrary power. There are two aspects to this principle: It is called liberty when it insists that the power of the state must be limited, and it is called equality when it defines a principle of resistance to the unequal distribution of economic or political resources. True, the fact that a political system allows us to resist the state does not necessarily make the system democratic; the limitation of power is no more than one of the constituent principles of democracy, although it is an indispensable component. If individuals are mere citizens, then there are no limits that the state cannot transgress; and if individuals are defined solely by their membership in a community, then they are unlikely to resist tyranny. Thus, the idea of basic rights—often described as "natural" in order to stress their universality—appears to be the sole principle capable of inspiring absolute resistance to a state power that is itself becoming increasingly total.

The Twofold Autonomy of the Political System

The idea of democracy is antithetical to that of revolution because the latter gives the state complete power in order to transform society. If we are to create democracy, we must, in contrast, make a distinction between state, political society, and civil society. If we confuse the state with political society, we will soon subordinate the multiplicity of social interests to the unifying action of the state. Conversely, if we confuse political society and civil society, it is no longer possible to see how we can create a political and juridical order that is not a mere reproduction of the dominant economic interests. The confusion of the two realms also might leave to the state sole responsibility for ensuring that society is managed coherently. In both cases, there is no space left for democracy. Democracy concerns political society, but it is defined both by the latter's autonomy and by its own role as a mediator between the state and civil society. A direct and unmediated confrontation between the state and civil society might lead to the victory of one over the other but never to the victory of democracy.

The separation of state, political system, and civil society obliges us to define the political order as a mediation between state and civil society, as did Kelsen when he wrote of "the formation of the ruling state will by a collegiate body elected by the people on the basis of universal and egalitarian suffrage, or in other words by a body that was democratic and adopted majority decisions" (Kelsen 1988 [orig. ed. 1920]). Democracy's mediating role means that we cannot define it in terms of a central principle or "idea," and obliges us to understand it as a combination of several elements that define its relations with the state and civil society.

In this context, the vocabulary of public life is a source of confusion rather than clarity as the same words designate very different realities in different countries. In the present context, I therefore understand *state* to mean the powers that build and defend the unity of a national society against external or internal threats and problems, against its past and future and, therefore, its historical continuity. It is both an administrative and an executive power. The *political system* has a different function. Its function is to create unity out of diversity and, therefore, to subordinate unity to the balances of power that exist at the level of civil society by recognizing the role of the political parties that intervene among groups and classes, and the state. In certain countries, such as France, the legal system is part of the state; in others, such as the United States, it is part of political society, as the law is made by the legislature and the judiciary. *Civil society* is not reducible to economic interests; it is the domain of social actors who are influenced by both cultural values and social relations that are often conflictual. The recognition of the autonomy of civil society—first achieved by the British and the Dutch—is the primary precondition for democracy, as it is the separation of civil society and state that permits the creation of political society.

Thus, democracy asserts the autonomy of the political system but also its ability to establish relations with the other two levels of public life in such a way that in the last analysis, civil society legitimizes the state. Democracy does not mean people's power—that expression is so confused that it can be interpreted in all sorts of ways, even to legitimize authoritarian and repressive regimes. Democracy means that the logic that descends from the state to the political system and then to civil society is replaced by a logic that moves up from below. This does not destroy the autonomy of either the state or the political system.

A national or local government that served public opinion directly would have deplorable effects. It is the state's responsibility to defend the long term against the short term, to maintain the collective memory, and to protect minorities and encourage cultural creativity, even when such acts do not correspond to the demands of the public at large. It is also essential that there be no direct correspondence between parties and social classes or other interest groups. Large popular and mass parties throughout the world have always been democracy's foes rather than its defenders. One of the strengths of American democracy is that it has maintained a distinct separation between civil society and the political system. It has strengthened the power of the "representatives of the people" to resist not only the state but also society. The principal function of the political system and in particular of its central institution, the parliament, is not to collaborate in the management of the country or to train statesmen but to make and modify laws in such a way that they correspond to public opinion and interests. The political system must establish principles of unity on the basis of a diversity of social actors. It sometimes does so by invoking the interests of the state; at other times by arranging compromises or organizing alliances between different interest groups. Expressions such as "popular democracy" or "plebiscitary democracy" are therefore meaningless. Democracy is an institutional mediation between state and society, with the latter's freedom depending on the sovereignty of the state.

This mediating role means that the political and judiciary systems must be autonomous. The development of democracy can be understood as the continuous but difficult and embattled process of winning the autonomy of both politics and law from the state and from civil society. To stress that the two systems do not merely represent constituencies or interest groups or even that they represent something more than the people—"the people" designates, after all, nothing but the social equivalent of the state and the nation, which are obviously political notions—is not to preclude the social representativity of political actors. It is social actors within the political and judiciary systems who create the law, and their decisions are implemented within a national territory. However, public opinion looks unfavorably on political personalities who appear to be defending particular social interests. When a political party such as the Greens in Germany drastically reduces the autonomy of its elected representatives by issuing binding mandates that make them delegates rather than representatives and by imposing a rapid rotation of parliamentary tasks among members elected under the list system, it demonstrates above all its inability to transform a social movement into a political force and thus succumbs in short order to internal tensions between "fundis" and "realos."

However, at the other end of the equation—in relations between the political system and the state—the boundaries are even more difficult to trace. So much so that in many countries, especially those with a French-style republican tradition, the distinction between the two notions becomes difficult to understand and accept. In France, a member of parliament is often a big-city mayor with ministerial ambitions. In that respect, the American-style presidential system has major advantages: It turns parliamentarians into legislators, whereas in France almost all the laws that are passed by parliament are government sponsored, and a high proportion merely harmonize national legislation with European directives. Under such conditions, how can we make a clear distinction between political system and state? We must, however, do so if democracy is to exist; it is largely because the separation of state and political system has not been clearly understood that democracy appears to have been weakened in so many Western countries. At a time when republican ideology was triumphant, it was possible for political thinkers and actors to believe that a country's government was the expression of its social life and its political philosophy; this was, however, an illusion, and confrontations on both literal and figurative battlefields were obvious enough to render a purely juridical and social conception of government unrealistic. Those who see the construction of Europe as transcending national interests and confrontations between nation-states are subject to an even more dangerous illusion, as are those who express pacifist ideas that are all the more readily acceptable in that they refer to threats that are now almost nonexistent, such as a possible conflict between the nations of western Europe. The Europe that is emerging is faced with state responsibilities, and if it does not shoulder them, it will prove powerless.

National political systems have been weakened in Europe. On the one hand, far-reaching powers have been transferred to Brussels; on the other, we are seeing the formation of interest groups and pressure groups of all kinds. Either they rely exclusively on the media because they expect nothing from the political system, or they bring direct pressure to bear on European institutions. The globalization of the economy may result in extreme particularism at the level of social and cultural demands, and that too will weaken the political system and the state. Democracy will survive and grow stronger in the European countries where it was born only if a European state is established and only if national political systems are recognized as being autonomous from that state. In this regard the Danish resistance to the ratification of the Maastricht treaty has had a positive effect, highlighting the fact that the treaty, although quite explicit where the creation of a single currency is concerned, is vague on the subject of social policies and has nothing to say about how responsibilities are to be divided between the European and national levels. In the United States, in contrast, the fall of President George Bush, who devoted himself to foreign policy, and the triumph of his Democratic opponent Bill Clinton can be explained primarily in terms of the success of the "politics of meaning" elaborated by Michael Lerner—as a reflection of the electorate's desire to breathe new life into a domestic political system that had been marginalized by the preponderant role of the state at the international level. The priority that the Bush administration gave to foreign policy was seen as detrimental to the defense of the immediate interests of the U.S. population, especially those affected by unemployment and the inadequacies of the social welfare system.

Now that the Soviet Union no longer exists, Russia's most serious problem is the absence of a political system. By contrast, in Poland, Hungary, and even the former Czechoslovakia, political systems have been reconstructed and have already demonstrated—especially in Poland—their ability to respond to social demands and therefore to fill the gulf between an economy brutally exposed to the laws of the market and a population swayed by defensive nationalism and populism. As we shall see, the weakness of the political system also explains the fragility of many Latin American countries, from Mexico to Peru and Venezuela, whereas the stability of the political system is contributing to Chile's success in every domain. Likewise, Brazil's political system has successfully avoided involvement in the crisis affecting the state.

The separation of civil society, political society, and state is a central precondition for the emergence of democracy. The latter exists only if the distinct and often contradictory rationales of civil society and state are recognized and if a political system exists that is autonomous from both and capable of managing the difficult relations between the two. We must recall that democracy is not a mode of existence for society as a whole but a mode of existence for political society and that the democratic character of political society is determined by its relations with civil society and the state. The hegemonic conception of the political system defended by the upholders of the social contract notwithstanding, these are relations of bilateral dependency; but they are also relations of autonomy that give political institutions a role far more important than that of an honest broker, as the central element in the integration of society and the preservation of public order. Functionalist theorists describe societies as comprised of institutions, all of which contribute to the integration of the whole. This gives the family and the school, mores and religion, as important a role as political institutions. The principal goal of state and civil society is not, however, the integration of society. The state "makes war" or, in other words reacts primarily to the country's international situation; civil society, for its part, is dominated by social relations of conflict, cooperation, or negotiation. The political system alone has responsibility for making society function as a whole by reconciling the plurality of interests with the unity of the law and by establishing relations between civil society and state.

Two conditions are necessary in order to limit state power: political society must be recognized and it must be autonomous from both state and civil society. Political society has long been confused with civil society and was assumed by

Talcott Parsons to fulfil one of the latter's functions, that of defining goals. If we understand the role of political society, then we should be suspicious of calls for the democratization of state or society. The state is not in itself democratic, as its primary function is to defend the unity and strength of a national society against foreign states and in the face of long-term historical changes. The state has an international role and a role in defending a collective memory, just as it has a role in long-term forecasting and planning. None of these basic functions in itself results in democracy. Similarly, the social actors and movements that are the lifeblood of civil society by no means act in a democratic manner, even though a political system is democratic only if it represents the interests of social actors. It is the political system that is the site of democracy.

The Limits of Liberalism

Liberal philosophy, in rejecting any identification of the state with religious faith or with another system of values that transcends the sovereignty of the people, allies itself with democracy. Its distrust of the state, ideologies, great popular mobilizations, and what Ralf Dahrendorf scornfully described as the "steam bath of popular feelings" (Dahrendorf 1990: 10) has been so often and so tragically justified that liberal philosophy deserves a place within democratic thought. Indeed, the expression "antiliberal democracy" is a contradiction in terms; it designates an authoritarian regime rather than a particular type of democracy. These facts do not, however, make liberalism and democracy synonymous; for although there are no democracies that are not liberal, there are many liberal regimes that are not democratic. Liberalism sacrifices all for the sake of a single aspect of democracy— the limitation of power—and it does so in the name of a conception that threatens the democratic idea as much as it protects it.

Liberal thought is based on a distrust of values and of the forms of authority that ensure that certain values are respected. It separates the realm of impersonal reason, which should be that of public life and utility, from the realm of beliefs, which should be confined to private life. It does not credit the existence of social actors defined both by values and by social relations but rather validates private interests and preferences, seeking as much leeway for their exercise as is possible without infringing on the interests and preferences of others. "What," asked Isaiah Berlin (1969: 121–22), "is the area within which the subject—a person or group of persons—is or should be left to do or be what he is able to do or be, without interference by other groups?" This question suggests that if private interests and preferences are to be reconciled, then each subject must renounce its claim to absolute right or in other words, must allow its values to be reduced to an interest or an opinion that cannot be forced on others. This implies an image of social life that excludes both believers and basic social conflicts, and therefore the very idea of power. The ideal liberal society, thus, is a marketplace. This view does not preclude the intervention of the law or the state, but envisions them intervening only in order to ensure that the rules of the game are respected, that transactions are honest, and that all are free to act and express themselves as they see fit.

Liberal thought establishes the greatest possible separation between subjectivity and public life, and, more concretely, between personal demands and the rationality that must govern social exchanges. The liberal conception of democracy is restricted to the guaranteed freedom to choose rulers, and it is not concerned with the content of their actions. Like so many liberal thinkers, especially British ones, before him, Ralf Dahrendorf expresses this clearly: "The important thing is to check and balance ruling groups, and to replace them from time to time by peaceful means, such as elections" (Dahrendorf 1990: 10). But what gives these ruling groups their legitimacy? Liberals insist that it is their competence and their concern for the public good; their opponents stress that the economic or cultural power of capital influences the selection of leaders. The two interpretations are less contradictory than they might at first seem, and liberals have no qualms about stating that wealth, property ownership, and education are all essential characteristics of the high-minded individuals who display a concern for the public good and rational action.

Liberal elitists readily accept that *gentlemen* can have the strangest tastes and can express them quite freely, but they are suspicious of popular passions. This is so because like all forms of rationalism, liberalism is based on a dichotomy between reason and passion, and therefore between a rational elite and social categories that are ruled by their passions. The latter group would include women as well as the popular classes or colonized peoples, who must submit to the authority of the *sanior pars*. Liberal thought denies that elected representatives represent actors and social movements. It even denies the existence of a social domain, for it recognizes only political organization and interests. Liberal thought thus condemns itself to having very limited practical importance, although its critical importance has been and is considerable. For liberalism is a permanent element in democratic thought; but it is no more than an unstable intermediary zone between opposing political forces when the latter are defined in clearly social terms, particularly in terms of social classes and interest groups.

Liberalism opposed absolute monarchies; but after they were overthrown, it soon came into conflict with popular movements. There is less and less room for liberalism in contemporary societies. How can we defend liberal agnosticism at a time when nationalism and religious creeds are sweeping so much of the world? And in societies that are ruled by the market economy, how can private interests and tastes be prevented from fragmenting society into a series of self-contained communities that are bound together only by a market dominated by financial interests no longer subject to any political control? Can we still describe as liberal a society that is rocked by waves of speculation, dominated by financial empires, and manipulated by the perverse charms of a mass consumerism that prioritizes individual demands for commodities over collective consumption and the desire for fairness and equality? The welfare state and the new brands of nationalism are equally alien to the liberal conception of society, for liberalism divorces private interests from public regulation. Sociology has offered a more powerful image of a society that is driven both by cultural aspirations and by social conflicts, which in combination produce social actors and movements; but liberalism strives to ignore such models of action and analysis.

Liberal thought paved the way for democracy by criticizing autocratic power, but it also opposed and fought democracy until such time as the rise of totalitarianism reconciled liberal and democratic thought, which have in fact always been mutually independent throughout their changing relationship. After the French revolution, liberal thought took on an increasingly conservative tone, as we can see from Tocqueville's violent response to the revolutionary *journées* of 1848. Taine expressed similar views in a more systematic way. So too did Mosca, at first harshly and later apparently in more moderate terms: In the American translation of *Elementi di scienza politica* (Mosca 1939 [orig. ed. 1896]), "political class" became "the ruling class," and much of the expanded edition of 1923 was devoted to an analysis of this class. The divorce between the political and the economic creates a social barrier between those who are fit to rule and those who are unfit to do so. That barrier may well have seemed almost insurmountable in Mosca's native southern Italy; it was likewise very high in both Great Britain and France but less visible in the United States, even though Harvard and Yale had long supplied that country with most of its leaders. Such liberal rationalism is an extension of the Machiavellian tradition, as it gives the problem of governability priority over the problem of representativity.

In the late nineteenth century, however, trade and the law no longer seemed to be the principles governing the formation of the social groupings that Mosca described as social types; nationalism had taken their place. Modes of thought that prioritize the unity of social groups rather than their internal relations become nationalistic all the more readily when they are converted to the idea of class struggle—a social rather than a political idea. The prioritization of the political has at times been an expression of the spirit of freedom; the rise of nationalism, however, is adequate proof that it usually gives birth to authoritarian regimes because it rejects divisiveness in the name of unity.

In the early twentieth century, the explosion of revolutionary movements that led to revolution in Russia and Hungary, to attempts to create a revolutionary government in Germany, and to the great social crisis of 1920 that helped to spark the fascist reaction in Italy, transformed this liberal Machiavellianism into a more reactionary brand. Like Michels, Mosca, whose counterrevolutionary leanings are rightly stressed by Norberto Bobbio, supported Mussolini's fascism, but he supported it as a liberal. The young Mosca accepted Spencer's crude dichotomization of military and industrial societies and referred to them as feudal and bureaucratic, respectively; but in his maturity, Mosca looked more favorably on a combination of democracy and liberalism. His position during those years seemed moderate but was in fact antidemocratic, if only in that he defined democracy as a regime in which anyone could become part of the ruling elite; for when the social origins of rulers define democracy, then democracy is as far as it can be from government by the people. Like many liberals from Rousseau on, Mosca found the notion of a regime in which the majority governed and the minority obeyed contradictory.

The democratic idea emerged only after France adopted universal suffrage in 1848, thus mending the political and social rift that threatened to bifurcate society between active and passive citizens and linking political institutions to popular demands. In their battle against dominant interests, popular forces now resorted to the same technical and economic rationality that had so often been used as an argument against them. The labor movement provided democracy with a solid foundation; even though socialist ideology later helped to establish antidemocratic dictatorships, the labor movement itself did not. Democratic thought is as far removed from liberal ideology today as it is from revolutionary ideology.

In the contemporary world, dominated as it is on the one hand by the welfare state and on the other by nationalist or authoritarian regimes, liberal thought can no longer be content with a negative conception of liberty. At this point, we will look to Isaiah Berlin, whose name is associated with the theory that there are two contrasting conceptions of liberty. Berlin asserted that unlike the world of the rationalist Enlightenment, the modern world no longer believed in eternal truths or a timeless human nature. He claimed that systematic rationalism was the source of the utopias that always posed such a threat to democracy. Utopias were common in Greece and in the modern world's classical period, and they took on new forms with the historicist rationalism of Hegel and Marx; but utopian thinkers of all eras have posited the existence of a perfect and therefore immobile society. Such societies are uchronic as well as utopian; because they are "out of time" as well as "out of place," they afford no space to open political debate.

According to Berlin, the overweening pride of Enlightenment philosophy was swept away by Sturm und Drang, romanticism, and German philosophy from Herder to Fichte. The introduction of a pluralism of values now made it possible to create an open society. It was the appeal to the specificity, the *Eigentümlichkeit* of every culture that allowed a politics of the subject and of its authenticity and creativity to replace the authoritarian rationalist ideals of enlightened despotism. Some may find this starting point paradoxical, as it has so often been argued that rationalism facilitated universal communication, whereas the appeal to cultural specificity trapped everyone in a particular national culture and historical moment, in a *Volksgeist* and a *Zeitgeist;* but Berlin confronted these apparent contradictions directly: How can the modern world found liberty on the basis of cultural pluralism, he asked, and if it does, then how can it avoid lapsing into nationalism, which can take the most extreme forms? The only possible answer to these unavoidable questions is that liberty is threatened by all conceptions that identify individuals with the natural or historical community to which they "belong," as people say, because the role of the state is to liberate nations or classes and therefore to make individuals the slaves of those collectivities or of Rousseau's "general will." Although Berlin stressed the positive role of cultural pluralism, he also condemned the omnipotence of states that identified themselves with a specific community or moment in history. Once we have understood this principle, like Berlin, we can resist the tyranny of the majority and defend the personal subject—a creative, imaginative, and innovatory subject—against the dominant majority opinion and vested interests. We have come a long way from the deceptively clear dichotomy between negative and positive liberty, or *freedom from* and *freedom to*, as the English put it. We would do better to speak of two liberations, of two negative liberties: freedom from the state and freedom from social loyalties. Only in the presence of these freedoms will the appeal to the subject lead to liberty instead of repressive communitarianism.

The winding road to modern freedom, which is distanced from rationalism and thus always vulnerable to attack by nationalism or class ideology, is so difficult to follow that a liberal like Isaiah Berlin is constantly tempted to go back to his starting point in universalist rationalism, which would allow him to give a simple definition to negative liberty, in opposition to the power that speaks in the name of nature or history. His trajectory is, however, more interesting than that. I demonstrate that positive liberty, which can certainly give birth to popular dictatorship, can also be defined in "libertarian" terms as the defense of human rights against society as well as state. The liberty of the moderns is not reducible to a largely illusory individualism. It breaks with the Platonist integration of the individual into the natural and social order and instead promotes the cause of the personal subject by introducing social and cultural pluralism, which may destroy the subject but which is also the precondition for its self-assertion.

The strength of modern liberalism stems mainly from the fact that we live in a century in which democracy has been attacked by totalitarian or authoritarian regimes. Given that those states spoke in the name of cultures, adopted a dirigiste approach to the economy, imposed ideologies, and sometimes even claimed to be the military wing of religions, the defense of democracy implies a rejection of all hegemonic power and, therefore, a recognition of total separation among the various domains of social life, religion, politics, the economy, education, national life, the family, art, and so on. Yet although democratic thought has usually set itself against concentrations of wealth or power, Michael Walzer has argued that the task of redistribution can only be accomplished by a state that is so powerful that it can impose its hegemony on the whole of society. Our principal goal should therefore be to acknowledge and to ensure respect for the autonomy of every sphere of social life, while at the same time attempting to reduce inequality in all those spheres. "No social good X should be distributed to men and women who possess some other good Y merely because they possess Y and without regard to the meaning of X," (Walzer 1983: 20). Thus, in Walzer's view the most effective democratic struggle is one waged to prevent those who have wealth from also having power. This reasoning is predicated on the classic sociological thesis that in modern societies social subsystems become increasingly differentiated as holistic systems disintegrate and the autonomy of the spheres of art, economics, and religion is recognized.

It is, however, difficult to accept this conception, reminiscent as it is of the withering away of the state, an idea put forth by liberals as well as by Marx in the nineteenth century but negated by political experience, especially in democracies. Firstly, the withering away of the state would result in the identification of sphere of the political with that of speech, seduction, and the accumulation of such specifically political resources as votes and political alliances—an image that more closely corresponds to the parliamentary system of the nineteenth century than to the reality of contemporary states. Walzer, in this sense similar to Habermas, regarded politics as a world of argumentation and therefore of rational thought, facilitating the exchange of subjective visions. This conception is based on an excessive separation between the political system and state on the one hand and social actors and social relations on the other. Walzer's analysis, like that of many other liberals, is acceptable only as an analysis of one aspect of democratic political life. There is certainly no democracy in a total or absolute state, nor is there any democracy in the absence of any expression of popular sovereignty and majority rule. To adopt Walzer's own terminology, there can be no democracy unless it is defined as "*the political way* of allocating power" (Walzer 1983: 304). Rather than a specific *techne*, as Plato would have it, politics is thus elevated above particular activities and has a unifying role. Contemporary democracies, for instance, intervene in the distribution of national income by levying taxes and establishing social security systems, aid labor-union organizations, protect minorities, and bring legal standards into line with the demands of public opinion. In a word, they ensure that the various spheres of social life are at least interdependent, if not integrated—which should serve to remind us that the themes of the limitation of power and of citizenship are equally indispensable to democracy's existence.

We should never attempt to make too clear a distinction between liberalism and democracy; democracy is the principal victim of such an artificial separation. Norberto Bobbio rightly argued that "the mutual distrust that has existed between the liberal and socialist political cultures" is becoming a thing of the past (Bobbio 1988: 100). In this book I, too, have attempted to go beyond that dichotomy by defending the liberal political system against authoritarian threats; but I also have argued that social forces should compel the state to make voluntaristic interventions against an economic liberalism that could lead to a growing dualization of society.

4

Representative Political Actors

Democracy cannot exist unless it is representative; and the freedom of the ruled to choose their rulers would be meaningless if the latter were not able to express the demands, reactions, or protests that take shape in "civil society." But under what conditions do political agents represent the interests and projects of social actors?

Social Actors and Political Agents

If interests are multiple and diverse and if, ultimately, all voters have a series of particular demands concerning their professional or family activities, the education of their children, their security, and so on, it is impossible to define a policy that represents the interests of the majority or of a number of important and active minorities. If representativity is to exist, the demands that emanate from very different individuals and sectors of social life must be aggregated. If democracy is to have a truly stable social base, this principle must be taken to extremes, and social demand must be brought into line with political supply. To put it more simply, there must be a correspondence between social categories and political parties. If we depart from this situation and if political parties are coalitions of interest groups, some of them will, even if they are very much in the minority, be able to sway the balance in one direction or another and will thus acquire an influence that is out of all proportion to their objective importance. That is why democracy is strongest when it is based on social conflicts with a general import—for example, what the Western tradition once called the class struggle—and on an acceptance of political liberty. Just as the will to overthrow power by force, to eliminate dominant minorities that are regarded as antisocial, and to assert the triumph of the people reunited leads directly to authoritarian regimes, so the existence of a general conflict among social actors provides the most stable basis for democracy. It was in the country where social classes and their conflicts were most pronounced, namely Great Britain, that democracy achieved its most stable forms. The social democracy of northern Europe was able to bring about

51

the triumph of the democratic spirit because there was an open conflict between a workers' party and bourgeois parties, as the Swedes put it. However, where the state rather than the ruling class was simultaneously the main agent of economic modernization and the agent that perpetuated social hierarchies—as in the Latin countries of Europe and in Latin America—democracy has always been weak and has often been swamped by a more or less revolutionary political action that prioritizes the seizure of power rather than the transformation of the social relations of production.

When the aggregation of social demands takes this extreme form, political debate tends to revolve around a conflict between two parties. These parties are not necessarily defined in class terms, as in the cases we have just mentioned. One may represent the central social and cultural group, and the other a set of minorities made up of immigrants. This was the case in the United States, though it is less so today. In most countries, however, political life has not been simplified to this extent and alliances have to be forged between political forces corresponding to different social categories and political conceptions. Political representation becomes increasingly complex as the state strengthens its hold over social life; the latter becomes fragmented due to its dependence on the unitary state and its limited capacity for autonomous action. According to René Rémond's analysis (Rémond 1982), for instance, France has had three rights and at least two lefts since the Soviet revolution caused the French socialist party to split in 1920, with the majority supporting the Soviet Union and the minority refusing to join the Third International. The electoral system obviously has direct effects on the number of parties. Great Britain, in contrast, remains attached to a simple majority electoral system, in which votes are cast for individual candidates in a single round, because English society since the end of the nineteenth century has been dominated by the conflict between the gentry and the working class.

The second precondition for the representativity of political actors follows from the first. Social categories must be able to organize autonomously at the level of social life or in other words, outside political life. In the Western tradition, this autonomy has been achieved in a highly visible form. In the social democratic tradition, syndicalism led to the formation of labor or socialist parties representing the political arm of trade unions, as is clearly demonstrated by the British Labour Party, in particular, which was controlled by the unions affiliated to the Trade Union Congress. In Sweden, the LO union federation has similar links with the social democratic party. The situation is, or was until recently, little different in Italy and Spain, where union federations have links with specific political parties. In Spain, however, the Unión General de Trabajadores recently came into conflict with the ruling Socialist party (Partido Socialista Obrero Español). In France, the Confédération Générale du Travail has very close links with the Communist party, and members of the Confédération Française Démocratique du Travail are often sympathetic to the Socialist party. Force Ouvrière, which once had close links with the Socialist party, now draws much of its support from

right-wing and far left, militant voters. On the employers' side, professional organizations play an analogous role, but they are stronger because of the more direct
links that exist between members of the government and the most important economic leaders.

If the integration of social demands takes place at the purely political level instead, it is impossible to speak of representative democracy, and we come danger-
ously close to the antithesis of democracy, namely a mass political society. The
links between social life and political life are not always direct; they also involve
mediators, associations, clubs, newspapers and magazines, and intellectual
groups. These mediators influence political choices and at the same time help to
shape party policies in many domains of social life.

Political Representation in Crisis

In many Western countries there has long been talk, increasing in urgency, of the
crisis in political representation that is supposedly responsible for the falling level
of political involvement. Such talk is not unfounded, for the social basis of political life was weakened and dislocated as the West emerged from an industrial society that had been dominated by the conflict between employers and wage earners.
In these countries, the majority of the active population now belongs neither to
the working-class world nor to the world of business, even that of small-scale
craftsmen and shopkeepers. The world of office workers is not simply an extension of the world of factory workers. As a category, middle management has as little in common with wage-earning workers as it has with decisionmakers. Furthermore, mass communications and mass consumption, social mobility and
immigration, a wide variety of social mores and the protection of the environment, are all as characteristic of these societies as is industrialized production. Because it is impossible to base political life on debates and actors that bear little relationship to contemporary reality, political parties have become increasingly
independent of social forces and are reverting to the conception that dominated
the English experience at the time when the Whigs were in competition with the
Tories: that parties should be government teams and voters should be free to
choose between them. In fact, this is not an accurate picture of any existing political system. It is not true that the U.S. Republican and Democratic parties are
merely coalitions that are cobbled together for presidential elections; a significant
part of the electorate that votes for both parties is stable and identifies itself with
particular social and economic choices. It is in France and Italy, perhaps, that the
gap between political parties has narrowed most in recent years; in France, because the need for economic recovery led the Socialist left to adopt an orthodox
liberal policy from 1984 onward and because that policy was not greatly modified
in 1986, not to mention 1993; in Italy, because the Social Democrats and the Socialist party shared power for a long time, and this *consociativismo* bred corruption. The collapse of these two Italian parties has benefited both the former Com-

munist party (PDS) and the far right. Now it is precisely in these countries and in Australia, where the socialist government has adopted a liberal economic policy, that there is the most talk of a crisis in political representation. The explanation is that although there is no clear difference between the policies of the parties of the so-called left and right, public opinion remains acutely aware of the social differences between the two.

The extreme autonomy of political parties may have positive aspects when their social definition has become outdated and corresponds to rhetoric rather than practice, but the principle of party autonomy is more dangerous than it is useful. American democracy has been consolidated now that the Democrats have acquired a clearer social definition; and the heavy defeat suffered by the Socialist party in France will lead to still worse defeats if it does not quickly define more clearly what it sees as the most important social problems and its answers to them.

The necessary dependence of political forces on social demands is not changing, but the nature of social demands is. Parties once represented social classes; they now represent the projects of collective life and sometimes even social movements. The very idea of a social class derived its strength from the identity it established between a social situation and a simultaneously social and political actor. Class action and social relations of production were inseparable on the left, just as liberal ideas and market forces were inseparable on the right. If this "objective" definition of social actors has been undermined, that does not mean we need argue that there is no necessary connection between political choices and the interests or values of social actors who are defined by their position in the balance of power. The "objective" definition of social actors, in contrast, gave political parties a monopoly on the meaning of collective action; parties were the concrete expression of the self-consciousness of social classes. Conversely, when social action is defined as a demand for liberty, the protection of the environment, or the struggle against the "commodification" of every aspect of life, it becomes responsible for its own meaning and may even be transformed into a political party or at the very least, force any party it supports to adopt its priorities.

The collapse of socialism—from Leninist communism to social democracy—resulted primarily from the increasing subordination of the labor movement to a formerly revolutionary party that became the state itself. There can be no representative democracy if social actors are incapable of giving a meaning to their action rather than allowing political parties to define it for them. The difference between democratic thought, or at least the conception of democratic thought outlined here, and French-style Jacobinism, and especially Leninism, now becomes eminently clear. Their general outlook and their historical practices cause us to view Leninism and Jacobinism as antidemocratic forces. Leaving aside the revolutionary Soviet regime, which broke with democracy immediately, the major threat posed by French- and Latin American-style democracy is that political actors may be reduced to a mass—that is, to the status of political resources. They may even be destroyed if social action is subordinated to the political intervention of forces that, at the moment of their triumph, possess the weapons of power and unchallenged omnipotence.

Serious as they may be, these criticisms should not, as we have already said, lead us to mistakenly see the so-called French type of democracy as "exceptional" or marginal. This type of democracy would not have had the historical importance it has had if it did not have positive social implications as well as dangerous political effects. Its appeal to the people combined democratic action with a direct attack on social inequalities and capitalist power. The egalitarian spirit of French republicans has inspired the public school system that attempted to extend education to all children and that improved the social mobility of poor children. Governments inspired by this conception of democracy subordinated their action to the interests of the nation, understood not only as a political notion but also as a social one, with universal aspirations under the banner of liberty, equality, and fraternity. Even if we do criticize the ideology of both the Third Republic and national-popular regimes in Latin America on the grounds that they did not really attack social barriers and inequalities, we cannot argue that the French model of democracy has no positive value. It would be more accurate to say that in both Latin America and France it promoted the interests of a middle class of civil servants and social categories dependent on the state rather than those of the people or the workers, whom it treated with almost as much contempt or hostility as the old ruling elites. Yet cultural barriers between classes were still higher in Great Britain than in France. For a long time, English society was dominated by an aristocracy that had not been eliminated by a revolution. Each type of democracy has its strong points and its weak elements, and there is no justification for arguing that only one type corresponds to the nature of democracy in general.

Political Corruption

What happens when political actors are not subject to the demands of social actors and thus cease to be representative? The resultant loss of balance may lead political actors to take the side of the state and to destroy the first precondition for the existence of democracy, the limitation of state power. If, however, that situation does not arise, political society may free itself from its ties with both civil society and state, with the expansion of its own power being its only goal. In Italy, this situation is known as *partitocrazia*. Italians have denounced its ravages in terms that have been broadly echoed by public opinion in many European countries and a good number of Latin American countries, from Peru to Brazil and Argentina.

Public opinion in these countries speaks more plainly of *corruption*—a more accurate term, if we accept that democracy must be representative and therefore that political forces, and parties in particular, must serve social interests rather than their own. Corruption is widespread in Italy, exists on a more limited scale in other European countries, and is common in many non-European countries, from Japan to the United States, from Algeria to Venezuela. We will not dwell here on the personal corruption of political leaders. The form of corruption that poses the greatest threat to democracy is the corruption that has allowed political parties to accumulate such vast resources, so independently of the voluntary contributions made by their members that they can choose who will be on the ballots and ensure that a number of them will win elections. This makes a mockery of the principle that the ruled are free to choose their rulers. How can we speak of democracy when the outcome of elections is decided by "rotten boroughs," as in nineteenth-century England, or by the distribution of money in the rural constituencies of Japan? How can we speak of democracy when Italian parties take a major cut on most of the contracts that are signed by publicly owned companies? In April 1993, large numbers of Italians responded to Mario Segni's call for demonstrations against the system that was turning their country into a *tangentopoli*, or a land of bribes. Such gestures in defense of democracy cannot in themselves bring about the recomposition of a perverted political life, but they do make it possible to build political coalitions that offer voters a real choice.

No one denies that there can be no democracy without parties or without truly political actors. However, *partitocrazia* destroys democracy by taking away its representativity, and it leads either to chaos or to the de facto dominance of the most powerful economic groups until such time as a dictator intervenes. The threat is greatest when a country is emerging from industrial society and when its social actors become fragmented and weakened. At this difficult time, it is very tempting to accept a purely institutional conception of democracy and to reduce it to no more than an open political market. The outcome is a debased democracy. Protests against the party system, on the other hand, do have the virtue of reminding us that institutions must be representative if they are to be free. All too often they are not.

Social Movements and Democracy

Representativity also presupposes, however, that social demands are truly representable, or in other words that they respect the rules of the political game and the decisions of the majority. Many collective actions are not representable in this way. I refer to demands that meet with no response within the political system either because the system has been restricted, paralyzed, or crushed by an authoritarian state or because the demands in question are not negotiable but simply a way of mobilizing forces with a view to overthrowing the institutional order. The two situations and the ideologies that interpret them are very different: in the first case, collective mobilizations appear to be a residue that institutions cannot handle; in the second, collective mobilizations are manifestations of a radical or revolutionary upsurge against institutions protecting ruling interests and of the conviction that violence alone can overthrow them. Neither type of collective action is democratic in inspiration. This negative conclusion should help us make a clear distinction between these types of collective action and social movements, defined in the strict sense of the term as collective actions that attempt to modify the social mode of utilizing important resources and *cultural* orientations that are accepted in the society under consideration. An example of the latter is the labor movement, which fought capitalism in the name of progress and production. According to this definition, a social movement must have a political program that appeals to general principles as well as particular interests. This was as true of the labor movement as it was of national liberation movements, women's movements, ecological movements, movements that rebelled against the ancien régime, and religiously inspired social movements. We cannot describe as a social movement the nonnegotiable residue of demands or the element of rejection that is present whenever social pressure is exerted. In such cases, the collective action is no longer defined by its orientations but merely by the limited extent to which institutions can handle conflicts in a given situation. Similarly, a collective action defined by a break with the established order cannot define a political actor. Such actions define a situation in military terms. They speak of civil war, crisis, or arbitrary rule, and therefore inevitably generate a strategy for the seizure of power; and the social objective of that seizure of power is the creation of a homogeneous society, from which enemies and traitors will be excluded. Defining a situation and an action as revolutionary inevitably leads to the creation of an authoritarian power.

Far from being antithetical, social movements and democracy are, in contrast, indissociable. On the one hand, if a political system regards social movements simply as violent expressions of demands that cannot possibly be satisfied, it ceases to be representative and loses the trust of the electorate. This is happening in many countries, and not only the European countries, where the so-called demands of the international situation and the need for austerity lead to the rejection of most demands on the grounds that they are unrealistic and pose a threat to jobs or national security. A government that tries to legitimize its actions in terms of the constraints of the system loses its democratic character, even if it remains tolerant and liberal. On the other hand, a social movement can exist only if a collective action has social objectives, or in other words, recognizes that society has general interests or values. In other words, a social movement can exist only if collective action does not reduce political life to a confrontation between camps or classes, even though it organizes and extends conflicts. Social movements can only emerge in democratic societies, in which freedom of political choice obliges every social actor simultaneously to pursue the common good and to defend particular interests. This is why the greatest social movements have constantly used universalist themes that establish a link between a social actor and a political program from the outset. Such themes include liberty, equality, human rights, justice, and solidarity.

The link between the notion of a social movement and democracy and the defense of basic human rights becomes even clearer if we contrast it with the notion of class struggle. The notion of class struggle implies a reference to historical necessity or to the triumph of reason, with a popular uprising against irrational domination as its agent. This leads directly to revolutionary action rather than to democratic institutions. When the notion of a class struggle gives way to that of a social movement, it is a sign that a sociology of the actor, or even of the historical subject, is replacing a theory of history, that a sociology of liberty is replacing a sociology of necessity. For a social movement is always based on the liberation of a social actor, and not on the creation of an ideal or "natural" society. Nor does it suggest that we have reached the end of human history. As I demonstrated in my *La Conscience ouvrière* (Touraine 1966), working-class action reached its apotheosis and formed a social movement when it defended the autonomy of workers in the face of managerial rationalization. Those who believe in the class struggle speak of the contradictions of capitalism and of proletarianization and want to destroy what is destructive, or to negate the negation. In order to do that, they call for the seizure of state power. A social movement, in constrast, is civil and is an affirmation rather than a critique or a negation. That is why it can inspire reflection and discussion and lead to the deliberate reconstruction of a society based on the principles of justice, liberty, and respect for human beings—the very principles on which democracy is based.

A clear distinction must be made between the idea of a social movement and the idea of violence. Violence is antithetical to both democracy and social movements, but social relations are profoundly marked by violence because political power, like social dominance, is never completely governed by institutional rules. Political power has a capacity for arbitrary decisionmaking that cannot be completely suppressed. *Raison d'état*, the royal prerogative, the right of grace, favoritism, personal responsibility, and executive decision, are all attributes of a head of state or the head of a company, and they can, depending on the circumstances, be either positive or negative. Anyone who holds power is only partly involved in a system of social and political negotiations; such a person is also acting on a market or with reference to other states. It is because the state is not reducible to the political system and because a company is not reducible to collective bargaining that there is inevitably a violent dimension to demands emanating from dominated categories or categories that have been excluded from power. The characteristic feature of democracy is, however, that it reduces violence, just as it limits absolute power. Political violence becomes inevitable when a society is so locked into internal negotiations that it is quickly paralyzed by the search for a compromise that is rendered impossible by the absence of external constraints. Conversely, a direct confrontation between the violence of the rulers and the violence of the ruled destroys democracy, even if it results in compromises and truces; it also destroys social movements by trapping them in a strategy that forces them to reject any reference to a common good.

Overrationalized Democracies

Democracy is a system of political mediations between state and social actors, and not a rational way of managing society. Liberal thought is satisfied with the latter definition, the attractions of which are obvious given that we live in a posttotalitarian period in which there are still many authoritarian regimes. Such a restricted definition of democracy, however, is itself a threat to democracy. The wealthiest societies seem to have become incapable of analyzing and handling their most obvious problems, as they are no longer willing to speak of structural conflicts between antithetical interests or ideas. The dominant image of social life is one of an immense mainstream, of a huge middle-class majority that excludes marginal groups—the victims of unemployment and their own lack of qualifications—and rejects particular minorities and people living their personal crises. Society is seen as a marathon: in the center, a pack that runs faster and faster; in the lead, the stars whom the crowds have come to see; in the rear, those who, being badly nourished and badly equipped or having pulled muscles or suffered heart attacks, are out of the race. The dominant social model, which has triumphed in Latin America, postcommunist Europe, and the affluent West, externalizes and isolates violence and conflict. Our social imaginary abounds in criminal violence and aggressive sexuality, which are rejected by a majority that craves security and comfort. We have reverted to the image that bourgeois society had of itself in the early nineteenth century, when it felt threatened by the "dangerous classes" because it could not accept the demands of the "working classes." Democracy is weakened if we too drastically reduce the gravity of the problems it is mandated to address—if we indulge, for example, in humanitarian expressions when we should have intervened directly, as in Bosnia, in order to halt policies that are destroying the foundations of democracy.

We are so used to speaking of minorities, marginality, and even exclusion, that we forget that such terms help to promote an image of a society in which there are no basic conflicts. Democracy is thus reduced to the management of relations between weak and unfocussed social demands and technological or economic requirements that are impossible to resist if we wish to remain competitive.

Our democratic liberties are being debased because they are no longer a way of dealing with acute social problems. This self-critical comment might prove useful if it brings grist to the democratic mill and encourages us to identify the most serious conflicts in our society and to understand the nature of the social movements that political parties must eventually address. If the democratic idea means anything to us, how can we be satisfied with a rich, open, and diverse society that excludes from public space the very demands that may prove to be the most important of our day? In the same way, the nineteenth-century European debates between conservatives and liberals, secularists and catholics, or monarchists and republicans weakened democracy because they were unrelated to the demands of the workers and to early manifestations of women's demands.

During this difficult period, the most urgent task—for intellectuals even more than politicians—is to demonstrate that in a democratic culture, new social and cultural issues are at stake. The association of social movements and democracy is a new theme. Until very recently it was contemptuously rejected by agents of the dictatorship of the proletariat, authoritarian nationalists, and supporters of revolutionary war, as well as by those who believed that economic growth would do more than political debates and social demands to promote social integration.

The most urgent problem is to channel into the political system the demands, protests, and utopias that might make our society more aware of its orientations and its conflicts. Our political systems today are suffering from an almost universal absence of internal conflict, though they are surrounded by belts of violence. Those within the system think peace has been achieved because internal demands have subsided into external threats and because they are more concerned with law and order than justice, with adaptation than equality. Democracy is capable of defending itself only if it can improve its capacity to reduce injustice and violence.

Democracy and the People

A democratic government must represent the interests of the majority. This is primarily because democracy must be an expression of "the most numerous classes" and because it must be defined by its links with popular categories. Those categories are not only the "most numerous"; they are also more dependent than others on the decisions taken by elites. It is essential to state that there is a link between democracy and the people, if we are to curb attempts to define democracy without reference to representativity or purely in terms of the freedom to choose our rulers. If we do not do so, there is a danger that democracy will be reduced to a contest between ruling teams that are all part of the ruling elite, otherwise known as the *sanior pars*. The democratic idea is in fact never socially neutral. One of the first great democratic debates was that held by the Estates General of France in 1789, which ended with the decision that votes should be cast by individuals and not orders. When it takes place democratically, the transition from hierarchical and holistic societies to individualistic societies works to the advantage of those who do not have access to material or spiritual wealth or power. The idea of the *sanior pars* and the related idea of the tyranny of the majority, which were so central to debates about the U.S. constitution and to liberal interpretations of the French revolution, are in principle opposed to the democratic spirit. These ideas soon came to be identified with a regime in which the right to vote was conditional on the ownership of property, but they were later swept aside by the implications of universal suffrage. No one would now describe as democratic a regime that restricted universal suffrage; we can no longer retrospectively accept a restrictive definition of the electorate that excludes women. That definition necessarily marked the entire political workings of our societies as nondemocratic by creating a sharp demarcation between public and private life: Public life was inhibited by its limitation to men, while women were confined to the world of culture and of the shaping of personalities—a world into which democracy was not supposed to penetrate. Today we might likewise question the exclusion of young people under the age of eighteen. In various domains of consumption, such as the cinema, music, television, or clothes, they account for a large share of the market, and their exclusion from political life thus gives our public life a nondemocratic character. It is of course difficult to estimate the extent to which public life is nondemocratic because the excluded have not become political actors. Women have succeeded in entering public life only to a limited extent; young people have yet to do so. In countries like those of Mediterranean Europe, where the rate of unemployment is much higher among young people than in society as a whole, it is inconceivable that giving youth the vote at the age of fifteen or sixteen would not have an effect on the economic policies that were adopted.

It is by resisting social inequalities in the name of a principle of equality that democracy acquires a "popular" tonality. Abolishing social hierarchies—which often claim to be natural—in the name of equal rights does more than create a political realm distinct from the social realm; it also transforms the social realm, because equal rights would be no more than a hazy notion if they did not result in pressure for actual equality or for "a certain equality of condition," as Jean-Jacques Rousseau put it.

These points are an essential reminder that democracy is not simply a matter of procedures. They explain much of the political history of the old continent and of other parts of the world, and to a lesser extent of the United States, a country founded on the idea of equality and the absence of any feudal and monarchical heritage.

We must, however, take our analysis a step further and ask ourselves whether or not political ideas and forces that appeal to the people are always democratic, and we must do so in more specifically political terms. As we know, the answer to this question has to be "no." Democracy has often been destroyed in the name of the left, the people, the working class, and even democracy itself. The political left in Europe and Latin America has been profoundly divided, even to the point of open violence, by debates about democracy. For a long time and in many countries, the word "democracy" was anathema. There was talk of bourgeois or formal democracy. Communist parties struggled to establish the dictatorship of the proletariat, while the guerrillas of Latin America and Africa rejected mass action and concentrated their efforts not on mobilizing the people or even on creating a Leninist-inspired vanguard party, but on a direct attack on the state, which they saw as the weakest link in the chain of imperialist domination. In Europe, Italian- or German-style urban guerrillas adopted the same analysis and tried to terrorize leaders so as to weaken them and unleash the hypothethical revolutionary will of the masses. The left is democratic only if it believes in endogenous development and relates modernization to social and political class relations, whether in Marxist, social democratic, or liberal terms. As Lenin himself reminded us, only when the institutional road to change is blocked does revolutionary violence become necessary. Similarly, when the "national bourgeoisie" is weak, industrialization is overseen by a Bismarckian, authoritarian state. In both cases, the key question is whether the recourse to violence is a detour on the road to democracy or whether what was once a means is to become an end in itself, with economic moderniza- tion serving to supply the resources needed to build absolute power. To pursue the above-mentioned examples, post–Bismarckian Germany did achieve endoge- nous growth and democracy, at least for awhile; the Soviet regime never at- tempted to do so, at least not until Gorbachev's perestroika.

The appeal to the people ceases to be democratic and becomes antidemocratic whenever it makes the state—a voluntaristic agent of historical change—more important than social actors and their relations, whether the latter be conflictual, negotiated, or cooperative. The same analysis applies to left and right alike. The right has often evoked the threat of revolution in order to perpetuate dictator- ships. The appeal to the people has also been used against democracy to perpetu- ate or reestablish embattled social hierarchies and forces promoting cultural inte- gration or to launch an authoritarian process of modernization. Salazar, Franco, and Pétain exemplify the first tendency; the *Científicos* of Porfirio Díaz's Mexico, South Korea, and the Brazil of the *Estado Novo* and military dictatorship the sec- ond. All authoritarian regimes invoke their country's lack of maturity, or the in- ternal and external threats that loom over it. They all claim that only the state can save the country from chaos or invasion. Authoritarian regimes thus reveal the extent to which democracy is inseparable from the structuration, and therefore the representativity, of social interests. Authoritarian regimes have always invoked the disorganization of social actors, the weakness of labor unions, the corruption of parties or the splits within them, the gravity of economic crises, or the threat of foreign invasion in order to justify their own actions. Their existence and their ac- tions are an implicit demonstration of the strong link between democracy and the existence of constituted social actors. In Europe, too, democracy has been enfee- bled or destroyed whenever debates about social reproduction have been more central than struggles over the social relations of production. Marx saw the pri- macy given to the political, or in other words relations with the state, as the major sickness of postrevolutionary French political life, and it became worse with 1848 and the Paris Commune. We now refer to this exclusive preoccupation with poli- tics as Jacobinism. It is the source of the weaknesses of French democracy, which has often been overthrown by plebiscitary regimes and which would have been overthrown once more in recent times, had not General de Gaulle been such a sound democrat. Those who fight over religion and education, the monarchy and the republic, or in other words the overall orientations of society and culture, dream of a homogenizing model. Their ultimate desire is to cleanse society—to adopt the horrible phrase coined by Milošević, who suited action to words with arson, bloodshed, and rape. The political system is a way of liaising between civil society and state. If the pendulum swings toward the state, then the system becomes authoritarian, no matter whether it takes a bureaucratic, repressive, or military form; if the pendulum swings toward civil society, the political system is democratic, but it may lose its ability to control the state. If that happens, it may provoke an antidemocratic, oligarchic, technocratic, or militaristic backlash on the part of the state. Democracy demands both freedom of political choice and leaders who represent the interests of the majority. It is pointless and dangerous to give priority to one or another of these elements. In the past, those who claimed that popular power emanated from a people or nation had to be reminded that there is no democracy without political pluralism and free elections. In many countries today, the weakness of the links between social actors and political agents should be cause for concern. There are two main reasons for this weakness: either social demands are muddled and poorly aggregated, as is the case in the many countries that are living through an accelerated transition from one society to another; or government and public opinion are preoccupied with international rather than social problems. In both the South and the East, many authoritarian regimes have taken power in the name of struggle against the "imperialist camp." Western democratic countries have to some extent drifted into a similar authoritarianism: Nationalism, colonial conquests, the preservation of empire, or the quest for hegemony have at times posed an antidemocratic threat to Western countries, especially Great Britain, the United States, and France. The antidemocratic tendency was of course limited, even during France's wars in Indochina and Algeria or the U.S. war in Vietnam; but it throws into relief the importance of the link between political power and the social demands of the majority.

The existence of strong links between social actors and political actors and of socially representative rulers allows democracy to develop fully—provided, of course, that representativity goes hand in hand with the limitation of powers and a sense of citizenship. Democracy is never reducible to the victory of one social or political camp, much less to the triumph of a class.

Citizenship

There can be no democracy without a sense of belonging to a political collectivity. In most cases, the collectivity is a nation, but it could also be a township, a region, or a federation such as the body into which the European Union seems to be evolving. Democracy is based on the responsibility of the citizens of a country. If those citizens do not feel responsible for their government because it exercises its power in a territorial space that seems to them artificial or foreign, their leaders cannot be representative and the ruled cannot be free to choose their rulers.

Citizenship and Community

The term "citizenship" refers directly to the nation-state. We can, however, give it a more general meaning, as did Michael Walzer when he wrote of the right to membership, of belonging to a community (Walzer 1983). Irrespective of whether the community in question is a territorial or a professional one, membership determines the formation of democratic demands. Membership in a community is defined in terms of rights and guarantees and involves a recognition of the differences between those who belong and those who do not. It is not in itself democratic; there is nothing democratic about a soldier's experience of membership in an army or a Toyota worker's awareness of being part of the company. At the same time, however, membership is not dependency, for it is defined in terms of rights. Membership in a community is one of the necessary preconditions for democracy.

There are two complementary aspects to the sense of belonging. The sense of being a citizen, which emerged during the French revolution, was essentially connected with the will to escape servitude during the ancien régime. The sense of belonging to a community goes hand in hand with acknowledgment of the need to limit power, for an absolute power uses individuals and collectivities as resources and instruments and not as aggregates that have a managerial autonomy and a collective personality; membership in a community is the defensive face of democratic consciousness, helping to free the individual from social and political domination. That is why there was such a close connection between membership in a national community and the creation of free institutions in the United States, Great Britain, and France; the idea of community membership was closely associated in those countries with the democratic spirit.

Many countries have yet to build their national unity because differences between ethnic groups, religious groups, or regions are more important to people than their membership in a single national community. Even in countries with a high level of national integration, individuals may in certain situations identify more strongly with particular collectivities or minorities than with the nation. The common feature in both cases is that individuals are defined by what they are rather than by their conception of collective life. The recognition of minorities within a democratic society is desirable, provided that those minorities accept majority rule and are not entirely absorbed in asserting and defending their identity. A radical multiculturalism, as it exists in particular in the United States, eventually destroys membership in political society and the nation. How can democracy be preserved if African Americans, Native Americans, and women define themselves primarily in terms of their being and see institutions merely as instruments promoting the interests of an elite or, alternatively, their own interests? This cultural leftism takes us back to the divisive tactics of political leftism: "Election, treason!"—as the Maoists and Trotskyists used to say in 1968. In France, that slogan was merely an expression of the leftist fear of a huge conservative majority; but although it had only a marginal effect in French and U.S. politics, in Germany and Italy it did lead some to engage in terrorist action. In all these cases, the break with a majority that was seen as alienated and manipulated posed a threat to democracy, which presupposes a certain trust in majority votes. Democracy is not compatible with the rejection of minorities. Nor is it compatible with the minorities' rejection of the majority or with the assertion of countercultures and alternative societies that do not define themselves in terms of their conflictual position within society but in terms of their rejection of a society they regard as the discourse of domination. The Jacobin conception of citizenship and the extreme multiculturalism that rejects all forms of citizenship threaten democracy with equal force. For there can be no democracy unless we recognize the existence of a political field where social conflicts can find expression and where decisions taken by a majority vote are accepted as legitimate by society as a whole. Although democracy is based on the idea of social conflict, it is incompatible with a radical critique of society as a whole, be it extreme multiculturalism or *foquismo,* which in the name of an extreme theory of dependency rejected all mass social action in favor of violence directed against the pseudo–nation-state that it saw as an agent of imperialism.

The Communitarian State Versus Democracy

Modern democracy is closely associated with the nation-state. Social democracy and industrial democracy were defined by the nation-state's intervention in eco-

nomic life. In France and the United States, the birth of democracy was closely associated, or even identified, with the assertion of the nation and of its independence and liberty. Yet modern democracy has also been threatened and sometimes destroyed by nationalism. It is therefore not enough to recall that
democracy presupposes the existence of a unified political space, be it polis or nation-state. Democracy is bound up with one conception of the nation-state and
opposed to others. When the state defines itself as the expression of a collective
being that is political, social, and cultural—the nation, the people, or worse still, a
god or a principle—and claims that the people and the nation are its privileged
agents and therefore have a vocation to defend it, then there is no room left for
democracy, even if the economic context does allow for the preservation of certain public liberties. Democracy is based on the free creation of a political realm,
the sovereignty of the people, and therefore a political freedom of choice that exists independently of any cultural heritage. Democratization transforms a community into a society governed by laws, and the state into both a representative of
society and a power that is limited by basic rights. The opposite conception,
which we might call popular or *völkisch* (the word the Nazis used to describe their
regime), imposes the idea of a basic unity that exists over and above any possible
choice and it thus founds a nationalism that is incompatible with democracy. Instead of establishing a direct link between people and prince, democracy transforms the people into citizens and the prince into a magistrate, to adopt
Rousseau's terminology. If we describe this state as republican, the republic is an
indispensable component of democracy, even though it can turn against democracy, subordinating society to political power and thus establishing republican authoritarianism. The latter's ultimate result, from the French revolution to the cultural revolution in China, has always been terror. The prerequisite for citizenship
is not an all-powerful, republican state but the existence of a national society, or
in other words, close links between civil society, political system, and state. The
road to political modernity was paved by the abolition of absolute monarchy in
Great Britain and heralded by many texts and deeds that are still of fundamental
importance—the U.S. Declaration of Independence and Constitution and the
French Declaration of the Rights of Man and Citizen, as well as other decisive acts
such as the transformation of the Estates General of France into a National Assembly and the oath of the Jeu de Paume. In different forms in Great Britain, the
United States, and France, political society asserted that its legitimacy derived
from itself and from the sovereignty of the people instead of from a god, tradition, or a race.

   This trend, which has spread to many parts of the globe and whose most lucid
representative in the twentieth century was Tomáš Masaryk, founder of the
Czechoslovak republic, has always been opposed by the popular-nationalist tradition mentioned earlier. At times the trend has been associated with national liberation movements, but they have not always been democratic: Some were inspired

by the will to achieve popular sovereignty and to create a free society; but some were associated, often simultaneously, with a struggle against foreign domination in the name of a territory, language, history, or religion. Reference to a historical being does not lead to democracy; and revolutions born of national liberation movements have almost always split as the democratic tendency comes into conflict with the tendency that leads to popular or nationalist dictatorship. The meaning of democracy is certainly not reducible to the peaceful workings of societies experiencing endogenous development or becoming wealthy because of their technological superiority and their dominance over the rest of the world. Democracy is also present in revolutionary situations; but its presence can be recognized only if we make it quite clear that the subordination of political action to a nonpolitical principle or a metapolitical principle such as a god, land, language, or race, is incompatible with democracy. Democracy is neither black nor white, neither Christian nor Islamic. All democracies privilege freedom of political choice over the "natural" categories of social life. That is the ultimate meaning of democracy: the freedom of the ruled to choose their rulers.

We must, as liberals insist, clearly distinguish between the political society that gives birth to democracy and the prophetic state that destroys democracy. We must fight those who speak only of the sovereignty of the people and who transform it into a principle as absolute as God or race, turning society or the general will into a collective consciousness that exists over and above individual consciousnesses. At best, they will take us back to the liberty of the ancients, which is based on the subordination of the individual to the polis and its civic religion.

The idea of citizenship proclaims that everyone has political responsibilities and thus defends the voluntary organization of social life against the nonpolitical logic (which is claimed by some to be "natural") of the market or the national interest. When defined in this way, citizenship can no longer be identified with the national consciousness, which, as we have seen, has both negative and positive effects on the democratic spirit. Citizenship is not synonymous with nationality, even though the two are legally indissociable in certain countries. Nationality means membership in a nation-state, whereas citizenship confers the right to participate, either directly or indirectly, in the management of society. Nationality creates a community of duty; citizenship confers rights. The idea of the nation-state was liberating so long as it meant that the state and individual social and cultural actors were united within a free political society, that is, within a self-instituting nation; but it became a threat to democracy when the state came to be seen as the sole guardian of the interests of society and as therefore having boundless legislative powers. When political society is completely divorced from civil society, there is a great danger that society will be subordinated to the state. When that happens, political society cannot but merge with the state. Social actors then become subordinate to the state, and even politicians claim that they are the prisoners of social particularism and special interests.

Democracy must, therefore, always be social; universal human rights become effective when they are concretely defended in particular situations and in the face of forces of domination that are defined in equally concrete terms. In France, the democratic spirit was forged in the struggle against the ancien régime. Similarly, the English and Spanish colonies in America won their independence in the face of the economic and political dominance of the metropolis. The labor movement won recognition of social rights because it established a close connection between class consciousness and the struggle against social domination on the one hand and the defense of general principles such as freedom and justice on the other. Those rights were at once particular in terms of their content and universal in terms of their principles.

The British tradition has from the very beginning, particularly from the revolution of 1688 onward, defended the representation of particular interests, but Britain was very slow to extend the right to vote; not until 1884 did all adult males gain that right. Democracy is inconceivable unless the absolute assertion of human rights characteristic of the American and French examples is combined with an English-style defense of legitimate particular interests. This means that we must reject the elitist, property-owning democracy of the Whigs and Guizot, but also that we must refuse to identify democracy with the republican state. Just as the existence of a national consciousness can reinforce democratic action, so democratic action presupposes that actual social relations can be transformed by defending universal human rights and mobilizing actual social groups against dependency and injustice. The call to defend the republican state, which is heard with particular force in France, often comes into conflict with the democratic spirit because it promotes the ascendancy of the state and its social supports over social actors, be they rulers or ruled, innovators or those excluded.

The Decline of the Nation-State in Europe

The countries of western Europe are losing much of their sovereignty to an emerging federal European state. This trend is weakening their national consciousness and threatens to destroy the universalist element that made the republican idea so great. Yet many people think that on the contrary, the weakening of the nation-state in Europe may give political society and civil society still greater autonomy. The real danger is in fact that a globalized world market might become divorced from introverted local communities. A better alternative would be to combine a European state with the attributes of sovereignty—a currency, the ability to make war or peace, and the responsibility for macroeconomic policy—with a highly diversified social life and to strengthen the national political systems that implement social policies ranging from social security to education, from justice to national and regional development, the integration of immigrants, and the protection of minorities. I hope someday to become a European national while remaining a French citizen.

The weakening of the European nation-state demonstrates the need to separate things that have all too often been confused. State and society have merged into the idea of the republic. The fact that we live in a less and less republican situation, in which the nation-state has less and less sovereignty, does not mean that we cannot build a democratic society. On the contrary, the crisis affecting the idea of nationality may encourage a new notion of citizenship. We can already see what this might mean, as nationals from other countries in the European Community can now vote in elections in their country of residence if they have been living there for a certain period of time. There is no reason why all countries in Europe should not follow the example of those that have granted immigrants the right to vote at least in local elections, no matter where they come from and provided that they have been living in Europe for a certain number of years. Stressing the positive aspects of its decline does not mean that we have to forget the historical greatness of the nation-state. What the extreme supporters of republican unity forget is that there has never been a perfect match between state and society. For a long time a centralized state coexisted with local societies. Roads and long-distance networks of communication crisscrossed regions that were affected by wars, brigandry, epidemics, and feudal taxation and dues. They were relatively isolated and small-scale communities, and both information and regulations were slow to penetrate them. Such stimuli and constraints remained relatively external to societies and cultures geared toward the reproduction of a traditional order rather than the production of change. This equilibrium began to break down from the late nineteenth century onward. Its breakdown accelerated with the two world wars, and it was at that point that the idea of a homogeneous and highly integrated national society emerged. As Dominique Schnapper has pointed out practice was always out of step with the discourse of national integration, which is so pronounced in France (Schnapper 1991). That discourse is, however, taking on an increasingly nationalist form throughout the world and has less and less to do with the open theme of citizenship. Today, the great danger is that of an enforced correspondence between state, culture, and society. Both citizenship and democracy cease to exist when minorities are destroyed; that is why the idea of citizenship is so indispensable to democratic thought. The idea of citizenship is based on the separation of civil society and political society, which guarantees that all citizens of a country have the same legal and political rights, regardless of their social, religious, or ethnic background.

The increasing distance between economic exchanges and cultural communities may strengthen democracy, but it may also lead to the complete fragmentation of national societies. That nightmare has become a reality in many parts of the world and even in the heart of Europe, where ethnic cleansing has been imposed in parts of Croatia, Bosnia, and to a lesser extent other parts of the former Yugoslavia. The reduction of society to the status of a marketplace and its subordination to the unifying and homogenizing dream of one state are antithetical to democracy. The latter tendency takes us back to the principle of religious territoriality that dominated Europe from Catholic Isabella's expulsion of the Jews and destruction of Arab civilization to Louis XIV's revocation of the Edict of Nantes in 1685 and the massacre, deportation, and internal and external exile of French protestants, especially in the Cévennes.

There is little point in thinking about democracy today unless we do so in order to defend it against its most dangerous enemies: the obsession with national, ethnic, or religious identity on the one hand and a craven surrender to the economic forces that mold mass consumerism on the other.

The nation-state has often been identified with the republic and with democracy. This was particularly true in the United States and France and, more recently, in Italy, where the meeting between Garibaldi and Victor Emmanuel symbolized the alliance between nationbuilding and the democratic revolutionary spirit. However, the identification between the two was more ideological than real, and nation-states have just as often, from Richelieu to Boumedienne, been built in an antidemocratic spirit. Democracy's twofold struggle against the totalitarian state and the colonization of the planet by the world market must now be led by social actors. It must be inspired by their ability to organize themselves and to defend public and private liberties. The theme of citizenship means the free and voluntary construction of a social organization that can reconcile the unity of the law with the diversity of interests and respect for basic rights. Rather than identifying society with the nation, as during the headiest moments of the American war of independence or the French revolution, the idea of citizenship gives the idea of democracy a concrete meaning: the construction of a truly political space that belongs neither to the state nor to the market.

Three in One

Democracy is not simply the sum of the three principles we have so far analyzed; nor are those principles the attributes of a type of government whose general nature can be defined at a higher level of abstraction. To fully understand democracy, we must examine the relationship among the limitation of state power, representative political leaders, and citizenship. It should first be noted that each of these elements is defined negatively in terms of resistance to a threat: The first resists a state that is often authoritarian or totalitarian; the second, the reduction of society to a set of markets; and the third, the obsession with communitarian identity. However, the truly important thing to note is that these forms of resistance would be ineffective without the support of the other constituent principles of democracy. How can we limit the power of the state without appealing to "social forces" and asserting the autonomy and responsibility of society? How can we prevent democracy from being reduced to an open political market if we do not posit the existence of basic rights that are not subject to the judgment of the market and if we do not defend the idea of citizenship, which is equally alien to the market? The struggle against the segmentation of society, finally, requires an analysis of its overall social dynamic and a recourse to universalist principles. The unity of the three components is therefore practical rather than theoretical. It is impossible to defend one without defending the others. I earlier identified three elementary types of democracy not because I assume that a democratic system can be based on only one of these principles but simply to remind readers that various historical experiences have emphasized their respective importance in different ways.

Democracy exists only by combining different and partly contradictory principles: It is a mediation between state and civil society. An excessive emphasis on one pole strengthens it at the expense of the other, and that is dangerous. Specialists in constitutional law and jurisprudence usually have a better understanding of this than do political philosophers, who seek to define the spirit of democracy, whereas democracy is in fact primarily a set of guarantees and processes that establish a relationship between the unity of legitimate power and a plurality of social actors.

The explanation for the apparent weakness of democracy is that it cannot exist unless it constantly produces and recreates itself. Democracy is a form of action rather than an idea. Democracy is present whenever rights are asserted and recognized, whenever a social situation is justified by the pursuit of liberty and not by social utility or the specificity of an experience.

Democracy's main strength lies in its citizens' will to act responsibly in public life. The democratic spirit shapes a collective consciousness, whereas authoritarian regimes require everyone to identify with a leader, a symbol, or a collective social being—usually the nation. Some describe as democratic the prioritization of social realities over political decisions; others, in contrast, insist that it is democratic political action that forges the social bond and, therefore, a collective identity. Democracy is in fact defined by the complementary nature of these assertions. If they are not complementary, the world of power and the world of collective identities drift further and further apart; democracy brings them closer together by shouldering both society's demands and state's obligations. This brings us back once more to the three constituent elements of society, as citizenship is bound up with the unity of the state, whereas representativity is a reminder that social demands take priority. The principle of limiting state power by appealing to basic rights is therefore of central importance; merely by formulating it, we are speaking of the two spheres that democracy tries to bring together without fusing them into one.

The way in which the three constituent elements of democracy are combined into pairs complements the interdependence of rights and the limitation of power. Any democracy therefore has three main institutional mechanisms. The first combines a reference to basic rights with the definition of citizenship. That is the role of democracy's constitutional instruments. The second combines respect for basic rights with the representation of interests. That is the primary purpose of codes of law. The third combines representation and citizenship. That is the primary function of free parliamentary elections. We can, therefore, speak of a *democratic system,* whose constitutional, legal, and parliamentary elements implement three principles: the limitation of the state in the name of basic rights, the social representativity of political actors, and citizenship.

Liberty, Equality, Fraternity

Attempts to reduce democracy to procedures or even to the rule of law always end in failure; although it is possible to contrast rational-legal authority with charismatic authority, as did Max Weber, neither is synonymous with democracy. Weber himself therefore imagined that a plebiscitary democracy could reconcile respect for the law with the role of a charismatic leader. Democracy exists when the forces of social liberation intersect with the mechanisms of institutional integration. If it is suspicious of the disorders and pressures that accompany the rise of social demands, democracy is rapidly transformed into a mechanism for reinforcing established dominations; conversely, when social demands are overwhelmed by the institutional mechanisms of negotiation and law, then authoritarianism is not far away. Democracy cannot be identified with the power of a leader, a popular party, or judges, for it is based on the strength and autonomy of the political system in which the interests and demands of the greatest possible number of social actors are represented, defended, and negotiated. In a democracy, the heat of movements and ideologies is tempered by the cold impersonality of juridical rules.

The motto of the French revolution anticipated the conclusion of this analysis by more than 150 years, and it has been adopted by all democrats: Liberty, equality, fraternity. The motto recognizes that democracy has no central principle because it is defined by the combination of three principles. This famous motto is therefore vulnerable to apparently realistic criticisms, but they miss the essential point. It is true that a regime that privileges liberty can lead to greater inequality and, conversely, that the pursuit of equality may require the sacrifice of liberty. It is, however, even truer that democracy cannot exist unless it reconciles equality with liberty and unites the two in the name of fraternity. This book might be regarded as a commentary on the slogan, to which history has given incomparable grandeur. As declarations of human rights remind us, equality means equality of rights. Given the existence of de facto inequalities, the call for equality must have both an ethical and a political basis. Some take the view that all human beings are equal to the extent that they are all rational beings; for others, equality is born of participation in the social contract or in democratic institutions. The two views are not mutually exclusive.

Liberty, for its part, would be ineffective if it did not produce a diversified and complex society built on relations, conflicts, compromises, and consensus. The principle that leaders must be representative is therefore merely one expression of the general idea of liberty. Fraternity, finally, is almost synonymous with citizenship because the latter is defined here as membership in a self-regulating and self-organizing political society. All members are both producers and users of the political organization, both citizens and legislators. The motto "Liberty, equality, fraternity" provides the best definition of democracy because it reconciles truly political elements with social or ethical elements. It demonstrates that although democracy is a type of political system and not a general type of society, it is defined in terms of the relations it establishes between individuals, a social organization, and political power, and not only in terms of institutions or functional modes.

PART 2

A History of the Modern Democratic Spirit

PART 2

A History of the Modern Democratic Spirit

6

Republicans and Liberals

The evolution of modern democracies has been interpreted in two contrasting ways. According to the first interpretation, the history of democracy is that of its gradual extension. The right to vote was extended to new categories of men and then to all women. The age of civic majority was then lowered. Democracy was further extended by the appearance of what has been called economic or industrial democracy and, more recently, by the introduction of democratic modes of decisionmaking into many areas of social life. The second interpretation, in contrast, worries about the loss of autonomy of political life in a society that is increasingly dominated by either economic interests or the state's administrative rules. Many people think that we have undergone a transition from the rule of politics to the rule of economics and, therefore, from the proclamation of liberty to the management of needs. The first interpretation is too superficially optimistic to be convincing, but the second seems to me profoundly mistaken because what was invented, in both theory and practice, in Europe between the mid-eighteenth century and the mid-nineteenth century was not so much democracy as the modern state. The modern state was created by reason and a general will; it was the rational replacement for traditional society's pyramid of ranks and privileges. The invention of the political, from Machiavelli and Bodin to Hobbes, Rousseau, and the great liberal figures of the early nineteenth century, did at times have a democratic dimension, but it also took oligarchic forms and was sometimes associated with the formation of absolute monarchies. We can describe as republican a modern state that, even when headed by a monarch, gives governability new foundations rather than concerning itself with representativity. When such a state speaks of the people or, better still, the nation, it is employing a political and not a social category, designating a political community rather than a social one defined by its dependency or poverty.

The formation of the modern democratic idea coincided with the decomposition of this image of the modern republican state and, therefore, with the emergence and growing importance of the idea of representation. The classic dichotomy between direct democracy or self-management and representative regime originated because a Rousseauesque popular government was consonant with the philosophy of the Enlightenment, being founded on the principles of political rationality, individual interest, and universal integration, and thus defining a state that could be identified with society. The idea of representation, in contrast, institutes a divorce between representatives and those they represent, with the distance between the two at times being envisioned as the difference between supply and demand in a political market. Bernard Manin (1985, 1992) has clearly demonstrated the weakness of this metaphor, but it does have the merit of stressing the central tendency toward a separation between social and cultural demands on the one hand and the functions of government on the other. It was universal suffrage and the rise of working-class demands that brought about the transition from republican regimes, which were at that time often ruled by liberals, to democracies, which some described as bourgeois and many of which evolved into industrial or social democracies, especially in northern Europe.

Then came the triumph of mass parties, whose role was to establish a correspondence between social interests and government programs; but their victory was hollow, as the subordination of the political to the social weakens political power. Many are predicting the final demise of political power, as the nationalism of newly industrialized countries increasingly dominates decomposed political systems.

In rich countries, the internationalization of the economy and culture, which became obvious at the end of the long postwar period of modernization, was associated with the rapid growth of mass consumption and mass communications, and it did more to fragment the republican model than did the "social question" of nineteenth century Europe. The international system of production is now regulated by international markets and is becoming divorced from national political systems, which are being overwhelmed by social and cultural demands that have ever less to do with the agenda of governance and more to do with the problems of particular groups and with the opportunity for individuals to be recognized as subjects. Manin has shown that the crisis affecting the party regimes does not prefigure a general crisis in representation or the triumph of politics-as-spectacle but rather should be interpreted as a transition from one form of political representation to another. It may even be seen as a victory for democracy in that it permits a more direct and diversified expression of social and cultural demands, and more generally, a greater differentiation between state, political system, and civil society.

The Republican Spirit

Democratic thought's starting point is of course the idea of the sovereignty of the people. So long as power finds its legitimacy in tradition, right of conquest, or the will of God, democracy is unthinkable; democracy becomes possible only when the holders of power are regarded as representatives of the people. They are responsible for implementing the decisions of the people, and the people alone holds sovereignty. This idea marks the birth of political modernity, the reversal by which power is recognized as the product of human will rather than something imposed by divine decision, custom, or the nature of things. Although the English Bill of Rights of February 1689 did not explicitly proclaim the sovereignty of the people but instead referred to the traditional freedoms of the Commons and the Lords, the American and French revolutions did proclaim the principle of the sovereignty of the people and rejected the monarchy that stood in their way. These founding acts were the culmination of the liberal political tradition, which, from Hobbes to Locke and to Rousseau, asserted the foundational nature of the willed creation of the social bond, described by Hobbes as a covenant, by Locke as a trust, and by Rousseau as a social contract.

There is no possibility of democracy without the idea of the sovereignty of the people; but can one be identified with the other? Can we regard the sovereignty of the people as an adequate definition of democracy? No, for to do so would take us too far in the opposite direction: One cannot consider Hobbes a democrat; indeed, he has been classified as a theoretician of absolutism. As for Rousseau, although he had a republican soul, he believed democracy possible only in small collectivities. What Rousseau called the general will was not, according to Rousseau himself, to be confused with the will of the majority, for the general will was both voluntary and constraining. The idea of the republic and of the sovereignty of the people in which it is founded goes beyond the legal state that Montesquieu identified with monarchy as opposed to despotism. In a monarchy, the king governs in accordance with the law and not as he sees fit. Yet neither the idea of the republic nor that of the sovereignty of the people provides a definition of representative government. The republican idea gives birth to the autonomy of the political order but not its democratic character; on the contrary, for the republican idea, present from the beginning of the French revolution and long before the overthrow of the monarchy, gave rise to the absolute power wielded by the Convention, the Clubs, and the Comité de Salut Public; and this absolute power later was transformed into the Terror. Most revolutions have proclaimed the sovereignty of the people and have overthrown old regimes but have led to authoritarian regimes rather than democracies. As Pierre Rosanvallon reminded us, the French revolution appealed to the nation, patriots, and the republican spirit—not to democracy—because at this time, and until 1848, "democracy" referred to the ancient model, in which power was directly and collectively exercised by the people (Rosanvallon 1992: 11–29). The celebration of the republic in fact meant the seizure of power by the people, which led to the Terror and Bonapartism as well as to the overthrow of the ancien régime.

The idea of a voluntary social bond is synonymous with the idea of citizenship, assuming that the acceptance of a bond is voluntary only if it can be freely renewed or broken; but a collective identification with a leader or a nation means the loss of individual will in favor of merging with a higher collective experience, against which there is no possible recourse. That is why theorists of the sover-

eignty of the people recognize the right to resist oppression and define it as in-
alienable.

As we can see from the work of Sieyès, whose intellectual evolution was analyzed by Jean-Denis Bredin (Bredin 1988) and Pierre Rosanvallon (Rosanvallon
1992), it was in fact the abolition of privileges that gave democratic individualism
its meaning. The abolition of "orders" and privileges does not, however, make it
possible to build a new political society and instead may lead to grave crisis; the
Constituent Assembly, however, was aware that it was inventing a new society. I
therefore agree with Pierre Rosanvallon, who emphasized throughout his book *Le
Sacre du citoyen* that the intention behind the abolition of privileges was to trans-
fer the sovereignty of the king to the people. In order for that to be possible, "the
people had to be apprehended as an emblem of the social totality, or, in a word,
had to be identified with the nation" (Rosanvallon 1992: 60). Unlike the English
conception of democracy, which was dominated by utilitarian thought from the
end of the eighteenth century on, the French conception was dominated by the
idea of sovereignty and by the idea that all were equal before the absolute power
of the law as imposed by the monarchy. Confirming Tocqueville's classic analysis
(Tocqueville 1964 [orig. ed. 1856]), Rosanvallon wrote, "Political rights do not
derive from a doctrine of representation—to the extent that that doctrine implies
the recognition and celebration of the heterogeneity and diversity of society—but
from the idea of participation in sovereignty." The right to vote, he concluded "is a
key element in the symbology of membership in society and a way of collectively
reappropriating the royal power of old" (1992: 71, 452).

This conception of sovereignty is based on a rationalist and, one might say,
functionalist idea of social life: It is by participating in the shared tasks of the social body that the individual is educated, masters his passions and interests, and
becomes capable of rational action. As I pointed out in *Critique of Modernity*
(Touraine 1992), this conception has dominated social thought from Machiavelli
and Bodin to Talcott Parsons, despite the objections of many modern thinkers
who have identified individuation with socialization; hence the constant appeal to
a form of education that is at once scientific and civic and hence the convergence
between a Kantian democratic individualism and submission to the imperious
order of reason and the law. This republican conception holds, just as strongly as
the recent encyclical *Libertatis splendor,* that liberty must be subordinated to truth
because only by discovering and respecting truth can we become free.

The separation between active and passive citizens obviously did not reduce the
electorate to a small minority during the French revolution as it did under the
restoration; it did show, however, that the idea of universal suffrage was based on
an individualism that reserved the management of public affairs for those who
had the ability to act freely and to undertake the rational organization of society.
This led to an extreme divide between public life and private life, between the individual and the member of the community, which did not bring about democracy but rather a growing inequality between social categories deemed rational

and categories deemed irrational, be they "mad" or, more specifically, women. Republican politics assured the exclusion of the latter from public life, which explains why almost one hundred years (1848–1945) went by before suffrage was extended to women in France.

The whole of French political life until now has been dominated by a conception of democracy that subordinates political actors to the needs of society-nation-people, its collective consciousness, and its rational interests. When state power is weak and manifests itself mainly in a rejection of both religion and popular movements, this conception is merely "abstract"; but it becomes much more dangerous when it associates social progress with the victory of an avant-garde whose dictatorship must impose reason and the meaning of history on a civil society that has been perverted by private interests or tradition.

As a result of this republican conception, American society, according to Tocqueville, was exposed to the risk of being oppressed by the weight of public opinion and therefore by normality, and was long hostile to cultural innovations and minorities.

The idea of the sovereignty of the people, or the republican idea, gives the political realm such solid foundations that it destroys the idea of natural law, which Rousseau logically opposed; if the people is sovereign, the power it legitimizes has no preestablished limits and may become absolute. The republican idea therefore harks back to the liberty of the ancients instead of leading to the liberty of the moderns, although it did add one innovation—the extension of participation in civic life, which had been the preserve of a minority of the citizens of Athens, to a continually increasing majority of the inhabitants of a country. This new "liberty of the ancients" is not based on the idea of individual liberty or individual rights. If we contrast the two traditions of modern thought—the defense of reason against tradition and privilege, and the proclamation of the liberty of the individual—the republican idea is an integral part of the former tradition and is its primary political expression. In this tradition, the nation is not viewed as a collective being but as the expression of the will to create a rational organization, cleansed of all principles hostile to freedom of choice; however, freedom of choice is respectable only if it is guided by reason. The appeal to the general will and the appeal to reason are not merely complementary; they are one and the same—namely, an assertion that reason is the distinctive human characteristic. The domain of politics must be brought closer to that of science. This gives scientists and educators pride of place within the republic and justifies pedagogic methods dominated by the will to make rational thought triumph over feelings and particularities. In broadly similar forms this conception triumphed in most modern countries for a long period, spreading from the Jesuit schools or their protestant equivalents to the public schools that recruited their pupils on a much wider basis. The words "rationalization," "civic spirit," and "republican elitism" may inspire either admiration or criticism, but none of them are necessarily associated with the democratic spirit, freedom of debate, or majority rule. They can lend legitimacy to either an enlightened despotism or a democracy in which compromises are as inevitable as the formation of interest groups. Reason replaced God in the hearts of most republicans, at least in those countries that rebelled against the tradition bequeathed by the Catholic Counter-Reformation; but reason is as demanding as God and as the methods of industrial rationalization. The republican spirit replaces the authority of tradition not with freedom of debate but with the authority of truth and, therefore, science.

The republican idea contradicts the idea of human rights, which derives directly from Christianity. Although the supporters of the republican idea fought for liberties that the defenders of Christian traditions in many countries denounced until the end of the nineteenth century—led by a papacy that took its line from Pius X's *Syllabus*—we should not be deceived by this apparent paradox. The liberal bourgeoisie or even the republican bourgeoisie believed that its role was to act as humanity's guide because it had been enlightened by reason; this self-confidence was shared by all the great intellectuals, prophets, and beacons of humanity who fought established powers in the name of reason and liberty and who spoke in defense of those who, because of their lack of education and resources, were incapable of making use of reason and liberty. The republican idea implies the idea of a vanguard, which Leninists associated with the revolutionary idea of a liberating explosion that would allow the poor and exploited to shake off forms of domination as irrational as they were injust. Educated and magnanimous men would guide these poor people into the future. However, in actuality, while revolution makes democracy possible it may also facilitate the coming to power of an enlightened despot, be it a prince or a party. History was to make of this ambiguity such an unbearably oppressive reality that it is now difficult to understand the "progressive" discourse of politicians and intellectuals of such Jacobin persuasions.

The Tyranny of the Majority

Liberal thinkers and statesmen have always been convinced that democracy is dangerous. The tyranny of the majority was a continuous leitmotiv in the works of American thinkers who studied the regime born of their revolution (or, to be more accurate, their war of independence). Robert Dahl has shown that this wariness of majority rule was of central importance in the *Federalist Papers* and in the conservative thought of Madison and Hamilton as well as that of the more democratic Jackson. This same theme is just as central to the studies that Royer-Collard, Guizot, and Tocqueville devoted to the French revolution. How could matters be so arranged that the decisions of the *major pars* did not prevent the *sanior* or *melior pars* from governing? How could matters be so arranged as to ensure that popular pressure would allow reason to govern rather than leading to populist governments like that of Jackson in the United States, who so worried Tocqueville, or to terrorist governments as during the French revolution? Restricting access to power became the main preoccupation of those who defined democracy. The freedom of the ruled to choose their rulers was thus reduced to its narrowest meaning: the people must freely express their preference for a team or a manifesto drawn up, not by the people itself, but by educated and responsible men who were concerned about the public good and who moved in circles where rational plans could be drawn up and compared. This elitist conception of democracy enjoyed its greatest triumph in Great Britain, where it was upheld by great constitutionalists like Bagehot (Bagehot 1964 [orig. ed. 1867]) and encouraged by the social power of an aristocracy that had not been eliminated by a popular revolution and that had, on the contrary, played an active role in the abolition of the absolute monarchy. This explains why the country that gave birth to democracy was so late in extending the right to vote to less-educated categories and why it distorted the representation of the people by gerrymandering the boundaries of electoral districts so as to put the industrial population at a disadvantage. Like Latin America's conservatives and liberals, the Whigs and Tories were fractions of the establishment, and they made sure that political debate was confined to the political elite rather than opened up to conflicting interests.

Other democratic countries also restricted access to political power. In the United States, recruitment into the elite remained closed for a long time. A high proportion of the elite came from the Ivy League schools, and family background continued to play an important role. In France, republican elitism entrusted the *grandes écoles* with the task of selection. Although this method did allow many new recruits to join the political elite, it also had the side effect of divorcing the elite from the dominant categories who defined themselves in terms of the defense of religious, national, or economic traditions. These restrictive methods outlasted the property owner's vote, which could not withstand popular pressure, and, in the case of the United States, slavery, which was swept away with much greater violence.

Writing long after the English constitutionalists, Joseph Schumpeter took up the idea that one of the reasons for democracy's success in Great Britain was the existence of a political milieu that existed in England but not in the Weimar Republic. The argument derives from the general theory of democracy outlined by Schumpeter, a theory violently opposed to the classical idea that decisions should be made by the free will of the majority of citizens. Because he did not believe that individuals are rational, can understand problems, and are willing to concern themselves with the common good and to find rational solutions, Schumpeter redefined democracy as the freedom to choose a governmental team: "The democratic method is that institutional arrangement for arriving at political decisions in which individuals acquire the power to decide by means of a competitive struggle for the people's vote" (Schumpeter 1976: 269 [orig. ed. 1943]). This produces a nonrepresentative image of parties: "A party is a group whose members propose to act in concert in the competitive struggle for political power" (Schumpeter 1976: 283). This conception seems, rather, to describe an oligarchic regime, and it reduces the sovereignty of the people to the weakest possible role. This brutality has the merit of showing how far the fear of the people can go and how paradoxical it is to base the democratic idea on this fear. It is therefore preferable to reject this extreme view that eliminates almost all the real content of democracy and to go back to the thought of the liberals, which is so rich compared with the poverty of Schumpeter's.

No political thinker delved more profoundly than Alexis de Tocqueville into the novelty, necessity, and dangers of what I will describe as the republican spirit in order better to highlight Tocqueville's ambivalent attitude toward democracy. The predominant idea in his study of the United States (Tocqueville 1994 [orig. ed. 1835–1840]), is that the evolution of modern societies necessarily leads to the disappearance of hierarchical orders or estates (*Stände* in German), and that *homo æqualis* takes the place of *homo hierarchicus*. This implies a transition not to de facto equality but to de jure equality, and then to a certain equality of condition or, as Lord Bryce put it in his study of the American political system (Bryce 1893), to an equal respect for all that helps to restrict luxury, the display of wealth, and the conspicuous consumption described by Thorstein Veblen. According to Tocqueville, this is not a political transformation but a social evolution that can be either peaceful or violent. Tocqueville broadly approved of the effects of the French revolution but condemned its authoritarian deviations. In his view, historical necessity—the emergence of an egalitarian society—was at work in both the Terror and Bonapartism, as well as in the great parliamentary decisions of 1789. The removal of the ludicrous obstacles of tradition and institutional and cultural guarantees of inequality, such as the convention that votes were cast by orders and not individuals in the Estates General, was the work of historical necessity.

This belief in historical necessity allowed Tocqueville to concentrate on truly political problems: Once traditional hierarchies have been destroyed, how can the tyranny of the majority be prevented from founding an irrational social order? For, just like the Federalists, Tocqueville regarded the triumph of the masses—or what Serge Moscovici now calls the age of crowds (Moscovici 1981)—as the principal threat to democratic regimes. Tocqueville was not content with an appeal to natural rights. The example of the French revolution showed him that the modern world was indeed a world of positive law and that principles were powerless against crowds, princes, or armies. However, he did not side with utilitarians either, even though he preferred to speak of personal interest rather than of natural rights; Tocqueville's political liberalism was profoundly anti-individualist and did not imply economic liberalism.

Thus, Tocqueville remained closer to the liberty of the ancients than to that of the moderns. He asserted that the social order must be based on justice and that what prevents justice from being reduced to respect for personal interests or rights is analogous to what Montesquieu called virtue. For Montesquieu, virtue was the spirit of republican regimes; in other words, it was the civic sense that results both from respect for the social bond and from the laws that restrain human desires. Like Hobbes and Rousseau, and like Durkheim after him, Tocqueville thought that human desires were boundless and therefore dangerous. More concretely, he thought that democracy was based on a combination of the religious spirit and the civic spirit. The religion he saw at work in New England was a civic religion that guaranteed the social order rather than a recourse to transcendence in the face of the social order. Tocqueville believed in citizens rather than men, and the element of social Christianity in his work sensitized him to the theme of social integration. At the end of the nineteenth century, this became the theme of social solidarity; in his early work, Durkheim saw it as an important factor in overcoming the crises of modern society. Tocqueville was not satisfied with the overfacile dichotomy between *major pars* and *sanior pars*. As he put it in a note published by Antoine Redier (Redier 1925), he was torn between two conflicting tendencies: "I have an intellectual taste for democratic institutions, but I am an instinctive aristocrat; in other words, I despise and fear the crowd. In the depths of my soul, I passionately love liberty, legality and respect for rights, but not democracy." This is not, however, simply a matter of social origins resisting democratic equality; Tocqueville was afraid that equality would lead to revolution and then to despotism. Restrictions therefore had to be placed on the sovereignty of the people. It was the interests of the citizen, and not those of the individual, that would determine those restrictions and define justice rather than the interests of the individual. Hence the differences between Tocqueville and Benjamin Constant—whom he does not cite—or the defenders of individual self-interest.

Tocqueville was an antirevolutionary democrat; but it might be more accurate to describe him as a liberal rather than a democrat, as in his view democracy defined a social state rather than a political regime. He argued that the sovereignty of the people was not absolute, and he would have rejected Lincoln's definition of democracy. He concluded the first part of his book with the following assertion: "The power of the majority itself is not unlimited. Above it in the moral world are humanity, justice, and reason; and in the political world, vested rights" (Tocqueville 1994: 416). This is more a British than an American position; but Tocqueville later introduced the truly federalist, American theme of the importance of the local, and above all municipal, powers that protect individuals from the state. These powers are checks on the omnipotence of the state, rather like Montesquieu's separation of powers, and not an expression of the representative democracy defended by Tocqueville's follower, James Stuart Mill. Because he attributed such importance to the civic spirit, Tocqueville worried—especially in the second volume of *Democracy in America* (published in 1840)—about the pressure brought to bear by public opinion on ideas and innovations and about the possibility that it would lead to conformism.

Those doubts did not, however, distract Tocqueville from his central project of reconciling religion and the principles of 1789. He did not view that project in the same way as Auguste Comte, even though like Comte he was aware of the danger that society might disintegrate if its hierarchical order was destroyed. Tocqueville was a modern to the extent that he studied the revolutions that founded modernity; but he was also an ancient and remained a man of the eighteenth century and a reader of both Montesquieu and Rousseau in that he tried above all to create a new social bond that might prevent what Durkheim later would call anomie, or in other words, the collapse of the system of norms and social controls. The dichotomy between ancients and moderns therefore cannot be made to designate two successive stages in political thought and action. Durkheim is another clear demonstration of the intertwining of the two. At the end of the twentieth century as at the end of the nineteenth, the question of the social bond is once more on the agenda: It was because they called for reconciliation and not revenge that Chile's democrats won the plebiscite held by General Pinochet; their example adds to the significance of Spain's Moncloa pact, which so many countries dream of emulating. After the tragic exhaustion of ideologies based on class struggle or wars of national liberation, the ideas of justice, integration, and even fraternity are taking on a new importance in political thought.

Liberals and Utilitarians

The liberals brought about the transition from ancient to modern as they attempted to reconcile the civic spirit and individual interest. Dissatisfied with the liberty of the ancients, which identified man with citizen and liberty with involvement in public affairs and the common good, liberals also refused to place a boundless faith in either individual self-interest or the sovereignty of the people. On the whole, however, they were closer to the ancients than to the moderns; whereas the utilitarians, who were also attempting to reconcile individual self-interest and the common good, were closer to the moderns to the extent that they accorded a central importance to the pursuit of personal happiness.

The striking thing about Tocqueville is the way he emphasized political categories, as though civil society's evolution toward equality had eliminated old problems rather than providing new solutions. Like Rousseau, he was worried by the citizen's lack of interest in civic affairs; yet anyone who reads Tocqueville senses that it would be a mistake to overemphasize this, as, unlike Rousseau, Tocqueville also referred to natural law: "Providence has given to every human being the degree of reason necessary to direct himself in the affairs that interest him exclusively" (Tocqueville 1994: 418). This should not be interpreted in an individualistic way, for the freedom of the modern individual obliges our societies to define a new principle of social integration that can reconcile individual happiness with the collective interest. The utilitarians took up the same theme and, from Jeremy Bentham on, have defended the pursuit of individual happiness only because it promotes those forms of social and political organization that ensure the greatest possible happiness for the greatest number. Their argument is more analogous to that of the modern individualists, who try to justify the market as a principle for the allocation of resources than to the libertarians, who unstintingly sing the praises of the pursuit of personal interest.

Neither utilitarians nor liberals contrast individual interest with social integration; they regard the former as the best means of achieving the latter. They argue that the management of collective affairs should not be influenced by conceptions of man because such conceptions always lead to intolerance and discrimination. Their main objective is to strengthen the social bond in a society where egotism might otherwise prevail. Egotism must therefore be tempered by a respect for and a concern with the happiness of others.

Although they have much in common, the differences between the two schools are greater than their similarities. For the utilitarians, especially John Stuart Mill, the individual, and his liberty and demands, are central to the analysis. They therefore do not separate the social actor from the political system or the economy from institutions. Liberals, in contrast, are best defined by their acceptance of that separation of spheres and their wish to make it more complete. Whereas utilitarians refer to well-being, liberals are the servants of reason. They want the management of public affairs to be independent, protected from vested interests and passions; and therefore, as we have already seen, they seek to protect liberties from the tyranny of the majority by strengthening institutions. That is why the liberals in France supported an oligarchic republicanism that subsequently evolved into a more moderate republican elitism during the third republic.

Liberals distrust social actors to such an extent that they look for a principle of order that can replace religion. Their antireligious, often anticlerical spirit masks the search for a rational order, defined in as formal a set of rules as possible, that would oblige individuals to act rationally by sacrificing their particular interests so as to strengthen the institutions that organize and protect order. Utilitarians, in contrast, are more sensitive to the representation of interests. The fact that utilitarianism was more influential in Great Britain—where political categories always seem to be more important than social categories—than in France explains why trade-union action and industrial democracy developed much earlier in Britain. Liberal thought prevailed from Hobbes to John Stuart Mill, from Benjamin Constant to Tocqueville; but utilitarian thought became dominant with the advent of capitalism in the nineteenth century and the welfare state in the twentieth century. The difference between the two schools is not always clear; indeed, John Stuart Mill's thought combined the two, which explains both its strengths and its weaknesses. There is, however, a difference; and it tends to become ever more pronounced, mainly because liberals believe in the autonomy and centrality of the political, whereas utilitarians subordinate politics to the representation and satisfaction of interests and demands. Liberals generally are on the side of the system, utilitarians on that of actors; however, the demise of socialism and communism gave liberalism a new lease on life and led liberal thinkers to concentrate on incorporating the contributions of social movements and social democracy into their analysis of the political system. John Rawls's interpretation of social justice may be understood in this context. Rawls asked, How can individual liberty be reconciled with social integration when the latter always poses a threat to individualism? Rawls answered his own question with his second principle of justice, by which liberty, which may create social inequalities, is subordinate to the reduction of the burden borne by the least advantaged. This argument may be viewed as justifying the industrialists whose enterprises led to capital accumulation in the hands of a ruling class but who also improved the lot of wage earners at the bottom of the scale by increasing productivity, as symbolized by the Fordist policy of paying high wages. In Rawls's second principle of justice we can hear echoes of the declarations made by Montesquieu at the beginning of his preface to *The Spirit of the Laws*: "What I call *virtue* in a republic is love of the homeland, that is, love of equality. Therefore I have called love of the homeland and of equality *political virtue*" (Montesquieu 1989: 2).

This meeting of individual interest with collective interest, the combination of liberty with equality, is characteristic of the modern spirit. It is quite different from Edmund Burke's defense of the traditions and organic complexity of history as against the voluntarism of the French revolution (Burke 1955 [orig. ed. 1790]); but one can hardly describe it as "democratic," as it relies on the civic-mindedness of ruling elites to limit the nonegalitarian effects of liberty. This philosophy, congenial to philanthropists and businessmen such as Henry Ford, manifested its antidemocratic tendencies when the workers of Detroit organized hunger marches during the great depression. The remarkable wage increases Ford granted should be viewed in the context of an expanding country that had a shortage of workers despite widespread immigration—in other words, as a triumph for industrialism rather than democracy. The same criticism applies to the liberalism of the nineteenth century. How can one speak of popular rule or of the freedom to choose rulers when it is primarily a matter of avoiding the tyranny of the majority or an excess of popular sovereignty that might lead to an authoritarian regime? Can we rely on the moral conscience and civic-mindedness of the enlightened classes to protect liberty? Although he was sympathetic to them, Tocqueville understood why the American federalists were defeated and why Guizot's rational liberalism was rendered obsolete by the revolution of 1848. Even in Great Britain, the Labour Party was founded in order to challenge the limited democracy of the Whigs and Tories, and working-class demands and revolts paved the way for the industrial democracy that later spread to continental Europe.

In sum, the strength of liberal and utilitarian modes of thought is that they combine the theme of the limitation of power with the theme of citizenship that is defended by the republican idea. Yet both liberals and utilitarians have failed to elaborate a complete theory of democracy because generally they have not taken into account the representation of the interests of the majority. When they did so, it was in such an economistic way that it proved easy to use their arguments to justify authoritarian regimes by their success in improving the living conditions of the population. For a long time, this argument was used to prove that Fidel Castro's regime was democratic because it had improved the population's standard of education and health. Some results of Castro's policies were indeed very positive; but there are no grounds for describing as democratic a regime that was obviously authoritarian, if not totalitarian.

In the mid-nineteenth century, liberalism began to retreat before the advancing popular forces, which—thanks to the new industrialization—had been accumulating and mobilizing in the factories and working-class districts. At the end of the nineteenth century, that popular mobilization accelerated in a number of countries, especially Germany and the United States. Liberal ideas were not eradicated as a result, but historical reality meant that greater importance now had to be accorded to the representation of majority interests.

Opening Up a Public Space

Liberalism cannot be characterized as merely a defense of the interests of the bourgeoisie, nor socialism as the exclusive expression of the interests of the popular classes or the working class. Any such interpretation would reduce the realm of political life, including democracy, to the representation of social interests, which would be unacceptable. The contribution of liberal ideas to political philosophy is as permanent as that of republican ideas: There can be no democracy without the limitation of state power or in the absence of citizenship. But before we can understand why democracy cannot exist unless the interests of the majority are represented, we must first examine the nature of the personal rights that restrict state power and explore the nature of citizenship. For if personal rights are no more than a legal guarantee of personal interests, then political liberty is in danger of becoming simply a means of defending the strongest and richest.

The liberal idea is quite convincing when it combines a definition of basic rights with a recognition of the social obstacles and forms of domination that destroy them, which it has often done. In this vein the theme of the defense of majority interests has been developed by many liberals and utilitarians, not least among them John Stuart Mill. Like many of his contemporaries, Mill was obsessed with the French revolution, which he saw not as a government by the people but as a government by leaders speaking in the name of the people—an insight that led him to argue in favor of limiting "the legitimate interference of collective opinion with individual independence" (Mill 1991: 9). Despite his youthful differences with Jeremy Bentham and his father, James Mill, he adopted a utilitarian approach; yet at the same time he defended the interests of the dominated, including women—he was an early advocate of women's rights—and workers, which explains why some viewed him as a socialist. His main opponent was in fact Auguste Comte, who argued that society should have absolute control over individuals. For Mill, "The only purpose for which power can be rightfully exercised over any member of a civilized community, against his will, is to prevent harm to others" (Mill 1991: 14). It is this principle that justified state interventionism, especially in the late nineteenth century, for it introduced the theme of social relations and thus resulted in the definition of liberty as a way of resisting power both social and political. John Stuart Mill asserted that political realities take priority over social realities; he defended the unity of the nation and desired the creation of a professionalized civil society that would exist independently of parties. Yet he also authored the *Considerations on Representative Government* (Mill 1977c [orig. ed. 1861]). Although dominated by individualism, that text provides a purely political analysis and is inspired by a radical desire to do battle with the aristocracy. John Stuart Mill prefigured the politics of the liberal bourgeoisie, which in many countries of Europe and Latin America had to forge alliances with popular categories in its struggle against the oligarchy. This explains why the left wing of the radical parties became radical-socialist. It also explains the hasty adoption of social laws in countries such as Chile as well as Britain's more resolute transition from liberals to laborites.

The shift from a purely political analysis to a social and economic analysis has similarly transformed the idea of citizenship. The assertion of citizen and nation was made in the course of the struggle against the monarchy and, in the case of the French revolution, against foreign invasion. The people—the majority of citizens who were subject to the constraints of poverty and dependent labor and who were soon to be called proletarians—inevitably came to be seen as the social equivalent of the nation. France is the country where the transformation of the nation into the people, and of the people into a class, took place most openly and most smoothly. As a result, the theme of the struggle of the working class was for a long time associated, especially in the thought of Jean Jaurès, with the theme of the republic and the nation. In the late nineteenth century, wherever absolutism disappeared and the republican spirit triumphed—often in the shadow of constitutional monarchy—and wherever internal social problems prevailed over policies of conquest and the authoritarian mobilization of nations by militarized states, political life came to be dominated by the defense of social interests. So much so that there was usually a direct link between the conservative right and the interests of banks and industry, while the rise of social-democracy made parties the political wing of the working class. Parties were therefore usually controlled by labor unions. In France, however, the republican spirit shifted to the left, and revolutionary syndicalism, with its characteristic distrust of political action, therefore enjoyed a brief triumph.

This period seems far off, as we are now separated from it by the long period of postrevolutionary totalitarianism that transformed the reference to class and people into an instrument to be manipulated by despotic regimes, which were thus transformed into truly totalitarian regimes. But just as we cannot completely reject either the republican or the liberal heritage, and even though social struggles have dominated political life in recent years, it is impossible to argue that the debasement of the representative function means that it is not an essential part of the definition of democracy. We must, rather, look at why "class politics" sometimes strengthens democracy and sometimes destroys it. The answer to that question, which has dominated the history of socialist ideas and parties, follows from the analysis we have been pursuing. Class politics has a democratizing effect only if it is associated with the recognition of the basic rights that restrict the power of the state and with the defense of citizenship or, in other words, the right to belong to a political collectivity that confers upon itself the right to make and change its own laws. Democracy is, let us recall, defined by the interdependency of three principles: the limitation of power, representativity, and citizenship. It is not defined by the dominance of any one of those principles.

The first point is, in historical terms, the most important: If class relations are fully defined by the exploitation of workers reduced to the role of producers of surplus value and by the lowering of wages to the cost of the reproduction of their labor-power, then class action cannot be organized in defense of workers' rights but only in the name of the necessary overthrow of the social relations of production and the liberation of the productive forces they are holding back. There is no room in this argument for democracy; on the contrary, it is a call for revolution and for the seizure of state power, which shields capitalist domination. Force alone can defeat the violence of which the workers are victims. Democracy cannot be based on a purely negative definition of the people. All who analyze the situation of a class, a nation, or a gender purely in terms of the domination, violence, and exploitation inflicted upon it are turning their backs on democracy, which cannot survive unless the dominated play an active and positive role in the transformation of society. They must, that is, experience the sense of belonging expressed by the word "worker" but not the word "proletarian." I have twice demonstrated (Touraine 1966; Touraine 1988) that it is not the most dominated and least skilled categories that develop the highest degree of working-class consciousness. On the contrary, working-class consciousness is at its highest when there is a direct conflict between autonomous skilled workers and managerial methods that are destroying their autonomy, incorporating them into an authoritarian and centrally managed system of production and thus making them dependent. What is known as the labor movement is made up of two contradictory forces: on the one hand, revolutionary socialism, which seeks to take power in order to liberate oppressed workers and peoples, and therefore usually establishes an authoritarian regime; on the other, the true labor movement, which is based on the rights of workers who contribute their skills, experience, and labor to the process of production. A historicist logic is in conflict with a logic that might be called democratic in that it combines an appeal to rights with a sense of citizenship and the representation of interests.

The movement that defended workers' rights was intended to create what the English call industrial democracy. The principles of industrial democracy were established by the Fabians and later formulated in sociological terms by T. H. Marshall (Marshall 1950). However, it would be a mistake to contrast English-style trade-union action and French-style political action; the real dichotomy is that between democratic action and revolutionary action. Democratic action is based on the idea that workers have rights, and it defines social justice as the recognition of those rights; it therefore associates the idea of working-class autonomy with that of the political defense of the interests of the majority, or in other words the workers. The revolutionary program, in contrast, associates a negative definition of the interests that are to be defended—in terms of deprivation, exclusion, and exploitation—with the priority given to the overthrow of state power by popular forces and their organized vanguard. To employ a terminology that is now used less frequently than at the time when the influence of the communist parties was at its height, the revolutionary tendency makes a clear distinction between a class that exists in itself, and a class that exists for itself in identification with the Party. The democratic tendency, in contrast, refuses always to divorce situation from action or to reduce a class, nation, or any other social category to a mere victim of alienating and exploitative domination.

Democracy does not triumph when political action prevails over social struggle. On the contrary, it triumphs when class actors are defined in such positive terms that they are in control of political action and can legitimize their actions in terms of basic rights and the construction of a new citizenship.

The creation of the great social security systems, which has done more than any other political decision to transform west European society over the last half century, was the central expression of industrial democracy. In Great Britain, Sweden, and France, the goal was to extend the democratic principle to the economic domain by making labor unions and employers alike the social partners of governments and to create an economic citizenship. The English and especially the Scandinavians emphasized the need for industrial democracy; and the Scandinavians took the lead with the 1938 Saltsjöbaden Agreement between employers and unions, LO being by far the most important among the latter. The French social security system, in contrast, was the joint creation of General de Gaulle and the Communist-affiliated CGT and was more republican in inspiration. Its aim was to bring the working class, which had allied itself with the resistance to the occupation, back into the nation, and it worked to the disadvantage of the capitalist class, which stood accused of collaboration. These class differences are, however, less important than the differences between democratic creations and forms of action inspired by the desire to break the chains of a dependent population and those designed to defend workers' rights. Great revolutions always go through an initial phase in which the two tendencies merge; but as a general rule, the logic of the seizure of power prevails over the logic of the assertion of rights because the former uses effective strategies. In situations of apparently extreme dependency, the revolutionary dynamic is from the outset strengthened by the emphasis it places on the theory of the vanguard. Its Leninist expression is moderate; but the Guevarist theory of the *foco revolucionario* is more radical, as it accepts and even demands a complete divorce between the manipulated masses and a mobile and rootless guerrilla force whose sole goal is a seizure of state power that is almost indistinguishable from a coup d'état. People's revolutionary armies like the Khmer Rouge or Sendero Luminoso introduce a complete separation between political action and social actors: actors are denied any autonomous existence and are reduced to resources for use by politico-military leaders.

The weakness of social democracy stems from its failure to identify fully with either tendency—in other words, from its simultaneous emphasis on labor-union action and on state intervention, which creates the need to conquer state power. The split between the Second and Third Internationals clearly showed this confusion, pointing up the contradictions inherent in the very idea of social democracy.

Parties and Unions

These contradictions are, however, merely the obverse of important positive features—for example, the recognition of the need for party organization. Kelsen (1920) was defending the *Parteienstaat* when he asserted that parliamentary democracy was the only form of democracy. From the late nineteenth century until very recently, the central role of parties has been identified with the recognition that social struggles are basic to political life. Parties also give voters a degree of control over their elected representatives; although that control is obviously limited by the authority of party leaders, it is greater than it was in the republic of notables.

The defenders of the idea of social law, among them Georges Gurvitch, went even further to speak of juridical pluralism. The image of an integrated and coherent legal system, suspended like a pyramid from its summit—Kelsen's "basic norm"—is inseparable from the identification of the law with the state. The state in question may be national, republican, or authoritarian, but it is always sovereign and its supreme interest lies in the preservation of its territorial and social unity. This conception of the social order as though it were the state order goes hand in hand with a "normative" approach to the law. The idea of social law, understood in its broadest sense, leads, in contrast, to a much more fragmented view of both law and politics. Attention moves from system to actors as the normative conception of law gives way to a realist conception. The pluralism of centers of power and of legal initiatives gives an indirect power to associations and their leaders, although not to individual social actors. The representation of the interests of the majority results in the creation of associations, especially labor unions and parties, but also in the creation of cooperatives and friendly societies that allow the "masses" to enter political life, which was previously the preserve of notables or princes. Parties and unions thus come to be seen as essential elements of democracy. The more complex the society, the greater the number of interest groups. It is therefore increasingly essential that their demands should be aggregated by agents who can act as mediators between civil society and political society. A democracy without parties, governed by the views of an ever-changing majority, is almost inconceivable. The experience of countries such as France, where unions have lost much of their power, shows how difficult it is to manage the effects of major economic and international changes when the state is no longer able to negotiate with reliable social partners from both sides of industry.

The organization of parties made it possible to go beyond elitist politics. For a long time, Great Britain was the most stable expression of elitist politics because the aristocratic spirit remained as sturdy as the rejection of the absolute monarchy. In Moisei Ostrogorski's view (Ostrogorski 1993 [orig. ed. 1903]), the process of evolution that took Great Britain from Whig elitism to the Birmingham caucus's decision to found the Liberal Party should have ended with its central phase, or with the creation of the great leagues that defended the rights of Catholics, promoted electoral reform, and called for the abolition of protectionism (the Anti-Corn Law League). However, social mobilization around a single issue did nothing to promote the selection of rulers or the integration of different interest groups. Be that as it may, parties became a major theme for political philosophy only with the foundation of the socialist parties that claimed to represent a majority class and argued for the seizure of state power in order to overthrow a social order that affected every aspect of social life.

Ostrogorski, Michels, Mosca, and Pareto, writing before 1914, made two different critiques of parties. Ostrogorski's critique, which took its inspiration from liberalism and Tocqueville, was an attack on what one is tempted to call the "iron law of oligarchy" as seen in the workings of the English and American caucuses; the other critique, represented mainly by Michels—who in fact coined that famous phrase—tends, rather, to challenge the concentration of power within party-states. The first critique would later be directed against "screen-parties"; the second, which became more dramatically important with the creation of communist, fascist, nationalist, and populist parties, was directed against—and sometimes put forward on behalf of—the dictatorship of the proletariat and its equivalents.

The weakness of the first critique stems from its failure to recognize that political leaders must be representative. In that sense, it is an essentially liberal position. According to Ostrogorski (1993: 665–66),

> In a democracy, the function of the masses is not to govern, as they will probably never be capable of doing so. A small minority will always govern, in both democracies and autocracies. The natural property of all power is to become more concentrated. That is, so to speak, the social order's law of gravity. But the ruling minority must always be held in check. In a democracy, the function of the masses is not to govern, but to intimidate governments.

He concluded that the more restricted its aims, the greater an interest group's ability to exert pressure. The internationalization of the economy has given this argument new force, as the principal function of the state is, increasingly, to defend its country in international markets. It therefore pays less attention to social demands and tends to respond to them on an ad hoc basis.

Democracy becomes corrupt and loses its sense of direction both when the political system invades civil society and the state, and when the political system is destroyed by a state that claims to be in direct contact with the people or to be a direct expression of social demands. In countries that are considered democratic, the first threat, the party regime, is now the most obvious, but the twentieth century has been dominated by the opposite threat. Communism and fascism both defended the direct representation of the workers and opposed parliamentary democracy. Lenin's denunciations of parliamentarianism in *State and Revolution* were an extension of Marx's criticisms of French Jacobinism's "political illusion." Lenin called for direct democracy and outlined a pyramid of soviets that would give the workers—and only the workers—complete control over political power. Similarly, the corporatism of Mussolini, Franco, and Salazar contrasted real people's democracy with the power—described by Auguste Comte as metaphysical—of representatives chosen by parliamentary means.

Such antiparliamentarian regimes probably do not merit a theoretical critique, as their practices show that they organize the control of social groups through a party-state and not through the free expression of popular demands. On the other hand, it must be stressed that there can be no direct relationship between state and social actors; hence the need for an autonomous political system, of which democracy is the most highly developed and coherent form. Just as social demands must take priority over the internal needs of the government or political "games," so there can be no social movement that transcends the action of particular interest groups unless one particular social category takes responsibility for the general problems of social organization. The absence of free political institutions prevents the formation of social actors and facilitates the state apparatus's use of repressive controls over social protests and mobilizations.

The corporatist or totalitarian state is a threat to democracy; but a different threat emerges when the political system invades either the domain of the state or that of civil society. In Europe, parliamentary democracies have often weakened the state or brought about its decomposition. Italy in the early 1980s provided an extreme example. The public outcry that followed was inspired by the attempts of judges to put an end to the illegal financing of parties, mainly through public companies, and to the accumulation of personal wealth by so many political leaders. The invasion of civil society by parties poses an equally dangerous threat. Latin America provides the classic example of how collective action can be reduced to a political resource to be used by parties and their leaders. Albert Hirschmann has rightly emphasized the threat posed by great mass people's parties, which take the place of social actors, and I myself have analyzed how popular organizations in Latin America have been incorporated into party or state apparatuses. The classic example is Mexico's Institutional Revolutionary Party (PRI), a party-state that held direct control over labor unions, peasant unions, and urban organizations for half a century.

The nature of parties does not depend solely on the parties themselves or on the traditions of the state; it is also determined by the degree to which social demands are formalized and organized. As the most economically advanced societies are emerging from industrial society, the contradiction between the bourgeoisie and the working class, which was once the great principle behind the organization of their political lives, is losing its importance. Parties are therefore losing their overall sense of purpose. They are being invaded by factionalism and by struggles between tendencies that increasingly resemble clienteles. The Japanese liberal democratic party is an extreme case. After a long period of organized factional struggles, the Hata faction caused a party split in 1993. Indian democracy is also dominated by party factionalism, mainly because of the survival of social hierarchies, especially castes, and because of the regional diversity of a society that is at once holistic and relatively unintegrated. In France, the socialist party found itself in serious crisis after party unity was shattered by conflicts between the different tendencies dominating its Rennes Congress.

If there are no serious external or internal tensions, democracies can survive such crises of representation; but they are reduced to open political markets in which citizens are no more than political consumers. Although many people may be content with that situation, it enfeebles democracies by depriving them of active support and usually lowering the rate of participation in political life, including elections.

Totalitarianism

When a vanguard party feels that it need not obey the will of the social actor in whose name it is acting, whether because the party asserts the powerlessness of an exploited and alienated category or resorts to a nonsocial definition—such as a biological definition—of the actor, then democracy disappears and those who rely on democracy become totalitarian power's first victims. We have for so long identified totalitarianism with Nazism and, after Nazism's collapse, with communism, that we are usually reluctant to make use of the concept. It does seem too vague a concept to help advance our understanding of Nazism or of what we too cautiously refer to as Stalinism. Most people take the view that it is preferable to analyze nondemocratic regimes in their own terms instead of burdening ourselves with very general notions that mask differences that are often more important than similarities. The Nazi regime, in particular, seems to us an absolute evil that revealed its essence in the extermination of the Jews, Gypsies, and other categories it deemed inferior. The horror of the crimes committed in the deportation and death camps and throughout the societies enslaved by Nazism was so great and so unique that we are afraid of diluting it into a more general category, even though trustworthy analysts have convinced us that the communist regimes in Russia and China have deliberately murdered an equal or greater number of victims. We regard revolutionary communist regimes as social labor movements that have obviously been perverted and destroyed but argue that it is impossible to understand them without making reference to the original social movements. In contrast, we simply regard Nazism as the product of aggressive nationalism and racism and an irrational personality cult. Intellectuals, who have usually been hostile to fascism, have frequently been attracted to the communist appeal to the laws of history, material progress, and the people's state, and have seen those laws as forces that can liberate peoples from the poverty and ignorance perpetuated by despotism, oligarchies, or colonialism. Admittedly, the general political type known as "fascism" is more confusing than useful. It has little unity if it has to include political Islamism as well as other authoritarian regimes, not to mention the family of authoritarian counterrevolutionary regimes created by Franco, Salazar, the Greek colonels, Pétain, Pinochet, and their equivalents in Argentina, Uruguay, and Brazil. The situational diversity of these regimes should prevent us from considering them all as fascist. The concept of totalitarianism is much more useful.

Raymond Aron has identified five main characteristics of totalitarian regimes.

1. One party has a monopoly on political activity.
2. The party is animated by an ideology that becomes the official truth of the state.
3. The state reserves for itself a monopoly on the means of coercion and persuasion.
4. Most economic and professional activities are subject to the state and colored by the official truth.
5. An error in economic or professional activity becomes an ideological fault. There occurs "an ideological transfiguration of all the possible crimes of individuals . . . and in the end police and ideological terrorism" (Aron 1965a: 193–94).

Alessandro Pizzorno has provided a novel historical interpretation of the appeal that totalitarian regimes make to ultimate ends. In his view, the separation of temporal and spiritual power in the Christian lands of the West initially led temporal power—the mighty—to attempt to define ultimate ends and to wield spiritual power. It then encouraged the weak—nations, classes, and movements— "forcefully to establish explicit long-term goals in order to overcome their weakness" (Pizzorno 1993: 81). This interpretation presupposes that there is a high degree of continuity between the formation of the state in the Middle Ages and "absolute politics." As Tocqueville indicates (Tocqueville 1964), this is true in the case of the French revolution, but it does not appear to be true of contemporary totalitarian nationalism. The latter, instead, appears in reaction to crisis or to the challenge posed to communitarian values and norms by exogenous modernization. It was not the working class that gave birth to fascist or even communist totalitarianism but the ruling elites who spoke in the name of nations, classes, or religions. Totalitarianism is not the power of the weak; it is born of the disappearance of social actors.

These analyses suggest a more general explanation. Leaving aside the arbitrary nature of despotic power or the uncontrolled authority of the techno-bureaucratic ruling elite or the *nomenklatura,* the principal feature of an authoritarian state is that it speaks in the name of a society, a people, or a class, borrowing its voice and language. The term "totalitarianism" is well conceived, expressing the idea of total power. In this power, the state, the political system, and social actors merge, lose their identity and specificity, and are no more than instruments of absolute domination by a ruling apparatus that is almost always concentrated around a supreme leader and whose arbitrary power affects every area of social life. Modernity has often been defined in terms of secularization and the differentiation of social subsystems such as religion, politics, the economy, justice, education, and the family. The distinguishing feature of totalitarian regimes is that they destroy secularization in the name of an ideology that applies to every area of political and private life. The differentiation of social activities gives way to a partisan hierarchy in which the individual's personal bond with the prince or party determines his position. Those who fight totalitarianism are usually defending the independence of one of the activites that have been absorbed into the regime. Some defend the social or national movement in whose name the totalitarian power speaks; others seek to preserve the independence of religion, law, the family, or even the state.

So long as democracy was restricted to its republican or liberal elements, totalitarian regimes could not emerge, and democracy's main struggle was directed against the oligarchies and absolute monarchies of old. It denounced the separation of state and society and called for government of the people, by the people, and for the people, or for a people's government. Thanks largely to the labor movement, the transition from liberal democracy to social democracy was seen as such an important victory for the democratic idea that the left, especially in Europe but also in Latin America, rapidly came to be identified with syndicalism and with the twin goals of protecting workers and achieving social justice. The situation that allowed totalitarianism to emerge was, however, created by the notion that social forces had to be represented, by the very idea that representative democracy must make political action serve representable social actors whose existence and consciousness predate their political representation. Mussolini's labor union background, the very name of the German national-socialist (Nazi) party, the proletarian language of the Soviet communist party, and at a much less significant level, the presence of leftist or far-left political and union leaders in the Vichy regime in France are all reminders that totalitarianism was an inverted and perverted form of social democracy rather than simply the conquest of power by an authoritarian group resorting to violence. Totalitarianism triumphs only when a social, cultural, or national movement is reversed to become the *antimovement* that slumbers within it. Whereas a social movement combines awareness of social

conflict with loyalty to cultural values deemed central to the society under consideration, an antimovement transforms a social adversary into an external
enemy and identifies itself with the cultural values that found a community, or in
other words with a collectivity that coincides fully with its own values. An antimovement rejects its opponents as the enemies of society and tries to create a homogeneous society. It may take the form of a sect, but the most important anti-
movements are those that become states or counter-states. A totalitarian state is a
sectarian state, whose primary function is to fight its internal and external enemies and to ensure the greatest and most enthusiastic unanimity possible. An authoritarian regime may be content with crushing society or reducing it to silence.
The totalitarian state, in contrast, must make society speak. It must mobilize and
stimulate society. It identifies with society and demands that society identify with
it. Strictly speaking, there is no such thing as a totalitarian state or society. In a totalitarian regime, the state, society, politics, and civil society merge into an all-
powerful party or power apparatus. This fusion also exists in other regimes, such
as the national-popular regimes of Latin America, but only partially; it is therefore tempting, though erroneous, to describe the Perón regime in Argentina or
the Velasco regime in Peru as totalitarian or fascist. If an authoritarian regime
does not mobilize society or if its political and social action is repressive rather
than ideological, then it would be erroneous to call it totalitarian—General
Pinochet's dictatorship in Chile being a case in point.

Totalitarian regimes are not reducible to their self-image as a perfect harmony
among leader, party, and people. The proclamation of unanimity is important;
but so are the constant denunciations of the enemy, the surveillance and repression, and the transformation of the adversary within into a traitor who is working
for the enemy without. Revolutionary committees, the political police, shock
troops, and party militants are all constantly mobilized in an endless war against
an enemy who is as skilled at penetrating minds as at manipulating interests. Totalitarian regimes are always at war and never know the tranquillity of the despotisms of the ancient world. They are at once the heirs to social movements and the
creators of an order; they claim to be descended from social actors, but constantly
devour them, seeking to suppress their real existence.

This analysis is far removed from that of the Trotskyists, who denounced the
Soviet Union's new ruling class as a bureaucracy that had hijacked the battle for
the collective management of production. The image of a self-transparent society
in which there is a perfect correspondence between social reality and the political
will is, on the contrary, the ideology that best corresponds to the formation of a
totalitarian power, as it justifies the externalization of social conflicts. There can
be no democracy unless intractable social problems can be managed politically.
Claude Lefort has given a vigorous demonstration not only of the weakness of
Trotskyist analyses but of their collusion with the totalitarian spirit (Lefort 1981).
A critical analysis of totalitarianism can only lead to a recognition of the mutual
autonomy of state, political system, and social actors.

The twentieth century has seen totalitarian regimes of three general historical types. The first type is *nationalist* totalitarianism, which contrasts a national or ethnic essence with the rootless universalism of the market, capitalism, art, science, or a multinational empire. This antimodernist nationalism emerged in the late nineteenth century and largely replaced the rationalist and modernizing conception of the nation introduced by the French revolution. Whatever its particular features, fascism fits this general framework, and the fascist model proved attractive to authoritarian, corporatist, and traditional nationalists of the Mediterranean and central Europe. The breakup of the Soviet empire and the decomposition of Yugoslavia provoked a resurgence in nationalist totalitarianism, the most extreme example being the policy of ethnic cleansing pursued by President Milošević, a communist leader who converted to fundamentalist nationalism in the 1990s.

The second type of totalitarianism cries out for comparison with the first because it too refers to a historical being. In this case, however, the being in question is not a nation but a *religion*. This may lead to the sectarian state taking an even more absolute form of control over the whole of society. The Iranian revolution of 1979 began essentially as a social and democratic liberation movement, but it was very rapidly—especially after the outbreak of war with Iraq—transformed into a theocratic totalitarianism that used the Revolutionary Guard and its dense network of agents of surveillance, mobilization, and repression to control the population. Gilles Kepel has rightly drawn parallels between the authoritarian religious movements that have developed in Christian, Jewish, Islamic, and more recently, Hindu worlds (Kepel 1991). Because it is unacceptable to completely identify a religion of any kind with such movements, it is preferable to define them as totalitarian political regimes rather than as religious movements.

The third type of totalitarianism differs from the first two in that it is not subjectivist and does not speak in the name of a race, a nation, or a belief. On the contrary, it is objectivist and claims to be the agent of progress, reason, and modernization. Communist regimes are *modernizing* totalitarian powers, and their ambition is to play midwife to history. They are not a new form of enlightened despotism, for they demand social mobilization and an ideological discourse directed against a class enemy identified in peripheral countries with imperialist and colonial domination, against which communism joins forces with national liberation.

Totalitarian regimes of all types can have beneficial economic or cultural effects in the short or medium term: The German economy was badly hit by the crisis of 1929, and Nazism did aid its recovery. The postwar success of the Soviet economy was symbolized by the fact that the first man in space was a Soviet citizen. North Korea has enjoyed sustained economic growth, and Cuba raised its educational standards and improved the population's standard of health, even though many doctors fled the country. It is, however, time to introduce an idea that will be further developed in the last chapter of this book, namely that in the long term, development and democracy are inseparable. Totalitarianism is an insurmountable obstacle to endogenous development because it blocks the emergence of economic and social actors who are independent and therefore capable of making innovations. When totalitarian regimes are not destroyed by the wars they have unleashed, they suffocate because they refuse to recognize the autonomous existence of civil society and political society.

Such are the general characteristics of totalitarian regimes. Their most typical feature is that the state devours society and speaks in its name. This definition marks a departure from definitions that identify totalitarianism with militarism. The Soviet Union cannot be described as militaristic, as its military was always subordinate to political power. In contrast, imperial Japan, which occupied Korea and China with great brutality, was actually militaristic rather than totalitarian. Even so, we should not surrender to the opposite temptation of making too strict a distinction between the two: The military dictatorships that were established in Brazil in 1964, in Argentina between 1966 and 1976, and in Chile and Uruguay in 1973, were merely authoritarian and not totalitarian; General Stroessner's military dictatorship in Paraguay did, on the other hand, have totalitarian features, as the population was both mobilized and closely controlled by the *colorado* party.

Hannah Arendt's celebrated thesis is more extreme than the one I am putting forward. Taking up Le Bon's and Freud's ideas about crowd psychology, Arendt defined totalitarianism in terms of the dissolution of classes and the triumph of the masses: "The fall of protecting walls transformed the slumbering majorities behind all parties into one great unorganized, structureless mass of furious individuals" (Arendt 1962 [orig. ed. 1951]: 315). She then reformulated the same thesis in more convincing terms by demonstrating that totalitarian regimes use terror in an attempt to realize the law of nature or history, which is tantamount to abolishing actors and their subjectivity. "Totalitarian lawlessness, defying legality and pretending to establish the direct reign of History or Nature without translating it into standards of right or wrong for individual behaviour" (Arendt 1962: 462).

It seems to me, however, that it is dangerous to introduce such a sharp distinction between popular feelings and demands on the one hand and, on the other, the ideology of a regime that has supposedly made a complete break with a society that has been destructured, repressed, and manipulated. After all, Nazism's racist ideology was, to borrow a phrase from Michel Wieviorka, an "inversion" of a German nationalism that had been exacerbated and wounded by the defeat of 1918 (Wieviorka 1993), just as Fidel Castro's totalitarian regime was based on an anti-imperialist nationalism inspired by Martí, and as the communist regimes transformed the will to achieve social and national liberation into an apparatus of totalitarian domination. Nazism's main roots were not in the atomized and deracinated masses of the great factories and the big cities; on the contrary, it was the traditionalist and nationalist categories who, feeling threatened by the economic and political crisis, transformed a defensive nationalism into a nationalist, populist, and racist movement. It is, however, true that this movement was led by déclassé individuals who did not regard themselves as representing any particular social category and whose hatred of the Jews was an expression of a will to assert themselves as the defenders of their own racial purity. The Nazi regime identified with war and open violence to a much greater extent than did the communist regime. It was also much less integrated, and as Franz Neumann was already pointing out in 1944 (Neumann 1944) and as Karl Dietrich Bracher subsequently demonstrated (Bracher 1971 [orig. ed. 1969]), it gave more relative autonomy to the party, the bureaucracy, industry, and the army. Social actors could be transformed into a mass and manipulated by terror at the hands of political ideologues because, as Laski pointed out (Laski 1943), Germany was an industrial power that had not experienced the French revolution or the national unification from below that was so powerful in Great Britain and France. The traditional antimodernist elites therefore remained intact, and militarism was a very powerful force. In the case of Germany, and a fortiori the communist or Islamist regimes, it is impossible to divorce totalitarian regimes either from the social movements they simultaneously used and destroyed or from the factors that prevented the formation of autonomous social actors.

Although we can identify a totalitarian type of regime, there are great differences between the two categories I have outlined here, namely *objectivist* and *subjectivist*. The experience of the postcommunist countries recently has demonstrated that their totalitarian regimes—which were fairly aged and in an advanced state of decay into merely authoritarian powers—had penetrated the personality of their actors only superficially. The present weakness of neocommunist ideological movements, even in Russia, is adequate proof of that, as is the rapid disappearance of any reference to the old regimes in central European countries such as Serbia or Croatia, where communism has been replaced by nationalism. The similar ease with which statist ideology gave way to a complete infatuation with purely economic values is a striking feature in both Poland and Hungary (where large private sectors have been established) as well as Russia (where speculation, the black market, and the mafia, rather than true entrepreneurs, have prospered and provoked a populist backlash).

Subjective totalitarianism, in contrast, penetrates personalities much more deeply and can therefore reemerge after a long eclipse. The military defeat of the Nazi and Japanese regimes led to an American occupation—and to a joint Soviet, British, and French occupation in the case of Germany—one purpose of which was to initiate a profound social transformation. The occupying powers evidently believed that a thoroughgoing reconstruction of society and culture was necessary and feared a possible resurgence of totalitarianism.

It seems necessary to define totalitarianism in a book about democracy because for the past half-century resistance to totalitarianism has been the primary definition of democracy. This fact emphasizes the importance of "English" thinking about negative liberty, and especially recalls the work of Berlin and Popper. It also explains the influence of Sartori and Dahl in both the United States and Europe.

No one now divides the category of republican regimes into democracies and aristocracies or contrasts republican regimes with monarchies and despotisms, as Montesquieu did with such perspicacity in the mid-eighteenth century (Montesquieu 1989 [orig. ed. 1748]). The long half-century that took us from the great economic crisis of 1929 to Solidarity's rising in Poland and then to Gorbachev's perestroika has been dominated by the struggle waged by Western democracies against fascist and communist totalitarianism. We therefore must reject the argument that emphasizes the fall of colonial empires and national liberation movements during the same period. To regard the totalitarian phenomenon, which spread to part of the liberated Third World and to a huge country like China, as more significant is not to deny completely the importance of the fall of the colonial empires; it is merely to recognize that a truly political phenomenon was more important than the social changes that took place during this period. The liberals who constantly asserted the priority of the political, the above-mentioned English thinkers and France's Raymond Aron, have won an intellectual battle against Marxists of all persuasions who strove to apply Marx's idea, which was partly true in his day but false in ours, that politics is determined by objective socioeconomic relations. Thanks to Hannah Arendt, in particular, political thought has accorded central importance to the idea of democracy—and not that of revolution—because democracy is totalitarianism's real adversary. On the contrary, merely speaking, like Trotsky, of "the revolution betrayed" does not rid us of the political model that led to totalitarianism.

The Welfare State

Can the democratic critique of totalitarianism be extended to forms of the state that no one accuses of being totalitarian? Can we say that social democratic politics and the development of the welfare state give the state an increasing ascendancy over public and private life and that although the welfare state does not share the nature of totalitarian despotism it results in what Jürgen Habermas called the colonization of the life-world? Michel Foucault and those he has influenced have developed this theme with considerable force, arguing that the categories of state intervention are increasingly replacing lived experience and that we are what the state makes us through its controls and welfare programs. This trend is obvious in the domains of education, health, and welfare: Our identity is no longer merely a matter of demographic statistics about our sex, age, place and date of birth, or occupation; it is also constructed by administrative categories that have become ways of predicting how we will behave. The schools we go to, the way we pay for our housing, and even the hospital wards we are treated in are all indicators of our social status. In recent years, the files have grown fatter, often so as to facilitate scientific research, and the problems this creates are so serious that committees have been set up to protect the confidentiality of personal data. Is this deindividualization, characteristic of the scientific approach and administrative organization alike, a threat to democracy? Are our personal identities and lived experiences threatened by the classifications associated with the intervention of state, economic, or scientific administrations?

Such worries arise because of the dichotomy between strategic action and communicative action—or to use a more traditional terminology, rationalization and personal autonomy. Yet if we reject the extreme countercultural ideology that condemns the very principle of rationalization, then where are we to draw the line between the rationalized organization of society and the autonomy of lived experience? Do compulsory education and vaccination infringe on personal freedom? It is easy to reply, in this context, that we have to assert rights and find ways to overcome the obstacles to equality of opportunity created by poverty, ignorance, or prejudice; these obligations are therefore concrete forms of citizenship and are more readily acceptable than the duty to pay taxes or to perform military service, especially in time of war. Most social policies are designed to reduce inequality or to ensure a certain redistribution of wealth. The redistribution of wealth has reached a high level in western Europe and is still rising. In France, for example, indirect income has risen from one-quarter to one-third of household income within the space of a few years; and the proportion would be higher still if we took into account public subsidies of education. It is not, then, the action of the welfare state in itself that is disturbing but the heteronomy of those on welfare on the one hand and the ineffectiveness of redistributive measures on the other.

The directly social criticisms of the welfare state are less serious. It is true that free education has the effect of creating inequalities, as children from the wealthiest families study longest. In France, for example, students at the *grandes écoles* receive a salary because they will become civil servants. It is also true that health spending does not have a great redistributive effect, despite the creation of huge social security systems: The higher social categories are better at exploiting the system's resources and consult specialists more often. That criticism is justified but of limited relevance, as one could easily reply that more liberal spending on health and education has the result of creating even greater inequality, as can be seen from the American health system, in which tens of millions of people are not covered by adequate health insurance.

The danger of the heteronomy of welfare recipients, on the other hand, is real, even though we need not accept the hyperliberal talk of the need for individuals to take the initiative. Such talk takes no account of the destructive effects of poverty, unemployment, and illness on the personality. And this brings us to the real problem: Does not state aid to disadvantaged categories, which are usually those with the least capacity for individual and collective action, paradoxically weaken democracy, which is based on the active participation of citizens in collective life? Sociological conceptions of law highlight the interests of society and therefore solidarity. They give the state increasingly extensive powers, although their intention was quite the opposite. Social law, in the descriptive sense of the term, can be interpreted in a number of different ways. It can be seen as a means of protecting individuals and groups subjected to power relations; conversely, it can also be seen as a tool for promoting social and national integration.

The ambiguity of social policies can also be observed at the political level, where social-democracy has been described both as state intervention in economic relations, and as the subordination of political power to an organized social actor, namely the labor movement. The welfare state can belong to any one of the three main categories of legal norms. It may use the law as an agency of integration in an attempt to maintain order in the broadest sense of the term. Alternatively, it may use the law as a contract governing relations between the different or even contradictory interests of actors who must participate in the same social aggregate. Finally, it may use the law to protect individuals, minorities, and even majority groups from the power of the state or from various forms of social domination. It is the type of legal initiative that determines the relative importance of these tendencies. If the agent of intervention is the state, then the law is primarily a force for integration; if it is organized interest groups, then the law tends to be contractual; if mass opinion, organized or otherwise, is allowed to take the initiative, then the law may be more concerned with the protection of individual rights. It might also be said that the will to integrate is better served by measures that apply to particular categories, while collective agreements apply to more general conflicts, and the protective role of the law to general principles.

The best answer to the question "What should be the general direction of social intervention by the state?" is therefore that the assertion of rights and the search for general solutions should be given precedence over measures that apply only to certain categories. The "social" answer to unemployment has largely negative effects because financial aid and training schemes that offer no real prospect of work may marginalize their beneficiaries still further. Democratic debate alone makes it possible to draw up overall plans of action to fight unemployment by economic growth, job sharing, or some other transformation of employment and wages. It is not the increasing rationalization that impedes the formulation and implementation of such policies but the weakness of political thought and action. What we call the colonization of private life is merely an effect of our inability to express social problems in political terms and to find a political solution to them. Under these circumstances, the welfare state with all its weaknesses is preferable to the judgment of the market, which inexorably condemns a growing proportion of the population to social exclusion.

Democracy exists only when social problems are recognized as being the expression of social relations that can be transformed by the voluntary intervention of freely elected governments. Many problems and situations are not, however, recognized as being the result of a certain distribution of resources and, more concretely, of certain policies. If we contrast the life-world with rationalization, we weaken the political field still further; we eliminate all reference to social relations and to the possibility of formulating different policies. The countries that have been most severely affected by unemployment see it as inevitable, as the effect of an international conjuncture over which the country and people in question have little influence. It is argued that the yen and the dollar must rise or that the German or the French market must recover before economic activity and therefore employment can increase in Spain or Italy. The combination of a purely conjunctural analysis with a psychological description of the effects of unemployment creates a nondemocratic climate, for it denies all possibility of action and never gives public opinion a choice. The greatest weakness of democracy in Western countries is precisely this kind of depoliticization of social problems, which can be explained by a weakness in political thought and in parties, which cling to analyses and solutions that no longer correspond to the current situation.

It would be dangerous to put an end to the long evolution that has taken us from the idea of natural law to that of social rights or that has, more accurately, reinforced the idea of natural law by defending it in concrete social situations rather than solely at the level of general principles. The idea of liberty is strengthened when it leads to the recognition not only of civic rights but also of collective labor agreements, as opposed to the old subordination of individual wage earners to omnipotent employers. Defending basic rights in the domains of health and education is now a matter of urgency, but they must also be defended in urban life and in the vast domain of sexual behavior. In all these cases, it is not enough to contrast general rights with the administrative rules that are supposedly designed to normalize minorities and protect the majority. Above all, we must enhance the expressive capabilities of people, who must be recognized as actors and not merely as victims, and thus allow them to take the initiative. This extension of the political field will not come about through thought alone; it will be enforced by the action of the minorities concerned—as we have already seen with homosexuals who have been discriminated against in so many countries. It is not the life-world that must be protected and stimulated; it is the capacity for action on the part of dominated or excluded categories. It is not rationalization that must be fought but the degradation of the realm of opportunity into that of necessity and the disjuncture between economic policy and social welfare policy. When basic liberties are already respected, the fate of democracy depends primarily on the reorganization of social life through the formation of new social movements and the renewal of social and political analysis.

We have seen social-democratic policies degenerate into neocorporatism, strengthening interest groups within the state. We have seen them transformed into channels of public funding for rapidly expanding consumer sectors. We have to learn once more to look at our society in global terms and to see it as a productive society as well as a consumer and redistributive society. If we can do that, we will be able to identify new social and political actors and new issues, to define and evaluate them. The future of democracy depends not so much on the share of gross domestic product that is distributed by the state as on our ability to behave like the actors of a new type of society, to choose policies that reduce inequalities, and to breathe new life into political debates. The need for critiques of the welfare state is less urgent than the need to identify new forms of production and new social conflicts. If we achieve the latter, then we will be able to give social policy a renewed mandate of reform aimed at reducing inequalities and protecting the safety and liberty of the greatest number of citizens.

Democracy Weakened

What conclusions are we to draw from this glance at the history of democracy? Two contradictory ideas emerge. The first is optimistic: The emergence of the three principal dimensions of democracy—citizenship, the limitation of state power, and representativity—is a cumulative process that leads to ever more complete forms of democracy. The process began with the assertion of the sovereignty of the people and the creation of the nation-state, notably in the United States and France. The republican principle was then reconciled with the liberal principle in restricted democracies, the most complete example being the British political system of the nineteenth century. Finally, we see the emergence of a mass representative democracy that is at once republican, liberal, and social. The latter created the strongest images of twentieth-century democracy: Roosevelt's New Deal, the Popular Front in France, and the establishment of the British welfare state. This is the model toward which countries in eastern and central Europe and Latin America are striving in their attempts to democratize. It also serves as a reference point for India, the largest democracy in the world, and for other countries that have experienced and are still experiencing great struggles for democracy, such as South Korea and South Africa. Yet as soon as we advance this optimistic hypothesis, a more pessimistic question arises. Does not this progressive combination of our three components and the emergence of truly democratic thought in fact hasten the impoverishment of democracy? Wasn't democracy's heyday at the very beginning of its history, perhaps even in Athens? Or more recently, was it the moment of the drafting of the U.S. constitution or of France's Declaration of the Rights of Man and Citizen or the moment when Great Britain was basking in the light of the Bill of Rights? The eighteenth century saw the triumph of the republican idea; the nineteenth century, the success and then the demise of limited democracies; but the twentieth has seen the explosion of authoritarian regimes and then a growing lack of interest in politics in the richest societies. Does the universal verbal homage that is paid to democracy in fact mask, as John Dunn has ironically suggested, the degeneration of the democratic idea into an ideal of direct management that we admire precisely because we know it is impossible? Has not the trust that some countries, or rather their shrinking intellectual elites, once placed in the sovereignty of the people disappeared, and has not politics been invaded by consumerism and marketing? Can we speak of the triumph of democracy at a time when no one seems to have any faith in political action?

In answer to these questions, let us first of all affirm that a democracy that is not simultaneously republican, liberal, and social is now inconceivable, even though most democratic regimes do not fully meet these three criteria of existence. For a long time, we resorted to institutional methods to avoid the tyranny of the majority: limited suffrage, controlled access to the ruling elite, the creation of an upper chamber of notables, clientelism, corruption, and so on. Yet the creation of mass parties and unions, rising standards of education, and the spread of mass consumption, together with the development of the mass media, make it increasingly difficult to reconcile the political system's twin roles as an antechamber to the state and an expression of popular demands and feelings.

The intensification of national problems, the sensitization of the wage-earning majority to economic cycles of crisis and expansion, and the transnationalization of the economy all have shaken or even destroyed the social democracy created by the alliance between state and trade-union forces. The gulf between the elements of democracy is now quickly widening. Citizenship has come to mean cultural identity. The restriction of power by basic rights has been transformed into a divorce between private and public life, and the representation of interests has in many cases been so debased as to mean a neocorporatist fusion between the state and what were once social classes. It was the framework provided by the nation-state that allowed these three components to come together; but the nation-state itself has been weakened, particularly in those European countries that did the most to develop democratic action and thought. The republican state has gone into an irreversible decline. We no longer agree that particularisms should be absorbed into the universalism of state action, and we find such expressions shocking at the end of a century that has been dominated by totalitarian states.

However, it is not only the haughty modernizing state that is in decline but also the democratic nation-state, long exemplified by Great Britain and Westminster. The prominent role of parliaments gave this political system central importance in social life. The state was under the direct control of parliament and its administrative authority was restricted. Social actors were represented—not without major limitations throughout much of Great Britain's history—and parliamentary debates were society's debates. The political system, especially parliament, has now lost its central role. This is nothing new, as every critic of the excessive importance of parties since Ostrogorski and Michels has warned us of the demise of politics. What *is* new is that parties themselves are now in decline, while the state is preoccupied with responding to the constraints of the international market. Can we still speak of the triumph of democracy when the political system is declining, as is the case in most countries? The collapse of authoritarian regimes rarely increases the intensity of parliamentary debates.

The state in western countries has become less repressive and more concerned with growth. Its objectives for the most part are economic rather than political, and it relies more on foreign investment than on police to reduce social tensions.

In fact the drop in social tensions in the greater part of the world is striking; at a time when so many countries are experiencing serious difficulties, the political stage is deserted. The hopes that were once placed in political action, revolutionary or otherwise, have vanished. Some now place their faith in the hope of personal economic success; others accept a marginality they cannot hope to escape. Still others sink into lonely poverty, violence, or delinquency. Politics seems incapable of expressing or organizing demands, and the political system is becoming isolated from society. In the richest countries, youth culture, the messages of the media, and the attractions of mass consumption mean that social demands are now expressed in nonpolitical ways. At the same time, the state—and through it the international economy—is steadily increasing its hold over the lives of individuals. We should not allow the necessity of the republican state's retreat to blind us to the gravity of an extreme depoliticization that goes so far as to reject the "political class," negating the very substance of democracy. In the long term, we cannot be content with the illusion that equates democracy with restrictions on state intervention.

We do not yet know how to put a name to and discuss the great social problems of our day; therefore, we cannot express them in political terms. We still see them in moral or humanitarian terms, as did the philanthropists of the mid-nineteenth century, before trade unionism and socialist thinking came to the fore. A discussion of democracy cannot be restricted to an analysis of constitutional law, important as that may be; nor should it limit itself to seeking new means of linking state, political society, and civil society. A discussion of democracy should be primarily an investigation into the nature of the great social and cultural problems at stake in political debate and decisionmaking. Democracy will inevitably be weakened if it ceases to be representative and if social actors therefore become incapable of formulating their demands and hopes. We should, however, avoid the radical pessimism that is so quick to identify democracy with the particular form it took in the republican state inspired by the philosophy of the Enlightenment; for the correspondence between man and citizen has been destroyed, as has the more general correspondence between system and actors. That sort of participatory democracy, as earlier discussed, could lead to the state's authoritarian control over individuals as well as to an ideal popular sovereignty; so let us accept this new distance, within limits. On the one hand, all institutions are becoming increasingly autonomous—from science, which develops according to its own internal impulse, to production, which is regulated by the market. On the other hand, social actors no longer attempt to participate in the system but instead seek self-identification and recognition from other actors and institutions. The democratic order must be redefined to combine the internal logic of particular social systems with the self-proclamation of the subject, apart from any higher, unifying principle. In view of the threats posed by totalitarianism on the one hand and the rule of the neocorporatist or hyperliberal market on the other, democracy appears to be the only answer to the dangers of the fragmentation or the authoritarian unification of social life. One might even take the view that the separation of actor from system and citizen from state is strengthening democracy, whereas the republican spirit did at least as much to restrict it as to encourage it.

The Renewal of the Democratic Idea

An awareness of the most serious threats to democracy and of the means for combating them provides a first indication of where the solution lies.

Resistance to the totalitarian state and to the less dramatic dangers of mass consumption is based on the assertion of the personal subject and its freedom, memory, and cultural identity. Throughout the world, we find that workplace conflicts and class struggles are increasingly incapable of serving as a general framework for social demands; but that observation can lead us in two directions. First, we may accept the diversity of social problems and take the view that political life approximates the model of a political market where supply and demand may eventually match. The alternative interpretation is that the previous overlap of political, social, and personal concerns that once sustained the hope of a more efficient and fairer modern society has given way to a direct conflict between the constraints imposed by markets on one hand and demands for collective and personal liberty on the other. The market tends to maximize exchange and to increase the flow of commodities and information; social actors—individual or collective—seek to map out and preserve the meaning of their experience and to join their memories of the past to their present and future plans.

For a hundred years, democracy's space was to a large extent the space of economic activity and labor relations. In postindustrial society, where education, health, social security, and information play a more central role than the production of material goods, the fate of democracy is decided everywhere—in schools and universities, in newspapers and on television channels, as well as in the productive sector. This extension of political action means that the political space itself must be transformed accordingly. Democratic life was for a long time organized around parliaments. At a later stage it was organized around parties, which linked social demands and political action. The debates that are central to democratic action now take place in the vast world of the media. It is in the domain of health care that debates are most heated, ranging from campaigns in favor of abortion and contraception to arguments about genetic therapy, various methods of treating infertility and AIDS, and euthanasia. Neither political parties nor unions initiated these debates; they were initiated by associations, NGOs, shifts in public opinion, and in some cases social or cultural movements.

The weakness of such debates stems from the fact that they are increasingly divorced from the elaboration of economic policies. On the one hand, governments in both the North and the South are increasingly preoccupied with international economic issues. On the other, public opinion attaches increasing importance to the problems of personal life, to related environmental problems, and above all, to the survival of humanity, which is threatened by the uncontrolled effects of its in-creasing mastery of nature—now no more than a raw material for growth.

If we take the first path, which seems the more accessible, it is difficult to escape the theme of the decline of politics. Carlo Mongardini feared that the decline of political voluntarism, whose liberating aspects are real, might also reduce politics to self-interest and destroy the communitarian dimension of the pursuit of a common good (Mongardini 1990). Yet hasn't communitarian ideology itself been debased? Has not the pursuit of the common good become an obsession with identity and do we not need stronger institutional guarantees of respect for per-sonal liberty and human rights rather than more integrated communities?

We therefore have to look to culture and not institutions in our search for the foundations of democracy. *Democratic culture* is not merely the diffusion of dem-ocratic ideas—a set of educational programs and television broadcasts or publi-cations for the general public. Still less is it reducible to a discourse that, as we all know, is listened to all the more readily because it is so general that everyone can adapt it to suit his or her own ideas and interests. Democratic culture is a concep-tion of human beings that stubbornly resists all attempts to create an absolute power—even when it is validated by an election. At the same time, it stimulates the will to create and perpetuate the institutional preconditions for personal lib-erty. The central importance of the personal subject's liberty and an awareness of the public preconditions for private liberty are the two elementary principles of today's democracy. The identification of man with citizen was liberating in the late eighteenth century, but it has since become dangerous. The call for participa-tion usually leads to the rejection of outsiders rather than to the extension of the liberty of all. In a mass society, the obsession with homogeneity, which Toc-queville already found disturbing in the nineteenth century, leads to the exclusion of more and more people. The ever present threat of social normalization or cleansing obliges us to invent a democratic culture that can be initially defined as a recognition of the other. In embarking on a study of such a democratic culture we are not turning away from the central problems of democracy; on the con-trary, we are advancing toward the very core of political sociology.

PART 3

Democratic Culture

The Politics of the Subject

People generally have taken two different approaches to defining democracy: For some, democracy is a matter of giving form to the sovereignty of the people; for others, it is a matter of ensuring freedom of political debate. According to the first view, democracy is defined by its substance; in the second, it is defined by its procedures. The second definition is the more easily stated of the two: freedom of association and freedom of speech make it possible to hold free elections and to guarantee that they are fair. Law-governed institutions are also necessary to prevent the will of the people from being misrepresented, to ensure that deliberations and decision-making processes are open, and to prevent elected representatives and rulers from becoming corrupt. The primary goal is to protect parliament from the executive power, which has a greater capacity for data collection and decisionmaking. The weakness of this conception is that respect for the rules of the game does not prevent the players from having unequal opportunities if some have more resources than others or if only oligarchies are allowed to play.

This weakness is so obvious that few are satisfied with a purely procedural definition of democracy. Like Lincoln everyone expects a democracy to make decisions in accordance with the interests either of the majority or of society as a whole; but who is to judge where those interests lie? Sociologists tend to give very pessimistic answers to this perplexing question. The way people vote is heavily influenced by their situation and therefore their interests, and there is usually a large element of inertia in voting patterns; people tend to consistently vote for a party out of loyalty, tradition, or self-interest, and if they do change they way they vote, it is not usually because they have a clear vision of the general interest. Many observers of political life therefore conclude that elections encourage voters to make negative rather than positive choices; elections have become a way of expressing disapproval rather than preferences. I find this position too pessimistic, as it suggests that universal suffrage does not bring us any closer to a solution and that the initiatives taken by our rulers—or even the influence of ruling interests—still decide what political line is taken. We would do better to admit that democracy does not exist and that a government has only to rely on opinion polls and spin doctors to avoid public demonstrations of discontent or disobedience.

Those who brought about the triumph of the democratic idea and, above all, of universal suffrage had higher expectations of political liberty. They expected it to allow the majority to ensure that its rights were respected and that equality of rights and citizenship would prevail over the inequality of resources. Democracy's primary goal was to create a political society whose central principle was equality. According to this view, there is nothing to be added to Tocqueville's classic analysis. After the decisive acts of 1789 that transformed the Estates General into the National Assembly and later the Constituent Assembly by asserting the sovereignty of the people, nothing more needed to be done. Whereas civil society—in other words, the system of economic exchange—is dominated by inequality and conflicts of interest, political society must be a place of equality. The primary goal of democracy is to ensure equality of opportunity as well as equality of rights—that is, to exert every effort in order to restrict the unequal distribution of resources.

This conception of democracy was valid so long as the modern world was living under the sign of what Max Horkheimer called objective reason (Horkheimer 1947). While it was fighting a hierarchical society whose primary purpose was the reproduction of a social order, political society seemed an agent of liberation, like scientific reason; but when the success of modernization made more consumer goods available, increased mobility, and weakened traditional hierarchies, political society and its ethics of duty came to be seen as restrictive. The moderns therefore soon began to look to civil society rather than the state in their search for liberty. The liberal state was then invaded by social forces. Georges Burdeau wrote of the replacement of a democracy of the ruled by a democracy of rulers and, more important still, of the triumph of "socially situated man": "Not only is he a whole person, who is not required to detach himself from the determinisms that shape him in his daily life; he is also a perfectly actual man, whose aspirations all correspond to his condition and to the environment in which he finds himself. He is a situated man" (Burdeau 1972: 18–19). This new person completely transforms the relationship between the political and the social. "The appearance on the political stage of situated man results in such a total transformation of the relationship between the political and the social that the distinction between the two gives way to an identification of one with the other" (Burdeau 1972: 119).

Political democracy, according to Burdeau, has been replaced by social democracy and the triumph of the actual *people*. This necessarily involves a revolutionary break between the two, even though in Western countries an unstable compromise still exists between political democracy and a social democracy that takes the form of, for example, Roosevelt's New Deal. Strongly influenced by the experience of postwar political transformations and conflicts, especially the French experience, Burdeau has provided us with a remarkable documentary account of this stage in political history. The sixth volume of his *Traité de science politique* is devoted to the liberal state, the seventh to the democracy of rulers—in other words, social democracy—and the eighth to how that form of power entered its critical phase with the emergence of postindustrial society. We can accept this sequence of stages, but we should interpret it in the light of a study of political liberty. Burdeau gives a good account of the eclipse of the political, a topic that has long dominated social thought: Were not individual freedom and its legal guarantees destined to give way to the liberation of a class and the creation of a true people's democracy?

Yet political thought cannot mimic the continuity of the liberal thought that has supposedly always been identified with democracy; for liberalism has not always been democratic any more than social democracy has always respected liberties. Just as we cannot contrast the universalism of human rights with the particularist nature of social rights without destroying much of the content of the former, so the identification of the sovereignty of the people with government by the popular classes and their representatives destroys one of the founding principles of democracy: the limitation of state power and respect for the basic rights of individuals. Liberal thought was enriched by its struggle against absolute monarchy. In similar fashion, the struggle against the power of the bourgeoisie did much to promote the idea of social democracy. Yet both turned against democracy when they ceased to respect the combination of the three component elements that is essential to democracy's existence. Despite the existence of "people's democracies," it has been obvious to all for the past thirty years that democracy necessarily has a liberal content; one has only to think of the Hungarian revolution, October 1956 in Poland, the Prague spring of 1968, the action of Solidarity in 1980–81, Gorbachev's perestroika, the collapse of Mao's cultural revolution, the fall of the Berlin Wall, or the liberation of most of the countries that were once part of the Soviet empire.

Given the weakness of what Burdeau calls consensual democracy and the passivity of citizens in a consumer society dominated by great commercial, technical, and administrative organizations, we must attempt to reconcile the idea of social rights with that of political liberty. It seems to me possible to do so if we understand that in a postindustrial society where production centers more on cultural services than material goods, the idea of defending the subject and its personality and culture from the logic of apparatuses and markets replaces the idea of class struggle. The idea of class struggle has failed with good reason: Imbued with social naturalism and the idea that the triumph of the workers is the triumph of the rationality of history over the irrationality of capitalist profit, it left no foundation on which to base political liberty.

No one now admires the equality of condition that pertained in communist countries. No one envies the uniformity of the Chinese masses, dressed in high-collared jackets, trousers, and caps that transformed them into clones. We tend, rather, to be frightened by such uniformity and to see it as a sign of servitude.

The final transition from the liberty of the ancients to the liberty of the moderns is, thus, taking place. The republican spirit is growing weaker as the liberty of the ancients goes into decline. It is time to build new foundations for democracy.

Democracy first emerged when the political realm became divorced from the world order, when a collectivity resolved to create a social order that was no longer defined by its conformity to some higher law but by the body of laws it had created to express and guarantee the liberties of every individual member. However, the political realm was then invaded by economic activity, military might, and the bureaucratic mind-set. With increasing frequency it was destroyed by the reference to a superior power—by the idea that society itself was mind, reason, history, or even—and why not?—God himself.

The liberty of the moderns is a reformulation of the liberty of the ancients: It retains the initial idea of popular sovereignty, but it explodes the myths of the people, the nation, and the society so that they cannot give rise to new forms of absolute power; for it has discovered that only the recognition of the individual human subject can create collective liberty, or in other words, democracy. This principle is universal in significance but historically specific in application; it imposes no permanent social norms.

If there were no universalistic principles and human behavior were completely socially determined, no one could formulate laws. We would have to be content with social relativism—which may well satisfy ethnographers but which is powerless against conquest, domination, exploitation, and cruelty. We must pass judgments; moral relativism is simply irresponsible. The universality of moral principles means that we cannot view values in purely subjective terms. Psychology has given us such profound insights into the illusions of the ego that we cannot accept conviction and authenticity as justificatory principles. If we accept such subjective principles, we are in danger of tolerating all manner of fanaticism.

The consciousness of the subject and human rights have a history, and it is the history of modernity. The human subject's self-perception was originally mediated through a divine subject and then a political, or later a social, subject. The human subject was finally forced to discover its own face: the face of its freedom. The subject is not a prophet and does not formulate laws. The subject refers to neither social utility nor the world order and tradition. It is self-referential and refers only to the personal, interpersonal, and social preconditions that allow it to construct and defend its liberty—or in other words, the personal meaning it gives to its own experience by resisting all forms of dependency, whether psychological or political.

The relationship between religions and the idea of the subject is a contradictory one, as we can see from Pope John Paul II's recent encyclical *Veritatis splendor* (John Paul 1994). The Catholic church's fundamental teaching is that God forbade man to eat from the tree of the knowledge of good and evil (Genesis 2:17) and that although man was given the freedom to choose between good and evil, he was not given the freedom to decide which was which. Freedom must therefore be subordinate to truth, and the church is the guardian of truth. Like revolutionary parties, churches regard themselves as representatives of the truth. They are responsible for instilling a respect for the truth, like a schoolteacher who penalizes students for grammatical errors or mistakes in equations. Churches and parties are thus forced to resist democratic liberty as a matter of principle. Yet the same encyclical recalls at length that Christianity also has very different implications. If God did create man in his own image by giving him reason and freedom, then we have to agree with John Paul II that "The importance of this interior *dialogue of man with himself* can never be adequately appreciated"—although the pope immediately added, "But it is also *a dialogue of man with God*" (John Paul 1994: 131). We cannot, however, overlook the fact that many people in our secularized societies have long argued that God is man's heavenly reflection. There can be no democracy without a principle that places human beings outside the natural or social order of things. Religious belief did give this principle of externality a certain form, even though religious institutions subordinated human life to an order that was at once divine and natural. Similarly, in a secularized society, humanism has asserted that human beings are free, but at the same time has tended to dissolve liberty into needs that are socially, psychologically, and biologically determined. Thus, we never make the transition from a society of subordination to a society of liberty. We find in all societies both a clash between and a combination of the spirit of determinism and the spirit of liberty. If democracy therefore cannot be defined as either the subordination of the private lives of citizens to the public interest or as the restriction of public life to the defense of individual liberty, then we can only define it as a combination of the unity of law and technique, cultural diversity and personal liberty.

Conflicting Values and Democracy

If it is to be democratic, a political system must recognize the existence of insurmountable conflicts over values. It therefore cannot accept that societies can be organized around one central principle, such as rationality or cultural specificity. We have long been accustomed to the idea that the existence of insurmountable social conflicts makes democracy necessary; if the plurality of interests could be resolved in such a way as to allow the division of labor and vested interests to be managed rationally, there would indeed be no need for democracy. Democracy is necessary because economic development demands both the concentration of investment and the distribution of the economic product, and no technical rule can reconcile these requirements, which are contradictory as well as complementary. Only a political decision can decide the relative weight that is to be accorded these two components of economic development; and democracy is a recognition of that political process and of its accessibility and exposure to the public.

The modern world must recognize that the globalization of the economy and culture implies cultural pluralism. A national society that is culturally homogeneous is by definition antidemocratic. We do not witness the creation of a more and more homogeneous world. Social and cultural dualization is an international phenomenon, as are state policies designed to defend cultural specificities. Just as the liberty of the ancients was based on the equality of citizens, so the liberty of the moderns is based on the social and cultural diversity of the members of national or local societies. Democracy is now the means to safeguard that diversity, to allow increasingly diverse individuals and groups to live together in a society that must function as a unit. A political society cannot live without a national language or a legal system that applies to all, even if cultural diversity is increasingly accepted. The Europe that is emerging must be a federal state; at the same time, the nation-states that constitute it must have more rights and more responsibilities than do the states in the United States of America. Democracy is necessary because it is difficult to reconcile this combination of unifying and diversifying factors. Wherever conflicts exist over interests and values, a space must be organized for political debates and deliberations.

A Second Note on John Rawls

Political liberalism cannot accept that one general religious or political doctrine should determine the organization of society. However, it has sometimes surrendered to the temptation to make rationalism and the Kantian autonomy of the individual the principles on which society should be based. Yet this militant rationalism or secularism is as dangerous as any other variety of absolutist politics, as it too must rely on a state apparatus in order to implement its principles. In John Rawls's *Political Liberalism* (Rawls 1993), which brings together most of Rawls's own commentaries of the past twenty years on his *A Theory of Justice* (Rawls 1971) and on criticisms leveled against it, Rawls has refocused his argument on this central question: How, in a fair society, can we organize a lasting collaboration between individuals and groups that hold mutually irreconcilable convictions and beliefs? Democracy must be pluralistic. Rawls thus adds a new dimension to twentieth-century liberal thought, which has been criticized for not concentrating enough on the problem of the state and ignoring economics and ethics. Rawls's answer—which will be affirmed, at least in the first analysis and in general terms, by all who seek to identify the preconditions of democracy—is that democracy presupposes a specific but nonglobal agreement—an agreement that is not concerned with ultimate goals or conceptions of the good (Rawls 1993: 73–211) but rather with the political domain itself, or in other words, the preconditions for cooperation. This consensus is not global but is "a moral conception worked out for a specific subject, namely the basic structure of a constitutional democratic regime" (Rawls 1993: 175). Its focus is on "primary goods," or in other words, on the conditions of citizenship and free and equal participation in the management of society. It therefore is concerned with basic rights: freedom of conscience and of movement and access to power, income, wealth, and the social bases of self-respect (Rawls 1993: 181). The autonomy of the political field and the acceptance of principles of justice, according to *A Theory of Justice*, can constitute an "overlapping consensus" among individuals belonging to different categories because it affects only the specific domain of citizenship. The autonomy of the political further implies a process of communication, which Rawls defines in terms similar to those used by Habermas as the ability to establish "the sources or causes of disagreement between reasonable persons" (Rawls 1993: 55) and to recognize the authenticity of others' beliefs and consequently the particular nature of one's own—unlike a fundamentalist politics, which would relegate the other to such categories as devil, aggressor, or barbarian. Rawls described the ability to recognize the autonomy of the political field as "reasonable": "Reasonable doctrines endorse the political conception, each from its own point of view" (Rawls 1993: 134). Rawls's constructivism—which he contrasts with the intuitionist view that we must identify objective values—does not aspire to the building of a rational society, which was the dream of utopian rationalists, but to defining the minimal preconditions for cooperation and the limits of the political field. This theoretical argument is more in keeping than is *A Theory of Justice* with the growth of multiculturalism and of the autonomy of ethnic, religious, or ethical communities in American society. It is also an extension of Weber's notion of the pluralism of values.

However, Rawls's expansion of his analysis and his new focus on the theme of pluralism does not mean that his overall position has changed. His real concern is still to base social life on a contract that relates to the two principles of justice and that therefore is founded on a truly political mode of thought, separated from social interests by a veil of ignorance (Rawls 1971: 136f.).

Why does Rawls accept that the political realm should be isolated from social interests or cultural beliefs? We know of many societies that function differently, even apart from the two extreme cases that are rightly ignored by Rawls—namely, rationalist Jacobin societies and fundamentalist societies, both of which reject the very idea of reconciling citizenship and beliefs. I have already said on a number of occasions that the contemporary world, which is superficially described as globalized and unified, is on the contrary dominated by a hierarchical divorce between the world of international trade and the world of local identities; hence, the European-style nation-states that broadly conformed to Rawls's idea of the political system are in demise. Another example is the system of *consociativismo*, analyzed by Alessandro Pizzorno (Pizzorno 1993: 285–313). In this case, the political system is jointly managed by actors holding conflicting convictions or beliefs. In Europe, Italy is the most striking example of this arrangement: power there is shared by parties or social forces that define themselves as mutually hostile but that still coexist, thanks to some form of *compromesso storico*. Rawls's conception, in fact, presupposes the existence of actors who are reasonable and therefore tolerant and moderate; but although the recognition of the autonomy of the political field might be described as reasonable, rationality does not explain how or why this autonomy is recognized.

The argument I have outlined is rather different. It stresses that there is a growing dissociation between instrumental rationality and the cultural identities and it views the autonomy of the political field, and in more concrete terms, democracy, as the only possible means of restricting or perhaps reducing that dissociation. This can only be done by wresting both instrumental rationality and cultural beliefs from the power apparatuses that have appropriated them and that speak in their names. The strength of democracy therefore stems not from a rational construct but from a struggle that is waged against powers and in the name of interests and values. Democracy exists only insofar as it is a liberation from rationalist despotism as well as communitarian dictatorship—above all, from their extreme forms, which I describe, respectively, as the totalitarianism of objectivity and the totalitarianism of subjectivity. Democracy's space is not calm and reasonable. It is a space of tensions and conflicts, of mobilizations and internal struggles, because it is constantly threatened by one or another of the powers that loom over it.

In sum, there is a substantial difference between the efforts of Rawls and other key philosophers to refine the liberal conception of politics on the one hand and any attempt to elaborate a truly democratic but nonliberal conception of political society on the other. As I see it, democracy's raison d'être is to supply the indispensable institutional preconditions that allow the personal subject to act. As I have said elsewhere in a discussion of the emblematic figure of the immigrant, only the actor—individual or collective—can reconcile the universal with the particular and instrumentality with conviction. In my view, the idea of the subject determines that of intersubjectivity, and a fortiori that of democratic society. For Rawls, in contrast, it is the autonomy of political choice, based on the twin principles of justice, that defines the workings of democracy.

The difference between these two points of view is, however, limited: Both accept the autonomy of the political system and therefore reject the view, which is so dominant in the German and French traditions, that the political is reducible to the state. Rawls, in keeping with the Anglo-American tradition, takes as his starting point the individual and the interests and values of the individual. He thus accepts a utilitarian starting point, even though he criticizes it and goes beyond it by centering his analysis on a free *homo politicus* and on citizens, or in other words on individuals who can, throughout their lives, act as normal and fully cooperative members of society. This defines what Rawls describes from the outset as the "original position." Its twin components are what he terms reasonableness and rationality; they are distinct but also interrelated. Rawls argues that complete autonomy involves both the ability to be reasonable and the ability to advance conceptions of the good in a manner that is compatible with respect for fair social cooperation, or in other words, the principles of justice.

The emphasis should be placed on the complementary nature of these viewpoints rather than on the differences between them, as the political subject should be seen as simultaneously involved in relations of domination and power, as the defender of its own interests, and as a citizen and a force that can resist both the communitarian consciousness and ruling groups. This brings us back to the three dimensions of democracy that we described earlier, in Part 1: the representation of majority interests, citizenship, and basic rights that restrict power. I have attempted to demonstrate that these three cannot be reduced to a single principle: Revolutionary conceptions of democracy give greater importance to the first dimension; Rawls and Anglo-American liberals stress the second; and the theme of the subject, to which I accord a central importance, can be identified as the third; however, none of these dimensions can exist in the absence of the other two. Rawls's attempt to synthesize unity and plurality, or freedom and equality, is therefore open to criticism; his central themes are not.

Rawls's thought has dominated political philosophy for the past twenty years. More lucidly and more decisively than anyone else, he has addressed the central issue in the political debate by asking how the unity of political society can be reconciled with the plurality of convictions and beliefs. He occupies the middle ground; that is, he is at the crossroads of those who stress the themes of individual liberties and those who see the unity of the people and of citizens as the best defense against privilege and inequality. As Rawls's combination of the two principles that define justice as fairness demonstrates so clearly, his work is a meeting ground for those whose first thought is for liberty and those whose first thought is for equality. Yet although in intellectual terms he occupies a central position, is Rawls's thought truly a meeting point for and a synthesis of these ideas? Is a fair and equitable society capable of self-regulation? Can a combination of liberty and equality produce ideas and institutions that can mold social practices? One suspects not. We have a clear idea of what republican society is, even when it takes an extreme or revolutionary form: it follows Rousseau's conception that the political realm is divorced from the social realm and may have to fight it in order to force equality on the inequalities of social life. We also have a clear idea of what is meant by a pluralist society that respects a diversity of interests, opinions, and values; it follows Locke's conception. Yet although the Declaration of the Rights of Man and Citizen drew on the heritage of both Rousseau and Locke, it could not synthesize the two. Rawls likewise clings to both the idea of the social contract and the idea that individuals rationally pursue their own interests. He has reconciled the two principles at the intellectual level; and we can agree that American society has combined the corresponding sociopolitical models in practice. To combine conflicting ideas, however, is not necessarily to integrate or unite them. Rawls's ambition is indeed to integrate these two viewpoints; but despite his best efforts, there is in his work an ever present conflict between a pluralistic liberal society on the one hand and a republican society on the other. In Rawls's work, the individualist theme and the theme of citizenship intersect but never merge into one.

Yet we cannot rightly speak of a failure on Rawls's part. On the contrary, we must admit that it is impossible to reduce the constituent elements of democracy to a single principle. Even modest solutions—like that proposed by Rawls in his attempt to arrive at a synthesis of reasonableness and fairness, rather than the more ambitious synthesis of rationality and the good—are impossible. The dichotomy that runs throughout this book, between a republican democracy based on citizenship and equality and a pluralist democracy based on cultural diversity and liberty, is insurmountable. That fact should not prevent us from seeking combinations and compromises, but it does preclude the discovery of one central principle. Justice will not provide the desired (but impossible) synthesis of liberty and equality.

The Subject and Democracy

It is not enough to speak of a combination of elements, as though democracy were a synthesis of unity and diversity or of instrumental rationality and respect for individual and collective cutural identity. The logic of instrumental rationality and the logic of the defense of community are contradictory; they either clash or drift apart and leave the social world torn asunder. Such a rupture would be much more far-reaching than that between classes that fight over how the fruits of development are to be distributed yet share the same cultural orientations. It could lead to worldwide civil war and to a splitting of the individual personality, both of which would destroy civilization, were it not for the intervention of mediating forces such as the subject and democracy, which are the inseparable emblems of the individual and society.

The *subject* integrates identity and techniques to become an *actor* who can modify the environment and turn life experiences into demonstrations of liberty. The subject is neither self-consciousness nor an individual's identification with a universal principle such as reason or God. The subject is an attempt to bring together things that tend to drift apart—an attempt that is never complete and never successful. To the extent that the subject is its own creation, the social actor is self-centered rather than socially centered; the subject is defined by its freedom—not by the roles it plays. The subject is a moral principle that breaks with the ethics of duty, which associates virtue with playing a role in society. Individuals become subjects not when they identify with the general will or when they are a community's heroes, but when, on the contrary, they break free of the social norms of "duty to country," as the Christian moralists used to put it, and aspire to what Alasdair MacIntyre called "the narrative unity of a life." This corresponds to what John Rawls and many others have called a "life project." A life project is not to be confused with a "life idea," which is defined by its content, for that expression is as ambiguous as the notion of the "good life." It can easily be demonstrated that the notion of the good life is always socially determined and represents the internalization of dominant norms. A life project, in contrast, is an ideal of independence and responsibility defined in terms of a struggle against heteronomy, imitation, and ideology, rather than in terms of a specific content. We can therefore describe as a subject any individual who has never been content to cultivate his garden but who has fought those who invaded his personal life and forced him to obey their orders. The idea of the subject in fact brings together three elements whose presence is equally indispensable: The first is resistance to domination, which we have already mentioned; the second is self-esteem, which allows the individual to posit liberty as the main precondition for happiness and as a central objective. The third element is the recognition of others as subjects combined with support for the political and juridical rules that give the greatest number the best chance of living as subjects.

The idea of the subject marks a departure from the principle of natural law and the image of a conscious individual who is endowed with free will and whose social environment consists solely of similar individuals. That is to say, the idea of the subject is inseparable from social relations, from the forms of organization and, above all, social power, in which individuals and groups find themselves enmeshed. Those, like Jürgen Habermas, who replace consciousness with communication, and therefore, subjectivity with intersubjectivity, are right to distance themselves from an artificial individualism; but they do not travel the full length of the path that leads to a sociological analysis. For intersubjective communication does not bring individuals face to face with one another. It is as much an encounter between social positions and power resources as between personal and collective imaginaries. In any case, all individuals are more continuously caught up in relations of dependency or cooperation than in linguistic exchanges. An individual works, commands, or obeys and encounters scarcity or abundance. His private and public relations create around him an opacity that is never dispelled by debates and arguments. Knowledge of the other is always preceded by the quest for the self, as the individual is a subject not by virtue of some divine decision but by his efforts to escape constraints and rules and to organize his experience. All this produces a stronger and even more dramatic image of social life and the subject than is conveyed by the idea of communication between the individual bearers of different life-worlds. The individual is cut off from himself by organizational and institutional situations that are strewn with obstacles to the formation of an experience that later could be exchanged for others. The individual's relationship with himself—and it is this that allows the individual to be constituted as a subject—is more basic than are relations among individuals because it clashes with a lived dependency. Democracy can be defined primarily as an institutional space that protects the effort of an individual or group to emerge and to be recognized as a subject.

We can now grasp the difference between the evolution of political thought and that of sociology. Political thought takes as its starting point the image of reason enlightening individuals and transforming them into subjects by teaching them higher universal values. That image still dominates Horkheimer's antimodernism (Horkheimer 1947), although later political thought rejects it, mainly because it leads to a theory of language that prioritizes intersubjective relations rather than self-consciousness, which is now rightly suspected of being a false consciousness. Sociology took as its starting point the related idea that modern society was the incarnation of reason and that individual or collective forms of behavior should be evaluated in terms of their social utility—a criterion that leads directly back to rationality—for society is an organism or system that can function only if its organs are linked to one another by intelligible relations of complementarity and functionality. Unlike the history of philosophy, however, the history of sociology is the history of the gradual extrication of the subject from this systematic, functionalist rationality. Durkheim and Weber were merely disturbed by the modernity that Nietzsche and Freud called into question in a much more radical way. In the twentieth century, sociology has usually rejected the idea of a social system, as often in the interest of *homo œconomicus* or strategic analyses as of the study of social movements or the imaginary. As the actor escapes the system, the system begins to look more like a negotiated compromise than a rational order.

The idea of the subject marks the extremity in this transformation of sociology, and it completely overturns our conceptions of democracy. Democracy was once defined as participation in a political order, which acted as an Archimedean lever on social life, with reason as its fulcrum. It is now defined as the recognition of personal subjects and of the diversity of their attempts to reconcile instrumental reason with a cultural identity, personal and collective, which implies the greatest possible liberty for all.

The subject, as we conceive of it today, is not reducible to reason. The subject can be defined and understood only in terms of its struggle against the logic of the market and of technical apparatuses. At its most profound level, the subject is liberty and liberation rather than knowledge; at the same time as it shares collective identities, it seeks disengagement and liberation. *The subject is at once reason, liberty, and memory.* These three dimensions of the subject correspond to the three dimensions of democracy: The appeal to collective identity, or memory, translates into the representation of the interests and values of different social groups, or in other words, into organized politics. Trust in reason corresponds to the theme of citizenship. Finally, the appeal to natural law is directly related to the idea of liberty and to an individualist vision of society that places restrictions on the power of the state in order to preserve the basic rights of the individual. Those who reduce the subject to reason and contrast the subject with a troubled society are simply reverting to the illusions of the liberals of old and the defenders of republican elitism, who identified democracy with the rule of educated, wealthy, and respected citizens. The subject is no more to be confused with individual rationality than it is to be confused with the singular individual. The subject is primarily an attempt to combine reason, liberty, and belonging in the life of both individual and collectivity.

Democracy is indispensable if liberty is to succeed in managing the relationship between rationalization and identities. The reason why democracy is under threat and has been destroyed so often and with such brutality is that in the contemporary universe, the world of rationalization and the world of interests, of markets and communities, are increasingly alienated from one another. Democracy cannot exist in either world if the two become dissociated. The world of techniques and markets may well need an open political market, but it is scandalous to reduce democracy to a political market. In the opposite extreme, a world dominated by communities seeks only integration, homogeneity, and consensus and rejects democratic debate. These two halves of our fragmented modernity become debased when they are separated from one another, just as individuals lose their capacity to be social actors when they are reduced to cogs in a machine or defined solely in terms of their membership in a community. The subject is an attempt on the part of an individual or collectivity to reconcile the two aspects of being and of doing; and democracy is the institutional system that brings about their reconciliation at the political level. Democracy allows a society to be both united and diverse. That is why democracy is a *culture* and not merely a set of institutional guarantees. What makes an individual free and what makes a political system democratic can therefore be expressed in the same terms. At both levels, it is a matter of reconciling elements that are at once complementary and contradictory, and no one higher principle can reduce them to unity.

The democratic idea means that we have to accept cultural pluralism as well as social pluralism. Democracy must help individuals to become subjects. It must help them to succeed in both their representations and their practices, in integrating their rationality, or their ability to handle techniques and languages, with their identity, which is based on a culture and a tradition that they constantly reinterpret as their technical environment is transformed.

Using a different vocabulary, Alasdair MacIntyre also attempted to rediscover the unity of the subject by looking beyond individual behavior and arguing against the Sartrean idea of "a self separated from its roles" (MacIntyre 1985: 205). In MacIntyre's view, "The unity of a human life is the unity of a narrative quest. Quests sometimes fail, are frustrated, abandoned or dissipated into distractions; and human lives may in all these ways also fail. But the only criteria for success or failure in a human life as a whole are the criteria of success or failure in a narrated or to-be-narrated quest" (MacIntyre 1985: 219). MacIntyre therefore defines the subject not solely in terms of a project or *telos*, but also in terms of a family or national tradition, or even some other tradition. Rather than contrasting tradition with reason as did Burke, MacIntyre has combined the two in much the same way as I did in *Critique of Modernity* (Touraine 1995).

Democracy is no more reducible to negative liberty, or protection against arbitrary power, than to a form of citizenship that integrates and mobilizes individuals. Democracy is characterized by a combination of universals and particulars, a technical universe and a symbolic universe, signs and meaning. Thus, democracy is not merely a set of procedures, nor is it a popular regime; it is a form of work, an attempt to preserve the ever incomplete unity of complementary elements, which can never be allowed to fuse into a single guiding principle. A democratic regime is based on the existence of democratic personalities, and its primary goal therefore must be to create individual subjects who can prevent the world of action from becoming divorced from that of being, and the world of the future from that of the past. Rejection of the other and irrationalism pose equally deadly threats to democracy.

A Reversal of Perspective

The citizen was once seen as a product of institutions and civic education, a public man who subordinated his private interests and affections to the higher interests of the city or nation. Today, many of us live in a climate of hostile indifference toward public life, and we celebrate private life. Institutions retain their coercive power to a large extent, but they no longer have their old capacity for socialization. We live, on the one hand, in a world of markets, and we are attracted to their products because of the use we can make of them rather than because they belong to the culture or society they symbolize. On the other hand, we are retreating into our identity or identities, whether ethnic, sexual, national, religious, or simply local. Between the world of the market and the world of identities there is a black hole where the lights of social and political life once shone. Talk of socialization, social integration, or involvement in political life is no longer in keeping with observable experience, and this has forced us to reverse our perspective: Rather than believing that institutions can create a personality type, we now expect a personality type to make stable democratic institutions possible.

In the past, everything was based on the identity of reason and nation. Despotism itself was often defined as being enlightened by reason, as in the early Soviet Union or in the time of Joseph II of Austria; but the nation-state long ago ceased to symbolize reason, and it has been swept away by empires as well as the internationalization of the economy. The dream of the republic has vanished, even though it still haunts the speeches of a few politicians and a handful of intellectuals. Yet with what are we to replace this extreme unitary principle, if we are not willing to accept the dangerous consequences of a complete rift in the social fabric?

I see only one answer: the subject. Not because it is a new sun that can illuminate social life but because it is a network of communications between the worlds of objectivity and subjectivity, which must be neither completely divorced from one another nor artificially fused into one. The subject comes into being by criticizing instrumentalism on the one hand and communitarianism on the other; they are debased forms of the principles of rationalization and subjectivization, respectively. The subject resists the instrumentalism of markets and powers in the name of the individual and individual loyalties. The subject contrasts the image of mass society with the image of a society made up of individuals and groups who have a history, a memory, customs, and values. The subject also turns the analytic and critical functions of reason against reason itself—as have the many scientists who are critical of nuclear weapons, the destruction of the environment, or eugenics. It is in the name of science and not custom that subjects criticize technocratic or commodified instrumentalism. Communitarianism attempts to build suffocatingly homogeneous societies, and the subject resists by appealing to instrumental rationality and to culture. A culture is a powerful force that in many cases can resist the temporal power that speaks in its name. In many countries both traditional and modern communitarianism have been fought in this manner, in the name of Christianity or Arab nationalism—one example being the Palestinian nationalism that is now being forged in the face of the familial and tribal logic that once dominated the Arab world's traditional sectors.

The subject therefore fights its adversaries on the twin fronts of rationalization and subjectivization by invoking the antithetical cultural principle, but also by appealing to the very cultural principle that political power is trying to confiscate. The subject is above all the sum total of these resistances and these critiques of principles of order; but the subject also posits itself as its own end. It asserts its liberty and defends it against both the instrumentalism of the open society and the closure of the community—for both are threats to liberty, which presupposes the combination of an inherited sociocultural language with new technical and economic objects, words with things, the symbolic with the instrumental.

The subject cannot freely act on itself in this way if there is no *free institutional space* for its deployment. If the subject could achieve its own unification and could fully integrate instrumentality and the communitarian spirit of its own accord, there would be no need for political preconditions. The unification of the subject would mean either the triumph of individualism or the return of Greek tragedy, which Nietzsche defined as the union of Apollo and Dionysius. But that unity and that triumph never come about. The centrifugal forces that divide the instrumental world from the symbolic world always defeat the subject's centripetal efforts. That is why relations, conflicts, and compromises between the two worlds cannot be handled at a purely personal level. They must also be handled by democracy at the political level. If it were not primarily a way of constructing the subject, democratic openness would serve no purpose and would quickly be invaded by either the instrumentalism of the market or communitarian authoritarianism. A free society is built on free beings.

We have come a very long way from the liberty of the ancients. It is no longer a matter of replacing a hierarchical society with an egalitarian society, or even the communitarian spirit with the individualist spirit. Democracy was triumphant when it could trust in reason and labor to help it fight privilege and tradition. Democracy is now more uncertain because globalization is crushing cultural diversity and personal experiences and because the citizen is being transformed into a consumer. Democracy is particularly uncertain because it only recently emerged from a long period of domination by the totalitarian or revolutionary regimes that imposed their arbitrary power in the name of popular revolution, and even within societies that are protected from arbitrary rule, the forces that destroy democracy are still at work today. Public opinion can easily be transformed into the consumption of programs, and the defense of the individual can degenerate into particularism, sectarianism, or even an obsession with collective or personal identity. The growing rift between the world of objects and the world of culture is leading to the disappearance of the subject, which is defined by transforming activity into meaning and situations into actions, by producing itself.

Democracy does not mean the subordination of the individual to the common good; on the contrary, it makes institutions serve personal liberty and responsibility. Yet we find it difficult to perceive the space of the subject amid the surrounding masses that threaten to crush it—social and cultural loyalties on the one hand, the market and technical systems on the other. The crisis in modernity stems from the fact that we no longer feel that we are the masters of the world we have built. The world forces us to accept the logic of profit or power. If we are to resist it, we therefore have to appeal to what is least modern in us, or in other words to the things that bind us most closely to a history and a community.

And so we live—pleasantly in rich countries, and tragically in poor countries. In rich countries, our public life allows us to be part of an instrumental world, but we can preserve a private space that is full of memories and emotions, of narcissism, or references to an exclusive group. In poor countries, communities are mobilizing against a modernization that is allowing the interests and customs of victorious foreigners to destroy traditional forms of life. In both cases, democracy is losing its strength. At best, it is being replaced by an open political market. Where the confrontation is at its most destructive, democracy is being replaced by an open conflict between two cultures.

Democracy and Justice

If we are to defend democracy, we must recenter our social and political life on the personal subject; rather than being mere consumers, we must rediscover our creative and productive roles. Hence the growing importance of ethics, which is a secularized form of the appeal to the subject; the churches, in contrast, defend religious traditions and are usually on the side of forces involved in a battle that will destroy the personal freedom of the subject, no matter who wins. Ethics leads to debate because it does not refer to some metasocial principle that defines the good; instead, it helps to reconstruct the public space that lies between the technical or commodified world and a cultural heritage. When the existence of the subject is governed by the twofold struggle against the apparatuses of communitarian power and the logic of technical and commodified systems, the theme of the subject and the theme of democracy become inseparable.

Positive liberty does not result from political mobilization and the seizure of power. We can no longer place our hopes in the complete transformation of society; as we know only too well, that would pave the way for an absolute or even totalitarian power that would devour society. Liberty cannot, however, be purely negative. Negative liberty, without which nothing is possible, does not have the strength to defend itself. It must be brought to life by individuals, who through democratic debates and decisions produce a space in which each individual or each group can blend their cultural heritage with their technical environment, transforming the two into a project that is both particular and endowed with a universal meaning. Democracy is not an end in itself. It is the indispensable institutional precondition that allows particular actors to create the world. The actors are all different, but by working together they produce the discourse of humanity. That discourse is never completed, and it is never unitary. When it is unaware that its role is to serve personal subjects, democracy degenerates into institutional mechanisms that can easily be made to serve the most powerful apparatuses and groups, which have accumulated enough resources to impose their will on a society that is powerless to halt their triumphal march.

If we make democracy the servant of the personal subject, we distance ourselves from a major body of democratic thought. John Rawls, for example, has attempted to demonstrate that the interests of all are best served by the equitable or fair organization of society. The two principles he uses to define justice—liberty and equality—are in fact compatible only because the differentiation and integration of society are complementary. They are complementary because society is a system of exchanges, and it could not exist if every element in the system were not defined both by a social function and by particular goals, or if the actors did not both internalize values and norms and rationally pursue their own interests. If society is not seen as a differentiated community whose elements are bound together by an organic solidarity, then the liberty of each individual and the equality of all—or at least the reduction of inequalities—are more likely to come into conflict than to complement one another. This conception, which obviously inspires juridical constructs, and more generally, what we might call an institutional conception of social life, derives its strength from the direct correlation it establishes between the rational pursuit of personal interests and social integration, while it ignores social relations—as does Rawls voluntarily from the outset of his analysis. Individuals, society, and exchanges are the elements that make up social life, yet theory must ignore social relations, conflicts, and compromises.

In contrast, I emphasize two terms that are overlooked by this liberal functionalist conception—namely, the subject and the social relations of domination. The two are closely intertwined, just as there is a close link between individual and system in functionalist thought. It is because society is dominated by powers that democratic action is primarily a matter of opposing institutional practices and rules, which usually serve to protect the powers of the dominant. Democratic action mobilizes a collective and personal will toward liberation, which is by no means synonymous with the rational pursuit of self-interest. Democratic action upsets the existing order, destroys the institutional guarantees of domination, and appeals to universal cultural values in its struggle against a power that it accuses of serving particular interests.

These two conceptions are not totally distinct and may even be complementary. Historically, the British model of democracy is of central importance because in terms of the debate between fairness and liberation, it seems able to meet both demands and to be both institutional and social. What is more, the "liberating" model may lead us to make the same mistakes as the antidemocratic revolutionary model if it does not attempt to bring about institutional reforms. The European labor movement instituted reforms of this kind when it created the welfare state in Sweden, Great Britain, France, and almost every other European country, as well as in the commonwealth countries—Canada, Australia, and New Zealand. Similarly, a politics that reduces justice to fairness is implicitly conservative and may lead to a passive acceptance of power relations if it is not inspired by the spirit of liberation. In the United States, the spirit of liberation created the New Deal through union action and, a generation later, inspired the struggle for civil rights.

Democratic action means the institutionalization of social, cultural, or national liberation movements. But just as Rawls has insisted that the principle of liberty must be limited by the principle of equality of opportunities and the attempt to reduce inequalities, so the democratic action that is set in motion by the defense of the subject and struggles against domination must "lexically" govern the quest for social integration and the reconciliation of conflicting personal interests. Democracy is not based on the law. Democracy transforms the legal state, which can take the form of an absolute monarchy, into a free public space. Democracy is not primarily a set of procedures but a critique of established powers and a hope for personal and collective liberation.

Mass Society

Authoritarian and totalitarian regimes pose the most direct threat to democracy, but the existence of another threat must also be recognized. It does not come from an all-powerful power that reduces society to its mercy, but from society itself. This threat arises when society sees the political realm simply as an arbitrary or corrupt bureaucracy that must be reduced to a minimal state or a nightwatchman so as to remove all constraints on markets or the distribution of consumer goods and mass communications of all kinds. This narrow liberalism can be regarded as democratic, as it does respect liberties and does respond to the demands of the majority. In rich countries, marketing tends to replace voting; in poor countries, escaping from poverty is seen as the priority and talk of public liberties is criticized as elitist, inspired by dominant foreign interests. It is increasingly said throughout the world, albeit in different ways, that defending liberty means reducing state intervention. If democracy implies the separation of church and state, and if it is the regimes that reject secularization that pose the most direct threat to democracy, why not take the principle to its logical conclusion by making a case for the complete abolition of social norms and for pure tolerance? The strength of this argument is that it can quite rightly proclaim that markets are more tolerant than administrations or even laws and that the law must adapt to demands with as much suppleness—or in other words with as few principles—as possible. This is an attractive idea, as the consumer society is more diversified, less normalized, and above all more tolerant than any other. It does less and less to repress forms of sexuality that are considered deviant because it makes the very idea of deviance meaningless and replaces social norms with personal authenticity. As a famous slogan proclaimed in May 1968, it is forbidden to forbid. This spirit of tolerance is best respected not in a revolutionary society but by a market economy.

But must we really be content with mass society and rely on the law of supply and demand to ensure the greatest possible liberty? Does not a political and ideological void promote the most immediate and unthinking forms of consumption, and is it appropriate to refer to a situation as "liberty" in which everything that does not lead to the immediate satisfaction of a need is ignored? According to some, we need not fear that a mass society will produce a society of individualized consumers. As Michel Maffesoli, in particular, has shown, although many worried that the advent of an atomized and anomic society would result in individualism, isolation, and the disappearance of all social controls, what we are in fact seeing is the reemergence of "tribes" (Maffesoli 1988), for society is disintegrating. Social actors no longer define themselves in terms of economic goals and social relations but in terms of their cultural heritage and the groups to which they belong. New communities are emerging from the ruins of society and the political realm.

Clearly we cannot defend democracy by rejecting mass society: The dichotomy is artificial and a contradiction in terms, as an oligarchic democracy is inconceivable. Democracy is, on the other hand, in danger when a mass society fragments into a set of communities that are locked into the defense of their identity or transformed into sects that refuse to apply any social norm that interferes with their conception of the good life. But how can we prevent or limit the fragmentation of society without imposing civic or republican norms that are little more than secularized forms of a religious ethics that an increasing number of individuals are rejecting in the name of the freedom to live, think, and organize as they see fit? There is only one answer to that question: We must rediscover the social relations, and therefore the power relations, that are masked by mass consumption.

Debates about the media, and more especially television, are usually confused by the resistance offered by an elitist conception of culture. Culture supposedly puts human beings in touch with values that transcend their experience, such as the good, the beautiful, and the true, which sometimes fuse into a single divine form. Television, like the school system, must be educational. Such was the ambition of the *maisons de la culture* set up by André Malraux in France—to bring the general public into contact with the great works of world culture. This is an open and generous conception. A *Bildung* is seen as progress in the direction of universals. Intellectuals are given a mediating role. This vision has often gone hand in hand with the idea that the function of the media is to transmit a national heritage and to be agents of political socialization in the highest sense of that term. Visionaries have made a clear distinction between these noble tasks and the stress that was placed on the medium rather than the message—on winning audiences rather than producing quality programs. The most severe critics sometimes even talk of brainwashing and claim that light entertainment contains subliminal propaganda. There was, for instance, the astonishing book that accused Donald Duck of being an agent of American imperialism. The fables of La Fontaine and Florian could no doubt also be accused of promoting French imperialism, and the Grimms' fairy tales of spreading pan-Germanism!

The most important thing is not to become trapped in debates that have lost all meaning in a modern world defined by its action rather than its conformity to transcendent models. I am not suggesting that we should go to the opposite extreme and say the media are simply responding to consumer demand. That is a meaningless idea, as we have to begin by asking questions about demand. We have to look at how demand is shaped and defined. Demand can, that is, be either a positive or a negative response to what is on offer. In a society that is to some extent organized and that produces a certain self-image, viewers choose among the programs that are on offer.

We must replace the dichotomy between high culture and popular culture with one between two logics of action. The first is the logic of consumption. It privileges the material or cultural objects that provide the most direct response to a preestablished demand or reaction. One example is an image that provokes an emotional response because it supplies a clear and obvious image of good, or more usually, evil; such images have the same impact as representations of hell on the tympanum of a cathedral. The second logic is the logic of the production of attitudes. It encourages us to make judgments, supplies information, and either changes or reinforces existing opinions or attitudes. Studies of television show that the audience is not a mass that receives a program but a set of individuals or categories who use images and texts to construct representations and attitudes ranging from passive consumption to an active reaction or critical participation. As in the world of trade, supply is never equal to demand. The seller wishes to make a profit, while the buyer usually wants to acquire a symbol rather than a commodity. Similarly, mass communications involve two logics that may have nothing in common: The people who control channels and programs usually think in financial terms because they depend on advertising, whereas viewers react in terms of their personal concerns rather than as an audience. The simplest example is that of news broadcasts. At the moment, news is television's principal function, and it allows channels to demand very high advertising rates. No one imagines that a news program would reach a bigger audience simply because it was geared toward advertising. On the contrary, televised news must involve few judgments—moral judgments are the exception to the rule—if it is to be acceptable to all sectors of the population. The logics of consumption and of production, the behavior of viewers and strategies to mold public opinion, are as contradictory and complementary as are the respective functions of the capitalist and the wage earner in industrial society. The role of the state or of independent bodies is, like that of social law, to protect the virtual demands of viewers from the concentrated power of the distributors of consumable products.

There can be no democracy without a struggle against power. The objectionable thing about mass society is not the popularization of demands, which has more positive than negative effects; it is the way mass society prioritizes objects rather than social relations. Public life has been invaded by advertising. The distribution of objects has improved as a result, but political choices are relegated to a shadowy domain. It seems as though a society that sees itself as a consumer society pays the greatest and most constant attention to what are, even in economic terms, its least important activities. There is much more talk on television about detergents or cars than about schools, hospitals, or dependency; there is therefore less political debate.

The development of the market has very positive effects both because it allows diversified and changing demands to be satisfied and because it restricts the power of a state that is always tempted to control social life in its entirety. The consumer society is, however, no more than a representation or a way of looking at social life, and it gives priority to the production and consumption of commodities rather than to the forms of social organization, the policies, and the investments that mobilize our major social resources. Such policies are, however, a response to the most important demands: equal access to education and medical care, solidarity with the underprivileged, respect for the human personality, fair treatment for immigrants, and so on. Democracy must therefore be defined, not as the antithesis of a mass society but as an attempt to make the transition from the individual consumption of commodities to social choices that challenge power relations and ethical principles. As we make this transition, the individual consumer will give way first to the citizen—or in other words, a member of a political society who discusses principles of action and how resources should be used—and then to the subject, to the individual capacity and will to be an actor, to modify one's environment, and to extend one's zone of freedom and responsibility. A mass society is not in itself antidemocratic. On the contrary, it destroys cultural and social barriers that stand in the way of democracy. A mass society is, however, no more than the lowest functional level of a modern society. If a society remains at that level, it reduces its capacity for choice, debate, and development, and therefore turns its back on democracy—which cannot, as Herbert Marcuse asserted long ago, be reduced to meaning pure tolerance (Marcuse et al. 1969).

Recomposing the World

The transition from the individual attempt to integrate economic rationality and cultural identity to the democratic action that creates the institutional conditions for the subject's freedom necessarily implies a mutual recognition on the part of all individuals of the fact that they can all participate in this action. Democracy is impossible if one actor identifies with a universal rationality and reduces others to defending their particular identities; that is why Western modernization was often an antidemocratic process. The creators of modern republics and the modern economy were an elite made up of adult, educated, male property owners above a multitude of inferior groups, which were irrational. The self-proclaimed torchbearers of Enlightenment cast into the political darkness all those who appeared to them incapable of governing themselves because they were slaves to need, community, or their passions. The outcasts became passive citizens without the right to vote. Democracy, in contrast, is possible only if every individual recognizes that the other is, like him or her, a combination of universalism and particularism. If everyone is defined solely in terms of membership in a community, the question of democracy does not even arise, as society shatters into a number of mutually alien communities. By the same token, if we are all defined by our ability to think and to use the same rational techniques, then political decisions must be taken in the name of rational criteria, or in other words, in the name of truth and efficiency. This was until recently the dream of the Trotskyists and the anarchists before them. They were extreme rationalists who believed that a great machine, a central plan, or a supercomputer could reach the most rational decisions and eliminate power relations, and they thus paved the way for an all-powerful bureaucracy rather than democracy. Democracy, in contrast, presupposes both that I recognize my own particularity and that of my culture, my language, my tastes, and my taboos and that I behave in a way that is consonant with instrumental rationality. It presupposes that I recognize that everyone else is attempting to combine similar elements.

I describe as democratic a society that combines the greatest possible cultural diversity with the most extensive possible use of reason. We must at all costs reject the call for affectivity, tradition, and equilibrium to take their revenge on reason, modernity, and change. We must try to reconcile them rather than contrasting them or choosing between them. Ultimately, the divisive approach reinforces relations of domination and exclusion. The decline of politics and the fragmentation of the personality go hand in hand with the increasing divergence between world markets and particular identities. Francis Fukuyama (Fukuyama 1992) and others who claim that the world is moving toward unification and the end of history, thanks to the triumph of the market economy, liberal democracy, secularization, and tolerance, are blind optimists. They are victims of their own sociocentrism. Now that the Soviet system has collapsed, they believe that U.S. culture and society will become the universal model. They could not be more mistaken. Triumphal globalization goes hand in hand with accelerated segmentation. Throughout the world, embattled identities are becoming introverted. The most communitarian forms of nationalism and religious life are building barricades to resist the invasion of technologies and forms of consumption developed in the hegemonic center or are using them for the benefit of the political powers that are springing to the defense of their identity. Fundamentalism is at work everywhere in the radical multiculturalism and the sects of the West as well as in the Christian, Islamic, Jewish, or Hindu fundamentalism that exists in various other parts of the world. Likewise, there are no grounds for describing as democratic the triumph of the market, as the market also has made its peace easily with authoritarian regimes, like that in today's China and in Pinochet's Chile, and it is in the process of doing so also in Cuba and Vietnam. Compared to these antithetical political forms—triumphal hegemonism and introverted fundamentalism—a democracy based on the subject's will to exist and on the defense of personal and collective freedom seems weak.

Unity and Difference

It is not enough to assert that we have to reconcile the universal and the particular, or rationality and cultures; we must also be very clear about what such a reconciliation entails. How can we recognize others as different and at the same time preserve the unity of the law and of scientific and technical rationality? Our thinking spontaneously oscillates between two extremes. According to one view, all human beings are basically equal and alike because they have the same rights, but this view leads us to identify one type of social organization with the universality of reason. Others take the view that we have to recognize that every cultural creation contains universals; this, however, is the universality of conviction rather than of reason. In the aesthetic domain, for instance, we recognize that works of art aspire to beauty and to the representation of profound experiences or deeply held beliefs, even when their cultural content escapes us. This latter position cannot, however, take us beyond openness and tolerance. It is adequate if we wish to build museums, but not if we wish to create laws and institutions, which must have some coherent social and cultural content. If we define democracy as the understanding of the other and as the institutional recognition of the greatest possible diversity and creativity, then we also must understand how and why unity and diversity are interdependent.

The defining characteristic of modern society is the increasing divergence between rationalization and the assertion of the subject, or in other words the creativity of the social actor, which I term *subjectivation*. The subject asserts its existence in two complementary and contradictory ways. On the one hand, the subject is the liberty that overthrows social determinism and the personal and collective construction of society. On the other, the subject is a natural and cultural being that resists the power that controls rationalization. The subject is at once individuality and sexuality, family and social group, national or cultural memory, and membership in a religious, ethical, or ethnic group. The greatest threat facing the world today is that the world of instrumentality may become divorced from the world of identities. If that happens, the space where liberty once existed will become a void. It is, however, time to invert that pessimistic vision and to recall that modernity has constantly been characterized by an attempt to reconcile rationalization, liberty, and identity, and to make them complementary.

In the early stages of our modernization, we often believed that modernity meant sweeping away the past and our feelings and loyalties regarding it. Such was the spirit of triumphal capitalism and of revolution. Both have always taken society in an antidemocratic direction. Yet we did indeed have to free ourselves from the past, build a voluntaristic future, and liberate the exploited and the alienated. Today it is no longer a matter of sweeping away the past and overthrowing the old regimes. Our task is to prevent the fragmentation of the world and the disastrous divorce between the world of techniques, information, and weapons, and the world of ethnic groups, sects, and introverted individuality. We must *recompose* the world and recreate its unity. Some attempt to do so by returning to the past. The philosophers among them are, like Nietzsche, nostalgic for being, or, like Horkheimer, desperately aware of all the threats to objective reason. The militant ecologists are aware of the threats posed to the whole planet by the destruction of its biological and cultural diversity and by the irresponsible industrialization and consumption that are destroying the environment and that may lead to a natural catastrophe. Both groups tap into deep and increasingly disturbing feelings. But denouncing the present is not enough if we wish to define possible forms of action and an acceptable future. What is more important and more innovative is the attempt that has been made, ever since the beginnings of modernization, to bring together what has been separated, to unite what has been divided. In the earliest stages of accelerated industrialization, we witnessed the birth of a historical consciousness and a search for roots and origins as well as the pursuit of political liberty and individualism. From the very outset, democratic action has always been a combination of reason, liberty, and identity. And as the technical transformation of the world accelerated, many people saw it as increasingly necessary to defend everything in individual and collective life that could resist technical, political, or military life and to assert a collective will to be an actor of change and not simply a user, a consumer, or a victim. It is as though the industrial machine were plowing the land deeper and deeper, revealing previously undiscovered forces of resistance as it did so. The modern world is not the disenchanted, cold, technical, and administrative world we believed it to be during this early phase. Increasingly it is becoming "reenchanted," in both the best and the worst senses of the word. As techniques and markets are rapidly spreading, we see new and above all politicized forms of national or ethnic identity taking on more importance and becoming forces that can resist transformations experienced as invasions. We are also seeing a renaissance of things that had been destroyed. The museums are full, and travelers rush toward other places and into the past. In the intellectual realm, Freud plunged into the world of myths and dreams and overthrew the old dominance of the ego by recognizing the strength of the id. In contemporary culture, the relationship with the other is increasingly established outside social and cultural contexts, and personal life projects are becoming more diversified. At the same time, reproduction is becoming less and less important, and production is demanding more and more inventiveness and imagination.

We began by sweeping away the world of the past. We now have to try to bring together the old and the new, technique and emotion, the impersonality of the law and the individualization of punishments. Democracy is the political expression of this reenchantment of the world. Freedom of political debate and the conflicting values on which it is based are manifestations of this return of the repressed. Modernity was once authoritarian and repressive. A ruling elite seized power by claiming to be rational. Sometimes it was the bourgeoisie, sometimes the court of a prince, or more recently the central committee of a political party. For a long time, there has been a conflict between two different currents: One excavates the deep, narrow bed of technical modernization, increasingly destroying or repressing everything that is deemed archaic, in the name of progress, communication, and consumption. The other rejects the idea of a rationalized world. Seymour Papert has demonstrated that intuition and desire are essential if a child is to progress from one of the developmental stages described by Piaget to the next. In the same way, we have learned that we need the old to create the new and liberty to create organization and efficiency.

A culture of divergence thus gives way to a culture of complementarity and convergence, and a revolutionary political culture to a democratic culture. In a revolutionary culture, one class or group identifies itself with progress and attempts to destroy those it defines as obstacles to progress—sometimes by force, sometimes by relying on modernization to destroy witnesses to the vanished past. In a democratic culture, in contrast, elements that cannot do without one another enter into a debate. Democracy is inseparable from the centripetal movement that brings us closer to the things the rationalists had taken away or repressed, be it sexuality or madness, the unconscious or the colonized world, the labor of working men or the experience of women. These are not new liberation movements, promoting a new image of the totality, which always inspires the arrogance of revolutionary violence. On the contrary, they are *recomposition* movements. They represent the return of the stigmatized and the rehabilitation of what had been condemned as archaic or irrational.

Because it tries to increase its own diversity, a democratic society recognizes the work of the subject even when others see it as a transgression of norms. Take, for example, the insistent discourse that makes drug use a criminal act punishable by law: I have no intention here of discussing whether organized repression helps do away with the drug trade; I do, however, take the view that democracy is in danger when personality problems are seen as mere delinquency, as though the use of drugs were just a side-effect of *narcotrafico*.

I do not suggest that we make the rational calculation that recommends tolerance and benevolence toward those who have the least material, psychological, or cultural resources, as though we had to create the fewest possible inequalities so as to avoid extremely prejudicial situations. I am describing a principle—namely, the quest for the subject—that manifests itself in attempts to be a subject in situations that are by no means conducive to free and responsible action. This quest is so difficult that we have to prioritize compassion instead of punishment. Easing the crushing burden on the most underprivileged is preferable to giving the privileged even greater protection because they feel they are threatened. One criterion by which democracy is often judged is its ability to make decisions that go against the wishes of the majority, with reference to basic rights. The abolition of the death penalty is one example; this has occurred in many countries, often in defiance of the wishes of the majority.

Democratic Integration

Democracy is the political expression of a general tendency to recompose the world, and it affects every domain of social life: the economic, the cultural, and the national. It is in the national domain that recomposition is most difficult and that our analysis is most directly and urgently applicable.

The way in which we should behave toward *immigrants* is, in many societies, a subject of impassioned debate. We cannot describe as democratic the liberal position that invites immigrants to assimilate into a culture and become integrated into a society when that culture and society identify themselves as universal values. Immigrants are told to move from their closed world into our open world. One might as well ask them to strip off their culture and go naked into a new and foreign world. What arrogance and what contempt for different cultures and experiences! However, the acceptance of absolute differences and of the formation of communities with rules of their own is even more likely to destroy democracy. This pretense of egalitarianism is a poorly disguised way of segregating and excluding minorities that are regarded as absolutely different. As it was in the past, so it is today: The way to arrive at democratic solutions is to reconcile the defense of identity with integration. Mobility projects, to use an expression that I coined in a study of social mobility in São Paulo, are successful when they integrate a background culture and a host culture into a personal project, turning immigrants into subjects capable of saying both "we" and "I"—in other words, of integrating their cultural heritage and their goal of participation into a will toward free, responsible, and creative action.

The integration of immigrants is not a success if they must merge into the majority; it is a success when others respect their cultural identity because it seems compatible with membership in a common society. Immigrants are accepted only when they are accepted as immigrants, or when the fact that they are different is recognized as enriching society.

This is not what is happening in western Europe today. At a time when sections of the population, especially in East Germany or certain regions of France or Great Britain, are experiencing economic and cultural difficulties and are using poor immigrants as scapegoats, most protests are expressions of egalitarian republicanism, which is both eminently respectable and broad-minded. At the same time, however, that republicanism also implies a certain intolerance because it tends to condemn any attachment to traditional practices and beliefs, in the name of its own universalism. For the same reasons, despite their importance, Islamist groups in Egypt were for a long time either ignored or treated with contempt by nationalist modernizers, and later, by Marxists.

As Didier Lapeyronnie has shown, the dangerous dichotomy between de facto multiculturalism and nationalistic rejection can be overcome only by a combination of integration, personal liberty, and recognition of identities (Lapeyronnie 1993). We must encourage the capacity of individuals to construct a life project instead of emphasizing or repressing cultural differences. Retaining links with one's background, and especially one's family, is one way of resisting the obstacles and pressures that are encountered in the shifting tides of collective and personal life. That is what happened in the United States when immigration was at its height: All immigrants, from the Irish and Italians to the Croats and Jews, relied on their communities, their languages, and often their churches in order to enter the labor market and institutions of the United States. Techno-economic integration and exposure to mass culture may lead to psychological and social breakdowns if they are not offset by the support provided by a familiar cultural environment and by the preservation of elements essential to self-esteem and self-image, the absence of which saps the ability to shape projects and take initiatives. Where the emphasis on immigrant cultures versus host cultures implies that cultures are coherent aggregates, closed systems, or even conflicting sets of values, immigrants face very great and often insurmountable difficulties. Where the emphasis is placed on the individual, the family, or the local group and on their attempts to transform themselves—which implies both discontinuity and continuity, both integration into a new society and preservation of a cultural identity—the results are much better. We should therefore be talking less about clashes between cultures and more about the histories of individuals who are moving from one situation to another and who are taking from several societies and several cultures the elements that will shape their personalities.

Ecology and Democracy

If democracy is primarily a defense of the subject, and if the subject is an attempt on the part of freedom to reconcile reason and identity, then strengthening democracy goes hand in hand with rejecting the conquering pride of reason, which seeks to impose its law on nature and exploit its resources. It is true that appealing to the identity and survival of the planet and the environment we all share can lead to a naturalism that denies the liberating role of reason and science. Ecological campaigns have sometimes been marked by irrationalism and a zealous authoritarianism. Such deviations should not, however, lead us to accept only an environmentalism that sets itself more limited goals. Nor must we accept forms of environmentalism that attempt to reach a compromise with a system of production that is dominated by the search for maximal productivity rather than trying to restrict it. It would be a step backward to condemn all forms of communitarianism on the grounds that they are negative and to promote the extension of knowledge and scientifically guided action on the grounds that they alone are positive. To do so would be no more acceptable than rejecting all forms of national or religious consciousness on the grounds that they may lead to fanaticism. Fanaticism is obviously to be condemned, but it is not the only possible meaning of the appeal to community in the face of uncontrolled social change or forms of social change that are experienced as outside aggression rather than as liberation.

The importance of the environmental movement stems from the fact that it has raised social conflict from the level of the social utilization of cultural resources to the level of cultural orientations. It is not merely capitalism or bureaucracy but the obsession with maximizing production regardless of the costs that is coming under attack from this movement, which is greatly expanding the field of democratic action. For the first time, women are playing an important and often a dominant role in a broad social and cultural movement. Political ecology has also, albeit in tentative form, succeeded in reestablishing the broken link between political agents and social actors. It has reintroduced into the political system the hopes and fears of a society that now encompasses the entire human community. Even though "green" parties have experienced crises and defeats, the themes they defended have spread throughout the public space and have often taken the place, especially on the left, of the themes introduced by industrial society, which have lost their capacity to mobilize collective action. Luc Ferry quite rightly denounced the antidemocratic implications of certain aspects of *deep ecology* (Ferry 1995); but many tendencies within ecological action do converge into an attack on the dominant logic of technology and the market. It is not difficult to reconcile political ecology with the defense of national, ethnic, or sexual minorities, and therefore with respect for cultural diversity as well as for the diversity of animal and plant species.

Even the labor movement was not reducible to the defense of liberty; it also fought for the rights and interests of specific social groups and of communities defined by a trade or a region. Ecology mobilizes still more "natural" forces in its struggle against the untrammeled dominance of obsessive production. It mobilizes our existence as human beings and as living bodies. Democracy would be quite lifeless if it did not support a movement that is attempting both to protect natural beings and to develop an increasingly positive conception of liberty. Safeguarding human rights within the particular situations in which they are involved and threatened is a more than reasonable approach.

Our growing alienation from the Enlightenment concept of liberation does not imply a dangerous surrender to communitarian identity and to naturalism, which is hostile to any human action inspired by reason and technology; on the contrary, it leads to an ever more complete recomposition of the individual subject and the world. We can no longer accept modes of thought and action based on binary oppositions, obliging us to protect culture from nature, reason from emotion, men from women, and civilization from savages. We endeavor to bring together what has been sundered, to replace conquest with dialogue and a quest for new combinations. Insofar as it is a cultural movement, ecology is an important element in democratic culture—without which institutional guarantees are powerless to protect liberties.

Democratic Education

To define democracy as an institutional environment that is conducive to the formation and action of the subject would have no concrete meaning if the democratic spirit did not permeate every aspect of organized social life, from schools to hospitals, from factories to townships. Democracy was to a large extent born at the local level in a society that was experiencing the growth of both cities and trade. Today we expect to find it in all the large organizations that characterize our postindustrial societies. Public opinion makes this point forcefully when it demands the autonomy of towns and regions but remains attached to industrial democracy. Democratic action means resisting the growth of a mass society by extending decision-making sites and processes in such a way that the impersonal constraints on action come into closer contact with projects and individual preferences.

The task of resisting mass society is primarily a task for the educational sector. All conceptions of human beings and society imply ideas about education. *The*

Social Contract and *Emile* are inseparable, and the most powerful expression of Enlightenment culture is the idea that the role of education is to instill universal values into young people. The French developed an extremely rigorous version of this concept.

While Great Britain long retained a class-based system of education, France adopted a system of selection on the basis of merit—in other words, a talent for abstraction and formalization—and, in the spirit of the nineteenth century, attached great importance to a historical consciousness.

I previously argued that there is a difference between the democratic spirit and culture and the republican spirit associated with Enlightenment philosophy and rationalism; I now will explain why we need a new concept of education to replace the concept that made the lycée and the high school great and that the best American universities have tried constantly to revive and revitalize.

Education has three equally important goals: On the one hand, it should develop reason and the capacity for rational action; on the other, it should develop individual creativity and the recognition of the other as subject. The first goal echoes earlier ideals and should be maintained; the acquisition of knowledge must remain central to education. Nothing could be more ludicrous or harmful than a curriculum that emphasizes, instead of knowledge, proper interaction with one's peer group or appropriate responses to economic stimuli. Just as we must reject a purely rationalist conception of man and society, so we must reject any devaluation of reason. The endless struggle against the alliance of reason and power means primarily that we must protect reason and try to ally it with liberty.

The second goal of education is to prepare for rational thought: This means developing both a critical spirit of innovation and an awareness of one's own particularity, which is a product of both individual history and cultural memory. The third goal should be to understand and acknowledge others—individuals and collectivities—as subjects. Thus, education should be based on a curriculum that promotes the abilities to think scientifically, to express oneself, and to recognize oneself and others as subjects. In other words, education must promote an open attitude toward cultures and societies far removed from ours in either time or space and must help us to rediscover their creative inspiration—or what I term their historicity or their ability to create themselves by using models of knowledge, economic action, and morality.

A curriculum cannot in itself define a concept of education; the pedagogic relationship is also of paramount importance. We greatly need a new definition of teaching; for there is now, as François Dubet so clearly demonstrated in the case of France (Dubet 1991), a gulf between the world of teachers and the world of those they teach. The widespread violence observable among pupils brought up in a very disadvantaged situation is merely an external sign of the growing rift. A teacher is an agent of reason. A teacher is also a model who, like a father or a mother, helps children and young people to construct their own identity. And finally, a teacher is also a mediator who helps children to understand others.

Schools must be culturally and socially heterogeneous. A few years ago, an apparently minor incident led to heated debates in France on the subject of secular education. Three girls insisted on wearing Islamic headscarves to school, and the principal, who is now a member of the Parliament, refused to accept this sign of religious identity. Thanks to the Conseil d'Etat, tolerance finally prevailed; but a number of girls in a similar situation were later excluded from different schools. What is the point of education if it cannot instill the national spirit, tolerance, and the will to liberty in girls and boys from different social backgrounds and cultures? Why has the school system so little self-confidence that it must close its doors on boys and girls who are in some way different?

The rationalist West can no longer regard itself as having a monopoly on historicity and liberty. That is quite unacceptable, for it flies in the face of the West's own history. A refusal a priori to allow the free creativity of the human subject to seek alternative forms of education and self-expression is equally unacceptable. It is absurd to claim that religion in all its forms is the enemy of progress and liberty. Religious, national, and social movements are expressions of liberating force, and as it happens, they are usually also the first victims of authoritarian regimes. If we cannot recognize that, then our criticisms of antidemocratic actions undertaken in the name of a religion, nation, or class will be both unthinking and ineffective.

We ought to have learned this long ago. Let us recall that although the Leninist regime in Russia was by definition antidemocratic, it grew out of a socialist labor movement that did have democratic aspirations; and it is no accident that the workers' opposition was the first victim of repression after the authoritarian closure of the Russian Duma. What is true at the historical level is also true at the level of individual life: The personal subject is a combination of liberty and identity; the renunciation of identity is too high a price to pay for liberty. For the same reason, we must recognize that the family has an essential role to play in the formation of the democratic spirit.

"Progressive" thinkers were critical of the family and particularly of women, on the grounds that they were agents for the transmission of social and cultural controls. They argued that the education of rational and responsible citizens implied the eradication of particularism. That "progressive" ideal found its highest expression in Israel's kibbutzim because the stakes there were so high: the simultaneous creation of a nation, an economy, and a language. In a situation of dependency and struggle for liberation, the republican spirit may be likened to the democratic spirit; but the weaker the external obstacles and the more endogenous the process of development, the greater the need to recognize that the individual is a subject who can become an actor of social change, an agent of criticial thinking and innovation rather than a soldier who is mobilized for a collective struggle, be it defensive or liberating.

We must stop regarding parents who stay at home with their children as "traditional" and parents who are away for longer and longer hours as "modern." We must overcome the dichotomy between an open and gratifying public life and a monotonous and lonely private life. If integration is to come about, the collective or individual subject must be able to modify the social or cultural environment, and this means that we must place equal emphasis on participation and identity. In today's mass society, everyone talks of participation; but participation tends to mean dissolving into what David Riesman called the lonely crowd. Rather than contrasting the two, we must reconcile the goal of integration with the goal of the personal project or identity; for people must be integrated into a group or a system. How could people exist without the private space that is created or protected by the family or the national, ethnic, or religious group?

For a long time, individuals who privileged their participation in a family or a professional or local community found themselves excluded from the public space. Their identity was strong, their degree of participation low. The situation has now been reversed. Society's doors are open, and even the unemployed and other marginal groups take part in consumption, not to mention mass communications. Even if we play only a passive role, we all help to keep the wheels of the economic and social machine turning. We are, however, in danger of ceasing to be individuals or at least of losing the ability to control our individual lives. The established order once repressed those who attacked it; nowadays, it atomizes them and thus they lose their identity and can no longer attack the established order. They either try to maintain a toehold in society by taking refuge in defensive countersocieties or else they decompose under the influence of drugs that lessen their self-control and unleash energies, images, and sensations that undermine their ability to formulate projects and choices.

The most important image of democracy is that of the responsible citizen who cares about the public good. That is the image invoked by institutions. There is now, however, a widespread lack of interest in politics, especially in prosperous countries. Private life seems to have become divorced from public life, and fewer people are actively involved in politics. How is it that, at a time when so many countries are striving to introduce or reintroduce democracy, there is an increasing distrust of what we now call the political class in countries that have long had the good fortune to be free? Such a phenomenon, which should not be regarded as a recent and irremediable catastrophe, has multiple causes, and not all of them are structural. It is also associated with a decline in public-mindedness and often with a withdrawal into private life. In certain cases, that withdrawal can give rise to new political demands, as the women's movement has demonstrated; but it becomes negative when private life is nothing more than a screen onto which messages from the consumer society are projected. An individual who is no longer a subject cannot become a social actor and is dissolved into a changing flow of interests, desires, and images. Instead of seeking a separation between private and public life, we must understand that everything that strengthens the individual or collective subject makes a direct contribution to the continued existence of a vital democracy. It was once believed that being a good citizen, and a fortiori a good revolutionary, meant sacrificing one's personal interests; today, we have to say almost the opposite. People whose pattern of behavior has been reduced to passive participation in consumption can be manipulated by dominant interests; only individuated subjects can resist the domination of systems.

The One Disappears

Democratic culture is associated with modernity because modernity is based on the elimination of all central principles that can be used to define a unitary society. Democracy is based on the disappearance of the One. So long as we believe in an *ultima ratio*, or in the central role of the will of God, the national tradition, reason, or the meaning of history, we cannot be democrats, even though we may be tolerant and may defend public liberties. There always comes a moment when political debate reaches its limits and comes into conflict with a central principle that the authorities claim is not open to discussion. We cannot, they say, go against the word of God or the higher interest of the fatherland. Yet it would be ridiculous to give democracy a limited role, while requiring that basic problems be referred to a higher principle, and therefore to the decisions of those who represent that principle within social life.

I am not, however, one to take this argument to extremes or to see the autonomy of subsystems as the constituent principle of modern societies. If that were the case, only the rational pursuit of self-interest could ensure the coordination of the subsystems, according to the liberal conception. I merely posit that the disappearance of the One is a precondition for modernity and particularly for democracy. It removes the fundamental obstacle to democracy. Once we have dismissed the claim that society can be homogenized or totally controlled, the reconstruction of society becomes possible. This was initially done by making working-class struggles, labor legislation, and collective bargaining central to political life. It is in a similar spirit that I contrast the logic of the subject with the logic of the system—or to use what may be a more accurate formula, that I define the subject as an attempt to use creative liberty to integrate rationality and identities and to resist both communitarian confinement and the logic of rational choice. I assume, of course, that we have already laid to rest any thought of invoking the sort of historical inevitability that was used to legitimize the action of the working class and its revolutionary vanguard.

The absence of a central principle of order is not provisional. Some perpetuate the oldest tendency within social thought and argue that society should be centered, not on God, reason, history, or the nation, but on society itself, or more concretely, the law or the norm. It is, they say, the law that shapes society. This formula is, however, both less fresh and more dangerous than it seems. The appeal to law and therefore to the legal state was an essential feature of secularization, which made society rather than God the principle that regulated social behavior. But in today's "active" society, which has a high degree of historicity, the appeal to the national-legal authority leaves individuals and groups at the mercy of a power that is very concentrated and whose discourse and interests can permeate our very souls. The democratic field is one in which negotiated social relations prevail over the logic of the integration of the social whole and where respect for individual liberties and minorities provides a counterbalance to the central power of the state. Just as it is artificial to claim that the state can be dissolved into the market, so it is essential to define the democratic political system as the locus of tensions and negotiations between the unity of the state and the plurality of social actors. These tensions are essential, not only because they block the bureaucratization and militarization of society, but primarily because they prevent the dualization that leads to a centralized public life and an atomized private life that are entirely separate.

As the rich, industrialized countries approach the end of the twentieth century, the main danger is that democracy will degenerate into a political market in which consumers seek the products that suit them. Such a situation is not democratic, as it is dominated by a supply system disguised as a set of social demands. Society has been so greatly transformed that the social policies born of industrial society no longer have the meaning they had fifty years ago when the welfare state was created. Yet democracy is still closely interwoven with the defense of the state interventions that reduced social inequality and, more importantly, that prevented those stricken by illness, accidents, unemployment, old age, and disability from being expelled from society or condemned to loneliness and poverty. The logic of market forces by no means ensures a recognition of the other. There is no such thing as a laissez-faire democracy; all forms of democracy are voluntaristic. This was true when it was a matter of fighting the concentration of uncontrolled power; it is just as true now, as we protest the apparent triumph of private life as the acquisition of commodities available on the market, or conversely, the management of a cultural heritage. The role of social institutions is to simultaneously encourage two modes of behavior: free personal action and recognition of the other, who may be either a neighbor or someone who is far away in space or in time. Such are the two basic and complementary principles of democratic culture. Democratic culture is based on a belief in the private ability of individuals and groups to "live their own lives" but also on the recognition that others have the right to create and control their own existence. The two principles are not parallel to one another: the first determines the second. It is not a matter of recognizing the other as different, for that usually leads to indifference or segregation rather than to communication, but of recognizing the other as a subject, as an individual who is trying to be an actor and to resist the forces that rule either the market or the administrative organization. The transition from individual-as-consumer to individual-as-subject will not be brought about by thought alone or by disseminating ideas. It can only be brought about through democracy, through an open institutional space. That open space gives the most underprivileged groups, in particular, a voice; those who are in possession of power and money express themselves more effectively through the economic, administrative mechanisms and the media they control than through discourse or protests.

The Public Space

We can now explain the close connection between democracy and the freedom of association and speech that allows personal demands to enter public life and the decision-making process. If the media do not belong primarily to the public space, or if they abandon that space and become first of all economic enterprises whose policies are determined by profit or the defense of specific interests, then democracy has no voice. In the industrialized countries, there is a danger that parliament will be absorbed by the state and that the media will be absorbed by the market. If that happens, the public space will be empty at a time when the social movements of the industrial age have been exhausted and when new social movements are taking shape as slowly and with as much difficulty as did the labor movement of the nineteenth century. As Dominique Wolton has argued, the targeting of television programs at lucrative marketing segments—children, highly educated people, or religious, national, and regional communities—has impoverished the public space. Wolton's defense of popular television (Wolton 1993) points out that although the technical and cultural mediocrity of so many popular programs is obviously a matter for regret, the most important debates on television—for example, those concerning inequality, exclusion, segregation, unemployment, sexuality, old age, or education—are addressed to the general public, and the so-called quality programs that offer the public high culture or allow specialists to parade their knowledge do not always give creativity access to the media or encourage attitudes and modes of behavior that are tolerant of diversity and innovation.

Now that parliament is becoming part of the state's managerial action, the center of the political system must be displaced away from parliamentary representation and toward public opinion. In the early stages of modernity, bourgeois public space was a civic space. For a long time, intellectual circles, salons, cafes, and journals were the agents through which new ideas and sensibilities developed and were disseminated. We then entered a period when parliamentary debates and major negotiations with the unions were central to public life. Those institutions, which were characteristic of industrial society, are now in decline; and in their place, the media are taking on an importance they did not previously have and with a new and increasing independence since World War I. This development is obvious in countries where the crisis in the political system takes an extreme form, as in Italy, where judges and the press appear to be the defenders of democracy and where members of parliament are accused of having used this political influence for personal gain or to protect criminal interests. One can understand why politicians are both resentful of the media and eager to use them. In sum, it is no longer possible to assume that members of parliament are interested in the public good, while journalists are only interested in finding an audience that is greedy for sensation. In a consumer society, the links between public life and private life, and therefore those between civil society and political society, are increasingly important—and that works to the advantage of the media. In developing societies or societies in crisis, in contrast, politics is dominated by the problems of the state rather than by private demands.

Many observers denounce the worldwide absence of democratic culture, even in places where there is a certain political liberty. In many countries, economic constraints and the domination of foreign models prevent individuals from feeling that they are responsible for their own society. The outcome is the same when the internationalization of both the media and the economy, together with mass advertising campaigns, establishes a direct link between a globalized system and consumers who do not belong to any particular society or culture. Political space in both cases is invaded either by the state and economic constraints or by a private life that has been reduced to meaning the consumption of commodities.

Democratic culture cannot exist without a reconstruction of public space or a return to political debate. We have recently seen the collapse of a whole generation of voluntaristic states not all of which were totalitarian, notably, in Latin America and India. When we look at the ruins of communism, nationalism, or populism, we see either the triumph of chaos or a boundless faith in the market economy as the only method for constructing a democratic society. People no longer have any faith in their ability to make history and are falling back on their desires, their identity, or their dreams of a utopian society. Yet there can be no democracy unless the greatest number wish to exercise power, at least indirectly, to make their voices heard, and to be involved in decisions that affect their lives. That is why we cannot divorce democratic culture from political consciousness, which is not simply a sense of citizenship but a demand for responsibility, even if it no longer takes the form it took in small-scale and relatively simple political societies. More than ever before, the democratic consciousness is sustained by a recognition of diversified interests, opinions, and modes of behavior, and therefore by the will to create the greatest possible diversity in a society that must attain an ever higher level of internal integration and international competitiveness. In this book I have focused on the idea of democratic culture rather than on a purely institutional or moral definition of political freedom, not with the intent of accentuating the distance between culture and institutions and between public life and private life but in order to bring them closer together, and to demonstrate their interdependence. Democracy presupposes the acknowledgment of the other as subject; and a democratic culture is a culture that recognizes political institutions as the primary locus of that acknowledgment.

PART 4

Democracy and
Development

10

Modernization or Development?

The market economy and political democracy appear to many people as two sides of the same coin. Many argue that both limit the absolute state. Our century has been dominated by states that were at once authoritarian and economically voluntaristic, they say. In the last two decades of the century, we have witnessed the exhaustion of that model of the state, the triumph of the market economy, and the return of democracy to regions from which it had been driven out—as in several Latin American countries—or where it had never, or almost never, existed—as in postcommunist Europe, with the exception of Czechoslovakia, which was originally a true democracy. If we take away the state's direct power over the economy and separate political power and economic power, we strike a blow against the absolute state and thus make possible a free political debate.

There is an element of truth in this argument. We have to accept the idea that democracy is in great danger when the state is in direct control of the economy. The market economy is indeed a necessary precondition for democracy because it limits the power of the state. We therefore have to reject the ideology that identifies democracy with the will of the people as expressed by a state or a vanguard party that can overthrow a dominant class or ruling elite by violence if need be. This ideology is highly debatable, as there is no proof that the overthrow of *social* domination leads to the creation of *political* democracy. That the goal and desire of many revolutionaries was to extend democratic liberties is not in doubt, but it is difficult to see why a change of society should necessarily create a political democracy. We find the same analytic flaw in the liberal argument that goes beyond the established fact that freeing the economy from the state is a precondition for democracy and claims that it is a sufficient condition or even a determinant cause. It is not difficult to come up with a more balanced formula: There can be no democracy without a market economy; but many countries with a market economy are not democracies. The market economy is a necessary precondition for democracy but not a sufficient one. In many regions of the world, dictatorships are destroying voluntaristic states, forcibly introducing a market economy and relying on the world market to allocate resources. Regimes as authoritarian as that in the People's Republic of China have seized the initiative and are developing a market economy and encouraging foreign capital to penetrate one sector after another. In Latin America, military dictatorships proclaimed their economic liberalism in Argentina and Chile. Going much further back in time, we find that it was only with the reforms of 1884–85, or in other words many decades after it took the decision to open its market to international trade, that Great Britain introduced universal male suffrage, even though it was at the center of the world market throughout the nineteenth century. To function optimally, the market needs an efficient state, appropriate economic policies, good means of communication, and a high standard of education for the whole population; but why should it need democracy? To be sure, the liberal economy fears political control of the economy; however, a nondemocratic power can promote the accumulation of capital, whereas a democratic regime might forget the needs of the economy and concern itself with protecting its own vested interests or meeting particular demands rather than promoting social mobility or a coherent economic policy.

So we should approach the question from another direction: Rather than regarding democracy as the political counterpart to economic development, we should examine the preconditions for the transition from a market economy to development and the role played by democracy in this transition. There are three main preconditions for development, or more specifically for self-sustaining, endogenous development: large and well-selected investments; the distribution of the products of growth throughout the whole of society; and the political and administrative regulation of economic and social change at the level of the national or regional community in question. In more concrete terms, the transformation of a market economy into development presupposes the existence of a state that can analyze the situation and make decisions, as well as entrepreneurs and redistributive forces.

These three agents of development are closely related to the three components of democracy that we identified and defined at the beginning of this book. Firstly, there can be no democracy and no development without citizenship, or in other words, a sense of belonging to a national community that is ruled by law. Our analysis of development leads us to add that citizenship presupposes the existence of a state whose principal objective is to strengthen a national society through economic modernization and social integration. Secondly, the representation of interests is a component both in democracy and in development; it is or can be equivalent to a redistribution of the benefits of growth and therefore to social integration. Investment, finally, leads to development and industrialization because it destroys the mechanisms of social reproduction, promotes liberties, and replaces old principles of order with the principle of mobility.

Should we take this line of thought to its logical conclusion and state that development and democracy are synonymous? That is, in fact, the central idea of this chapter. The terms are not, however, completely inseparable because development, like democracy, is a process in a permanent state of disequilibrium. It is an open, asynchronic, and conflictual process, and its three components can become divorced from one another or come into conflict: For example, the accumulation of resources may require a high level of investment that places severe restrictions on redistribution and may even encourage speculation rather than investment. A counteroffensive designed to achieve a fairer redistribution of wealth may in turn reduce investment. Even in the highly controlled situations that pertain in western Europe, the complementary aspects of development have not always been in harmony, and citizenship has been affected by crises of varying severity. Democracy is a political system for managing social change; development is a set of social relations combined with an economic policy. The integration of the social and economic actors of development does not come about spontaneously; indeed, it is threatened by their respective rationales, which may conflict and thus disrupt society. By giving the political system the role of mediator between actors and the state, democracy makes the component elements of development cohere. *Development is the result of democracy and not its cause.*

Between State Voluntarism and Economic Rationalism

An obvious objection to this argument is that although these relations between democracy and development are observable in countries that are already close to endogenous development, they appear far removed from the reality of developing countries, or in other words, countries that are not in a position to achieve endogenous development. In such countries, only the voluntarist state—or sometimes foreign capitalism—can stimulate a takeoff and, more specifically, destroy the old oligarchies. Are we to conclude, therefore, that modernization is democracy's enemy, even though democracy is a precondition for the perpetuation of a level of modernity that has already been achieved? Many people take the view that dictatorship—either of the capitalist bourgeoisie or of the socialist or nationalist state—is necessary at the moment of takeoff and that only when cruising speed has been reached can political controls on social change be relaxed and democracy be introduced so as to bring about endogenous development.

This conviction was held by the enlightened despots of the eighteenth century and by the authoritarian but modernizing nationalists of the twentieth. Kemal's Turkey, Nasser's Egypt, Tito's Yugoslavia, and Vargas's Brazil are all cases in point. Voluntarist states played the leading role in these experiments, while democracy appeared to be the political banner of an oligarchy that was either foreign in origin or tied to foreign interests. This explains why democracy was reviled by the many revolutionaries in these countries, who wanted to free their peoples from the privileges maintained by political parties enserfed to the oligarchy.

We must, however, abandon this representation and take a more critical view of these voluntarist regimes. They played a modernizing role only when—as was often the case—they allowed political, economic, and social actors to become interdependent for the first time. The state was the main investor in most industrializing countries—for example, in Brazil and independent Algeria. The state also mobilized an emerging national consciousness or found a base in the urban masses, which had been swollen by economic modernization. The authoritarian state was likewise a modernizing force when it created a modern administration, fought corruption, and instilled respect for the law. The state cannot initiate a forced march towards modernization simply by freeing itself from particular interests; only a modernizing state that is an agent for the formation of economic, social, and administrative actors can play a decisive role in development. Such a state can put an end to the fragmentation of a society in which the economic goals of the oligarchy have nothing to do with the country's social and political problems and in which social actors tend to defend vested interests rather than use the mechanisms of social change for the common interest.

The breakup of traditional society is usually brought about by authoritarian means. We must, however, make a distinction between patrimonial states that are authoritarian or militaristic and mobilizing states. The latter may represent a stage in the formation of autonomous social actors and may therefore pave the way for a democratically based, endogenous form of development. It is when the strength of the mobilizing state is sapped by clientelism, corruption, or internal dissent that an antipopular and authoritarian state intervenes. Its action may, however, encourage development if its top priority is to free social actors from controls and agendas that are unrelated to the needs of the economy. Even when that is the case, it may be a matter of only a brief intervention. If, however, that intervention does not take place, then the whole process of development is blocked by a state that is defending its own interests rather than those of society, that is concerned with repression rather than openness and the relationship between investment and distribution. On the whole, development occurs only when the transition via the voluntarist state is a necessary detour on the road to endogenous development. If this enlightened despotism becomes an end in itself or its power becomes absolute, then development is paralyzed and suffocated, and the absolute state collapses eventually into chaos or underdevelopment. The state can be an agent of development, provided that development is a two-way process involving both state and society. Development is impossible if the state's sole concern is the accumulation of wealth, as is the case in certain oil-producing countries, or if it tries to control society rather than to guide its transformation.

It is usually the failure of the voluntarist state itself that provokes the return to society despite the resistance of the despotic state. In the case of Nazism and Japanese militarism, the state exploded; in the case of the Soviet system and Argentine militarism, it imploded. The collapse of an authoritarian state either leads to chaos or paves the way for the reconstruction of civil society, which is always a difficult process. In the case of Japan and Germany, which had reached a high level of technical development at the time of their collapse, U.S. intervention was a vital factor in the return to democracy and endogenous development. The collapse of national-popular regimes or the exhaustion of the military regimes that overthrew them forced other countries to submit to the dictates of the world market.

This brings us back to the argument put forward at the beginning of this analysis: The market economy, defined as the destruction of political controls over the economy, frees the economy from domination by a state or oligarchy and is a precondition for development. The transition to the market economy has often been brought about by authoritarian regimes, as was the case in Chile and in Peru, where Alan Garcia's failure led to Alberto Fujimori's coup d'état. But once the great transformation has taken place, the autonomy of political society is the most important factor in the creation of endogenous development. Endogenous development is, however, usually preceded by a long period during which the accumulation of capital and decisionmaking are monopolized by a ruling class or elite. The late twentieth century has not been dominated by the power of states born of national liberation movements or revolutions; it has been dominated by the exhaustion of such voluntaristic policies. In some cases, this was a rapid process, as in Nasser's Egypt and the FLN's Algeria; in others, it was much slower, as in Brazil and Mexico, where nationalism was tinged with populism.

The principal effect of democracy is to ensure the redistribution of the national product; but while it limits the power of the state, it also allows the state to act as an agent of development. This is the goal of Italy's democratic government as it struggles against corruption, the influence of the mafia, and the deterioration of public services; in the long term, those same goals imply the pursuit of a vigorous economic modernization. Democracy, finally, also strengthens national unity by giving the greatest number at least some access to decisionmaking and the public purse.

Democracy and development cannot exist unless they coexist. Authoritarian development suffocates and leads to increasingly severe crises. A democracy that has been reduced to an open political market and is no longer defined as the manager of historical changes is destroyed by partocracy, lobbying, and corruption. This conclusion is not a restatement of the classic thesis, which has been so well argued by Seymour Martin Lipset, of a correlation between economic modernization and political democracy and therefore of modernization's determinant role in creating a more modern and diverse society (Lipset 1960). It is, instead, an assertion that these two conceptions are at once contradictory and consistent. While modernization is defined as the increasing differentiation of subsystems, each of which is governed by a specific form of rationality, democracy is defined by the absence of any overall power, and therefore as the final product of an evolutionary process determined by the triumph of instrumental rationality and individualism. If, on the other hand, we define development as the political management of the social tensions between economic investment and social participation, then democracy will be seen as the precondition for that management and not simply as its result. That is the position I am defending here.

The idea of modernization triumphed after World War II and the collapse of fascist states and colonial empires. The idea of development was antithetical to this liberal trend; yet, Alfred Sauvy called the developing countries the "Third World" and thus identified them with the struggle for emancipation and progress waged by the Third Estate in France in 1789—a struggle that combined a will to achieve independence and equality with a belief in the beneficial effects of science and technology. Democracy and development came to be seen as forces that together could liberate human beings from the mutually reinforcing conditions of poverty, ignorance, and dependency. But this alliance between economic modernization and social and national liberation soon broke down. The level of social integration was too low, and in many countries, especially the former colonies, democratic hopes were replaced by nationalist mobilization, which destroyed the democratic forces and rendered their long-term development impossible, as happened in Egypt and Algeria. These new regimes, be they authoritarian or pluralist, readily adapted to dependency, as shown by the analyses of Celso Furtado and other Latin American economists. Dependency led to a structural dualization and therefore to greater social inequalities, which resulted—as early as 1964 in Brazil and 1966 in Argentina—in the fall of democratic regimes and the succession of military dictatorships. During this period, neither the defenders of modernization nor the radical dependency theorists made any further reference to democracy. The former were content to assert that growth would lead to the opening of social negotiations, as there would henceforth be a surplus to be parceled out; the latter called for revolution and for direct action against a pseudo–nation-state that was the economic agent of foreign domination.

Thirty years later, nearly all of these countries are turning to a liberal policy as a result of the collapse of the Soviet model and the triumph of U.S. influence. Authoritarian states are denounced as nepotistic or corrupt; frontiers have been opened up to foreign capital and to the orthodox economic programs of the IMF. A certain political pluralism has been established, and talk of democratization is everywhere, but it is as artificial as before, when a government of national liberation was automatically described as democratic. We seem to have fallen back on theories that reduce development to the sum of the social effects of economic modernization.

The link between democracy and development means, on the contrary, that there can be no development without an open management of the tensions between investment and distribution and no democracy without representation of social interests and concern for national society. Democracy and development are interrelated because both ideas introduce an integrated and overall image of social change and reject theories of modernization that describe society as a train whose social and political carriages are pulled by the locomotive of rationalization and material progress.

Democracy and development are interdependent notions: both simultaneously comprise economic, social, and political elements. This sets them apart from the liberal conception, which maintains that obstacles to the free workings of markets should be removed, and the revolutionary conception, according to which political and social mobilization lead directly to economic growth. Development and democracy stand midway between the objectivism of liberals and the subjectivism of revolutionaries, for both development and democracy prioritize the creation of an autonomous political system that can manage relations between economic change and social or cultural organizations. In any case, we must cling to a strict definition of democracy and refuse to equate nonauthoritarian regimes with democracies; for by that criterion we could describe as democratic any place where commodities or people are exchanged—a bridge, a station, or a subway train—as long as it has been stripped of political authority and reduced to a purely economic function.

Endogenous Development

There is a direct association between democracy and endogenous development. The link does not arise because a society has already been modernized and therefore has the capacity to introduce further changes without bringing severe pressures to bear on its members; it originates in the endogenous character of modernization, which implies the existence of a system for the democratic management of social relations. Countries in which modernization is exogenous are, in contrast, subordinated to an all-powerful external agent—a nation-state or a foreign state, foreign capitalism, or even international aid—that does not permit a pluralistic political system to form and that sooner or later becomes an obstacle to democracy and development alike.

The lesson we have learned from the century that is now coming to an end is that forced marches toward modernity and independence result in failure, underdevelopment, and greater dependency. How can we not be convinced of this after the fall of the Soviet empire and Soviet society, which tried in an authoritarian fashion to construct a new man and a new society on a modern technological and social infrastructure; and after the decomposition of the most extreme nationalist regimes, which in the name of identity or purity plunged their countries into economic crisis, from which they have yet to emerge successfully? The fact that they took place over a very long period of time makes it difficult to analyze these processes. It is true that the Soviet economy was still modernizing in the 1970s and that the People's Republic of China is achieving impressive economic results under a regime that is far from democratic; but the nationalist or revolutionary authoritarian state cannot be anything more than a provisional stage on the road to development. Either that state will promote the maturation and emancipation of civil society or it will devour society, making both development and democracy impossible. As this century closes, a number of countries are living in an intermediary stage, which should be recognized for what it is. China, Vietnam, and Cuba cannot in the long term reconcile an authoritarian government with an open economy; and the Chinese Communist party cannot be considered the principal actor behind the accelerated modernization taking place in a part of the economy. In the long term, democracy must be associated with development, even if in the medium term a high level of economic modernization can be brought about by— or despite—an authoritarian regime. Such regimes are no more than unstable compromises between the totalitarian state, which is incompatible with development, and democracy, which is associated with development but which can also degenerate and cease to liaise between state and social actors.

However, we also should recognize that this argument has its limitations, thanks to an apparent paradox in west European history. For centuries the center of modernization, western Europe, lived under authoritarian regimes. The absolute monarchy was associated with both a legal state and the growth of trade and industry. Neither Venice nor Florence were democracies; and neither Napoleon III's France, Bismarck's Germany, nor Stolypin's Russia could be described as democratic. To pursue the argument further: Can we, as Max Weber thought, describe as democratic the capitalist form of development, which is not only based on the power of merchants as the sole agents of development but which also explains their behavior in terms of private motivations such as the quest for personal gain, the acquisition of a family fortune, or a personal vocation? We are tempted to answer in the negative: If the ruling elite's mode of conduct explains economic modernization, then that modernization is not associated with democracy.

However, the European experience is distinguished by the fact that for a long time there was a very low level of social mobilization. Jean Fourastié has shown in striking fashion that it was only at the end of the nineteenth century, or in other words after a very long period of economic and administrative modernization, that the living standards of wage earners began to rise rapidly and on a sustained basis. This modernization took place in the context of a relative social immobility, which was more pronounced in eastern Europe than in the west and which in Prussia and Russia combined a market economy with precapitalist relations of production, as did the plantation economy in tropical regions.

That is the source of the unusual importance there of intellectuals, who for a long time indirectly represented "peoples" imprisoned in an imposed domination and denied freedom of political expression. In this time and place, democracy was a theory rather than a practice, an appeal to an absent people rather than an act by a people that was present. In the contemporary world these zones of popular silence, where democratic action is the preserve of intellectual and political counter-elites—such as the students in Beijing's Tiananmen Square—are shrinking. Both the Islamic world and the Latin American continent have, in contrast, recently experienced popular political mobilizations along nationalist, ethnic, or religious lines, but they have precluded democracy and have not allowed democratizing and revolutionary elites to play the important transitional role they played in European societies.

It was in the United States that the transition from the configuration made of a strong central state, a puritan capitalist bourgeoisie, and a hierarchical society to the configuration made of democracy, mass production, and conspicuous consumption took place. That is why U.S. philosophers have been so aware of the link between democracy and development, whereas those subscribing to the Soviet and nationalist models clung to the idea that development was the creation of a ruling elite, which although it looked after the interests of society at the same time retained a monopoly on power and its prerogatives. My critique of the liberal conception of modernization is therefore not intended to revive a statist and voluntaristic conception of development, but on the contrary, to provide an escape from too crude an opposition between voluntarism and liberalism by establishing a close link between development and democracy. Europe succeeded in creating precisely such a link under the twofold influence of social democratic policies and Keynesian thinking.

Crisis and Authoritarianism

The situation most conducive to democracy is one in which social movements clash over the management of a society's principal cultural resources. It is in such a situation that what I term a *historical system of action* exists in the strongest sense. Democracy is the result of a double orientation on the part of historical actors and social movements: They are in conflict even as they aspire to the same cultural values. That is why, as I have said, the strongest democracies emerged in those industrial societies that were most strongly structured around the class conflict characteristic of industrial society. In France, in contrast, social struggles have always been subordinate to more general struggles in which the state was the central target: struggles between republicans and monarchists, between clericalists and anticlericalists. Social struggles were therefore very ideologically charged, as though they all masked a more basic conflict between past and present, or between reason and culture, and as though no compromise were possible.

In crisis situations, we see the destruction of social relations, conflicts, and social movements. These are substituted by the defense of purely private interests or by a global relationship with the state, from which we expect everything or which we reject completely. When the adversaries can no longer openly clash, especially over how wealth should be allocated, social forces decompose and parties and trade unions are weakened. Some citizens sink into apathy or concentrate on protecting their immediate interests, while others put their faith in a charismatic leader who, according to Freud's classic analysis, establishes a direct personal bond with every member of a destructured crowd. Minorities either rebel or withdraw from public life.

Revolutionary theories have often asserted that class struggles break out in acute crisis situations. Ignoring what have now become pathetic political games, the collective actors of history enter the scene in preparation for the triumph of a popular revolution. That this conception is tragically mistaken has been demonstrated throughout this century. It is because Russia was in a state of crisis rather than a revolutionary situation in 1917 that a vanguard seized power and never handed it over to the people. It was immediately after the great crisis of 1929 that the majority of the German population allowed itself to be swayed by Hitler and supported the violent action of the National Socialist party, scapegoating the Jews for the national crisis. Eugenio Tironi is right to analyze the stability of the Pinochet regime, which remained in power for fifteen years and even adopted a constitution, in terms of the breakup of political parties and trade unions that resulted from the crisis of hyperinflation and the economic disorder of 1972–73. If the crisis is limited and if the society in question is stable, political disorder actually can be an expression of the democratic spirit. This was the case in Italy in 1992–93, when that country began to demand the construction of a true national political society and the destruction of the mafia, which Italians began to loathe when General Dalla Chiesa, Judge Falcone, and Judge Borsellino were murdered within the space of a few years. When the crisis is more serious, and when the majority no longer believes that the authorities can guarantee its situation and its future, democracy is threatened by the call for a leader—even when that leader is a democrat, as was General de Gaulle. De Gaulle could have become a dictator and the defender of French Algeria in 1958, but he chose instead to strengthen republican institutions and to prepare the way for Algeria's independence.

A crisis produces apathy, conformism, and an enthusiasm for saviors rather than active participation or intense political debate. Chaos does not give birth to a phoenix-like people, nor does it unleash the subterranean strength of society. Quite the contrary: Social movements take shape only in a society with a high degree of historicity, which is not reducible to rapid economic and social change. It implies the existence of collective actions and social conflicts that can be resolved at the institutional level because social relations are highly organized. A society in crisis does not have the capacity to deal with its problems or to handle change in a controlled way. It decomposes and waits for an external solution to problems it feels the political system cannot solve; and it often expects the solution to come from an order that has been imposed on it.

After World War II, much of the world believed in endless modernization. It thought that its historical actors would go on acting. Within the space of a generation, those hopes had evaporated—more abruptly in many countries of the South and more gradually in those of the North. In the 1980s, the sense of crisis became more acute in industrialized countries, especially in western Europe, while recovery was on the horizon or even rapidly accelerating in certain countries in the South.

In the rich, industrial countries, we then saw the rise of uncontrollable forces. Poor immigrants were turned into scapegoats. Law and order was breaking down. Riots erupted in underprivileged urban areas. The political system appeared powerless to ward off external threats, to organize an economic recovery, or to get the country out of a national crisis. At this point, the crisis of democratic representation and participation worsens. Parties are criticized and rejected, unions are undermined, and the voices of intellectuals are no longer heard. The local groups that were the bedrock of grassroots democracy in recent decades are disappearing.

In developing countries that have not yet reached the stage of endogenous development, the crisis is usually more acute as it exacerbates their underdevelopment. There is a great danger in these countries that the people will reject democracy and turn to an authoritarian helmsman to guide them out of the storm.

The link between crisis and authoritarianism parallels that between development and democracy. Yet it is not democracy that produces the crises that give birth to authoritarian regimes, and there are no grounds for describing as democratic the breakdown of a political system that has been invaded by interest groups, parties, or corruption. On the contrary, crises are a product of the political system's inability to handle difficult changes or to arbitrate between competing social demands; and authoritarian regimes find it easier to intervene in situations of crisis than do democracies.

This is why we democrats cannot be content merely to denounce all authoritarian regimes because some of them, in the course of responding to a crisis, destroy democratic regimes. We must also analyze the reasons for the defeat of democratic rule and the nature of the crisis signaled by the military collapse or economic disaster.

To pursue this argument still further: An authoritarian regime can, like a revolution—and the two categories of political action tend increasingly to overlap—pave the way for democracy even as it is hostile to it. This was the case in Perón's Argentina. Gino Germani well understood that this authoritarian rupture occurred at the very time when more people were suddenly allowed to be part of the political process (Germani 1962). Obviously, this does not mean that we should describe some authoritarian regimes as democratic. On the contrary, we should refuse to describe as democratic both populist regimes or any regimes that claim to be democratic simply because they hold elections while in fact those events are nothing more than contests between two clans within the oligarchy or between particular interest groups.

A country can be nondemocratic in many ways. Italy's *partitocrazia* and the corruption that once reigned in so many U.S. cities, especially in New York's Tammany Hall, were mere caricatures of democracy. On the other hand, we cannot overlook Lenin's democratic intentions, even though the regime he created was, in his own lifetime, antidemocratic. A strict definition of democracy means that we must be more critical of regimes that recognize specific political rights and less critical of those that recognize or embrace one or another of the constituent elements of democracy. While there can be no democracy unless basic rights are respected, the interests of the majority are represented, and citizenship is institutionalized, there are many different regimes whose action respects one of these principles even as it negates the other two. None of these regimes can be described as democratic: not those that merely organize relatively open elections, nor those that speak in the name of the people, nor those that reduce natural law to the right to own property. We must be prepared to condemn the antidemocratic elements in all regimes that claim to be democratic; but we must also recognize the presence in revolutionary movements, elitist regimes, and populist states of calls for democracy that undermine an order that is blocking the autonomous action of all social actors. An analysis of particular historical situations will help us both to criticize authoritarian action and to recognize the will toward liberation, without which democracy will never triumph.

Transforming Old into New

What agents control the transition to endogenous development and democracy? Scholars have suggested three answers. According to the first, which is close to classic capitalist thinking, the vital factors are the opening up of markets and the spirit of enterprise. According to the second, development results from a collective will and a collective mobilization, which are usually state inspired. According to the third, it is the existence of an open political system that plays the main role because it prevents rulers from becoming divorced from their subordinates and gives priority to the basic needs of the collectivity rather than to private interests. If the latter prevailed, there would be a crisis or a social breakdown. The idea of democracy would lose much of its meaning if we did not adopt the third thesis, which is consonant with the experience of the countries that were the main centers of economic development in the West—namely, the Netherlands, Great Britain, and then the United States. The existence of an open political system and the abolition of absolute monarchy do more than the protestant spirit to explain the success of these countries, whereas absolute monarchies reinforced by the spirit of the Counter-Reformation were an obstacle to development in Catholic countries.

This comment brings us to a still more general theme. Whereas the classic image of modernization depicts the triumph of reason against the obstacles of particularism, privilege, and private violence, what I have defined as democratic culture means transforming old into new. It means rejecting clean sweeps and enlightened despotism. It means mobilizing existing individuals and collectivities and their demands and memories. Social life is like a tree whose leaves draw sustenance from exchanges with their environment and whose roots take nourishment from the earth. We still contrast tradition with modernity, just as we contrast immobility and movement, or even, in many cases, religion and the family with exchange-oriented economic activity governed by calculation. Let us reject this vision and redefine development not only as a combination of democracy and growth but also, at a deeper level, as a combination of a cultural heritage and projects for the future. How can we speak of democracy if we take the view that the greater part of humanity must renounce its culture and identity in order to take the one road that leads to progress? Denying the majority of human beings the ability to be subjects of their own history is surely the ultimate denial of democratic liberty. If modernity is something we have to give people or force on them and if the only thing that can introduce modernity is an open market in which cultural heritages are destroyed, then we would do better to state honestly that poor nations are not ripe for democracy in the same way that children and young people are supposedly incapable of taking part in political life. Democratic culture is not restricted to defining how human beings must behave and relate to each other in a modernized society; it would be untrue to its central principle if it did not assert a continuity between past and future or the possibility of mobilizing a cultural heritage in order to create the future. The will to establish a break between past and present, between the old regime and "after the revolution," implies authoritarian modes of thought and action. If democracy consists in allowing different (and even mutually hostile) groups and individuals to live together in the same country and in combining unity and diversity, it must necessarily preserve as much as possible of the past, and even of past traditions, in order to create a future that is both particular and unique and yet built around the universal principles of rationality, respect for the liberty of human subjects, and equality before the law.

The globalization of the economy and of mass culture has given these problem areas central importance. It sometimes seems that we must now be either universalists or multiculturalists, just as we were once either defenders of capitalism or supporters of socialism. North America is a continent of immigrants, where multiculturalism and the communitarian spirit mutually reinforce one another; but the situation is very different in western Europe, especially in France. Europe and France remain more attached to a rationalism that is both individualist and universalist, which distrusts the communitarian spirit and suspects it of being sectarian or even racist. Yet we need not choose between universalism and multiculturalism. The real choice is between a hostile juxtaposition of these cultural tendencies and their reconciliation. Universalism and multiculturalism are two halves of a shattered culture, two levels of a society that has been torn apart by the conflicting rationales of objectivization on the one hand and identity and subjectivity on the other. The logic of objectivization governs markets, technical systems, political, military, and economic strategies, and mass communications; the logic of identity and subjectivity is increasingly divorced from productive roles and ways of participating in modernity. On the one hand, we act as both players and pawns in the great game of the world economy; on the other, we no longer construct our identities on the basis of our social roles but on the basis of our individuality, which is composed of sexuality and dreams, memories and transmitted norms, and beliefs and anxieties.

Memory and Project

Less than a century ago, the most important social contradiction was that between capitalists and wage earners, and it called into question what Marx referred to as the social relations of production. Employers and workers were defined, at least at the essential level, by what they did together, which both united them—they were all involved in industry—and divided them. In our day, the situation is much more difficult to analyze. The conflict is no longer one between social classes and interests—capital and labor—but between objectivism and subjectivism. Our objective and subjective realities are drifting apart and degenerating, respectively, into a mass society and an obsessional search for a desocialized identity. It seems the widening gulf between the world of the economy and the world of the personality has created a void where once there was the common good of Christians, the civic spirit of the ancients, and the solidarity of industrial society. Those who inhabit the heights of international society travel the world, accumulate wealth and information, and store fragments of cultures in their museums. They believe in science, technology, free markets, and the absence of authoritarian cultural controls. Those who live at the bottom of this society and those who have been excluded or relegated to its margins have no option but to defend their particularities against a universalism that serves the interests of the center so well. The dominated are indeed divided. Some hope to rise above their marginality, to enter the circle of light, to play their full part in mass culture, or to join in the economic contest; others, in contrast, are struggling to defend the integrity of a threatened culture. Some individuals belong to neither of these categories. Many are drowning in the whirlpools of the intervening waters, while others are trying to cling to two poles that are drifting further and further apart. Some immigrants, many of them women, wish to become assimilated and to break with what they regard as the intolerable constraints of their own culture; others want to drive out the invader and resort to violence in their struggle against those they demonize. Similarly, especially in the countries of the center, some women are demanding equal rights and the abolition of differences that produce inequalities; others wish to assert their cultural difference, and above all their biological and psychological differences. Mainly as a result of the influence of Simone de Beauvoir, the struggle of European women has been primarily for freedom and equality, for an end to legal and economic discrimination. North American women, in contrast, have been more forceful about asserting a female identity, and that may trap them in a dangerous quest for communitarian purity. Similar divisions can be seen in all dominated categories, from minorities such as homosexuals in the North to the disfranchised majority in the South.

We must refuse a choice between loss of identity and the ghetto, between assimilation and countercultures. The first choice is a complete denial of the autonomy of those who want to be integrated into a majority that claims to have a monopoly on universality. The second breaks off all communication and confines us within an identity—and usually one that has been artificially reconstructed. Neither choice makes any allowance for democracy. Similarly, eradicating the past in order to enter the future is as disastrous as confiscating the technologies of the present—those of the oil industry, for example—in order to preserve a cultural purity that serves as a pretext for the construction of absolute power. Democracy is not simply a political marketplace where conflicting interests negotiate; it is first and foremost an open public space where we can combine a memory and a project, instrumental rationality and a cultural heritage.

By fighting on both fronts, the subject may open up a clearing of liberties between two forests that usually merge and enclose it. Democracy would mean no more than the prudent management of political decisions, were it not regarded by all as the institutional precondition for the construction and liberation of the subject.

There is now a steadily growing rift between those who consider themselves entrusted with a divine message or a national heritage and those who define the subject solely in terms of the universalism of reason. It is a dispute of absolutists: "One law for all!" says one side in response to the other's cry of "One true faith!" This cultural conflict is reproduced in social conflict, dividing social movements as they orient particular actors toward general objectives such as liberty and justice. We are torn between contradictory positions.

I unreservedly uphold Salman Rushdie's right to publish his books and denounce the death sentence passed on him by Ayatollah Khomeni and his successors. I would also like to see religious beliefs taught in public schools. At the same time, I am a resolute defender of secular education. Am I being inconsistent or incoherent? I do not think so. We have to condemn communitarian, nationalist, or theocratic states because they do away with the separation of church (or culture) and state, which is one of the foundations of modern democracy. Yet, at the level of individuals and their lived experience or where the personal subject is concerned, we cannot force anyone to choose between rationalist individualism and a sense of belonging to a community and a collective memory. When ethnicity refers to membership in a community that is represented by a political power or directly incarnated in a territorial collectivity such as a neighborhood, country, or region, it poses a threat to democracy; when it is an element in a personal identity, it is a component of the subject. Our ideal should not be to aspire to the universal by shedding all our particularities; it should be to become both as universal and as particular as possible. We all need to be much more like the Jews, as they generally have been more successful than other groups at this dual task, participating in the universalism of art, science, and thought while remaining true to a particular people, tradition, and history.

This general principle can be applied to a great number of social problems. The integration of immigrants is one example. How are we to reconcile technical and administrative rationalization with cultural diversity without lapsing into a closed communitarianism or a colonizing Jacobinism? We can do so only by rising above identity and by integrating personal liberty and personal creativity with basic human rights. In the name of these rights, host countries must reject customs that make women socially dependent and inferior, just as they must condemn segregation and discrimination against immigrants.

Democracy is a battle against the One. It is a battle against absolute power, state religions, and the dictatorship of both the party and the proletariat. Neither a shared reference to rationality nor respect for the culture of the other will allow individuals and groups to communicate. Individuals will merge into that rationality rather than establishing a mutual dialogue; and respect for the culture of the other may be merely a recognition of difference. Communication is established by a joint attempt to create liberty for every individual. While we all cling to forms of universalism on the one hand and to particular practices, beliefs, and forms of social organization on the other, we also share the will to live an existence that is not simply a situation but an action. We also share the ability to recognize in others the same desire to be a subject, to say "I," and to feel responsible for oneself and those whose lives one shares. It is because we must make this desire for liberty central to existence that we can never accept a complete break between past and future or emotion and reason; nor can we accept a complete break between the worlds of men and women, even though women were long the chosen guardians of the private sphere of life, which was divorced from and increasingly subordinate to the male sphere—that of public life.

Religion and Democracy

A burning question of our day is how we are to interpret the return of the religious, or what Gilles Kepel called "God's revenge" (Kepel 1991). If religion were no more than a community's tradition and collective consciousness, if modernity and democracy were completely synonymous with the world of change, and if we therefore had to make a strict distinction between what Ralph Linton called ascription and achievement—or what human beings are and what they do—we would rapidly conclude that democracy and religion belong to worlds that are by definition as antinomic as tradition and modernity. Religion is not, however, merely a communitarian consciousness or a tradition that is handed down by a church. It is also the opposite—namely, a divorce between the spiritual and the temporal, regardless of whether the spiritual takes the form of an ethics of intention and purity or that of an appeal to one transcendent God. Likewise, we know that modernity is not merely a matter of rationalization and secularization but also of power and of social control. Thus, the relationship between religion and modernization is not reducible to a dichotomy but may take one of four general forms (see Figure 11.1).

In secularized modern societies, the religious tradition is transformed into a social ethics. Observers of American society, from Tocqueville to Robert Bellah

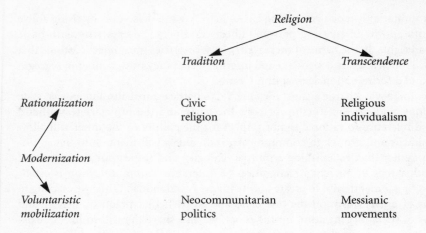

Figure 11.1

(Bellah et al. 1985), have stressed the importance of this phenomenon there. It also is present in France, in a republican form. Religious values and social norms have a lot in commom even when, as in the United States, the separation of church and state is recognized. Where modernization is not endogenous but is instead the goal of a voluntaristic policy, religion can no longer be traditional and may become a force for political mobilization, as in Iran. In that case, the conflict between religion and democracy is at its most direct; but even if a civic religion emerges, instead, one may doubt that it would always have a democratic effect, given that societies that are held together by ethical and religious values are generally conformist. There is, in contrast, a positive relationship between the appeal to a transcendent spiritual principle and democracy. In endogenously modernizing societies, religious individualism may encourage the growth of sects, but it also helps to defend the underprivileged and victims of the anomie of societies that are undergoing rapid change. In dependent societies, neocommunitarian action transforms movements that are struggling against authoritarian power into powerful and liberating forces. It is a mistake to concentrate exclusively on the negative aspect of the relationship between religion and democracy. Religions (especially Buddhism, Judaism, and Islam) can also often be seen as liberating forces.

It is true that the so-called fundamentalist movements that oppose secularization and attempt to reunite temporal and spiritual power and thus to fuse religion and politics, are more visible. It is also true that they have had more political impact in the Islamic world and in Israel. However, the role of such movements is more attributable to the national and nationalist struggles in which the countries in question are involved than to the nature of religion. We must make a distinction between the political implications of religious belief and the way an authoritarian nationalist power uses a religious tradition. The constantly repeated assertion that religions or certain religions—especially Islam—reject the separation of temporal and spiritual powers as a matter of principle is based on the unacceptable view that history is nothing more than a field for the realization of social, cultural, or political projects that have a metahistorical essence. We would do well to take a more cautious view and look at the historical conditions that allow the social order to be regarded as sacred, or conversely, that allow the spiritual and the temporal to achieve a degree of relative autonomy.

In the case of Christianity, two points should be recalled: The Christian churches defended the social hierarchies and controls of traditional societies by closely associating temporal power with spiritual power; but the dispute between pope and emperor, or the separation of powers, paved the way for democracy. One might also add that although protestantism encouraged democratic individualism, it also emphasized the social aspects of religion; and although Catholicism propped up absolute monarchies for so long, it also sustained a mystical life and a break with the social order that paved the way for liberation struggles.

We can no longer accept the extreme republican discourse such as that in Mexico, which went so far as to call for authoritarian state intervention to break the church's hold over rural society. Nor can we support the converse argument that the church has, in certain countries such as Poland, always been in the forefront of democratic struggles. The relationship between religion and democracy is always complex, even contradictory. The recognition that fundamentalism and democracy are in total conflict is now of vital importance. It would, however, be a mistake to fail to see that religiously inspired movements can also represent a democratic call for the liberation of the people, even though authoritarian regimes usually use such calls to consolidate their own power.

The most extreme defenders of Enlightenment philosophy believe that rational scientific thought alone can strengthen democracy, that a democratic society must be transparent and natural, and that any appeal to a people, a culture, or a history is implicitly nationalistic and promotes authoritarian forms of government. However, the recent history of a number of Latin American countries gives the lie to this argument. Religiously inspired popular movements in many towns waged a more effective struggle against military dictatorships than did the educated middle classes, who were often seduced by the promise of wealth and promotion offered by the authoritarian regimes that reestablished the rights of the market. We are well aware of the grave threats posed by all forms of communitarianism, and we should loudly proclaim that they are incompatible with democracy. We should not, however, confuse communitarian philosophies with religious or cultural reasons for resistance to oppression, which liberal thinkers regard as a basic right. If we go on condemning all manifestations of religious life as antidemocratic, we are in danger of becoming trapped into the extreme rationalism that ultimately denies social actors, their cultural orientations, and their social conflicts any role in the invention of democracy.

Revolutionaries and Democrats

The tragedy of revolutionary movements is that many of the democrats who become involved with them are transformed into leaders of authoritarian regimes or become actively involved in such regimes. It would be as erroneous to regard as democrats all those who have taken part in revolutionary movements as it would be to condemn them all as enemies of democracy. It would also be as wrong to describe as democrats all those who run mass-consumption or communications companies as it would be to regard them all as demagogues who are manipulating the people and leading them astray. The leaders who, acting in the name of popular forces, overthrew oligarchies and old regimes often believed from the outset that a dictatorship of the proletariat or an authoritarian nationalist government would be needed to lead the war of liberation. They therefore chose an antidemocratic path. Yet the democratic spirit was not absent from the social movements that brought them to power. Witness the appeal to liberty in the face of arbitrary rule, the decision to speak in the name of the people, and the demand that the ruled should be free to choose their rulers. It is always difficult to distinguish between the democratic spirit and revolutionary action because within every social movement there slumbers a social countermovement. The path to democracy is blocked by the negation of the social actor and the interpretation of collective action as an expression of the contradictions of a system of domination. On the other hand, when the action in question is intended to enhance a collective actor's capacity for action, the democratic spirit may be present—especially if the actor in question is a class or nation. There is a close connection between social movements and democracy; both are antithetical to the combination of a vanguard and a revolution. Even when endogenous development is a very distant prospect and a class or a political power exerts authoritarian rule or restricts or forbids political liberty, the democratic spirit is present as long as the hope exists that endogenous development can be made possible and that the role of the actors of civil society can be broadened. When struggles for development are bound up with a society's internal conflicts, when the talk is of the consciousness of the workers or of citizens and not merely of a generation sacrificed or alienated, democracy may yet be the goal of collective action, even though it will in many cases be sacrificed to the absolute power of the militaristic leaders of wars of social or national liberation.

Nowadays, none dare assert that democracy, revolution, and "popular" regimes are one and the same, and we have learned to distrust lyrical discourses about the meaning of history. We must not, however, go to the opposite extreme and say that the democratic spirit is never present in struggles where violence is used or where authoritarian mobilization is a strong possibility. The democratic spirit has often been present both in national liberation struggles and in social struggles, most notably in the labor movement. When the labor movement was weak and believed in the laws of historical development rather than in its own action, democracy was threatened or even nonexistent because the actors appeared to be no more than the instruments of necessity. In contrast, when a social struggle is defined as a social movement—as a confrontation between social adversaries who are fighting to control a society's resources and cultural models—collective action is bound up with democracy, as we saw in our discussion of the links between working-class unionism and industrial democracy, not only in Europe but in many other regions of the world.

The most serious threat to democracy stems from the depiction of society as a system of absolute domination that is not content with exploiting and excluding the dominated but also deprives them of their consciousness or instills a false consciousness. Sociology and historiography have been strongly influenced by the extreme image of a social order reduced to the language of domination and its reproduction. This image makes it impossible to recognize social movements; we see only the victims or agents of domination and never actors. This pessimism, which especially in the 1960s and the 1970s had a dominant influence in both Latin America and Europe, has usually weakened social actors and has always had a negative effect on democratic ideas, which are violently rejected or scorned as petit-bourgeois reformist ideas. It is because the hopes born of that revolutionary vision have been disappointed that the idea of democracy is so attractive in our fin de siècle. It is because most popular and national liberation movements were transformed into dictatorships, which rapidly became repressive apparatuses and obstacles to development, that we expect democracy to be a better manager of change and to reduce inequalities.

12

Democratization in the East and the South?

The mid-twentieth century, from Mussolini's fascism to Mao's cultural revolution, was dominated by the destruction of democratic hopes by the party-state and the authoritarian mobilization it forced on society. The end of the century has been dominated by the opposite tendency: the collapse or decomposition of voluntarist regimes and mobilizing states.

Postcommunism

States and regimes that were not willing to encourage the formation of a civil society foundered in bureaucratic routines, interclan struggles, a refusal to innovate, and inefficiency, because they refused to recognize the rationality of the economic world and because there was no political system capable of managing tensions between social groups. Perestroika now looks like a period of decay rather than an attempt to liberalize. Gorbachev could no more stop this process of disintegration than Kerensky could stop the decomposition of tsarist Russia. From Chernobyl to the war in Afghanistan, the Soviet regime demonstrated its inability to manage its own projects. Growth slowed down or ground to a halt. The U.S. "Star Wars" project, unrealistic though it may have been, revealed that the Soviet electronics industry could not achieve parity with the United States. At the same time, the nationalism that triumphed at the time of the Bandung Conference quickly revealed its weakness—not only in Egypt, where a military disaster exposed its flaws, but also in Algeria, despite the heritage of a war of national liberation and the economic benefits of oil, and even in Brazil, where, after the brilliant presidency of Juscelino Kubitschek, economic and political disorder set in and led to a military coup d'état.

It is usually difficult to challenge party-states because they have either destroyed society or control it tightly. In the communist world, party-states faced a serious challenge only where there was a strong sense of belonging to a national society. In Poland, for instance, the alliance between the KOR's democratic intellectuals and a national-popular movement that was strongly influenced by Catholicism, with Lech Walesa as its principal spokesman, meant that a high level of nationalist consciousness, a democratic consciousness, and workers' demands could coalesce after the Ursus and Radom strikes of 1975. Being social, cultural, and historical, this was a total social movement, but it was more symbolic than effective. It was, in other words, an expression of the democratic spirit; but it was unable to overthrow the antidemocratic regime, which finally declared a state of war in December 1981. When the Soviet Union lost its empire and its regime and then finally ceased to exist, the reconstruction of social life began, not with popular movements or new ideas, but with economic management. The first priority was to break the party-state's stranglehold on the whole of society. In order to do that, the economy had to be fully liberalized. Given that the Soviet regime had been totalitarian, economic freedom seemed to many people to mark an immediate transition to democracy and even prosperity. In most cases, and especially the Soviet case, that has proved an illusion, but the collapse of the Soviet regime was nonetheless irreversible. The communist parties of the East are disappearing.

This is the very opposite of a revolutionary situation: It is not a matter of a central will being confronted with a chaotic situation. It is a matter of doing away with aberrant political controls and liberating an imprisoned population. Hence the strange form taken by this historic mutation. A Polish friend who had been one of the major figures in Solidarity told me, when we met in Warsaw after 1989, "Ten years ago you came to see how we had created a social movement, and now you have come back to find out why we do not have one." He was not joking; no actors, social movements, or intellectual debates exist in the emerging postcommunist countries. Consciousness, politics, and social conflicts play a marginal role in the tumultuous changes that are taking place, while economic changes have absolute priority. The market is replacing the party-state as the absolute master of society.

There appears to be no room for democracy in these countries, and the extreme weakness of political life there makes it foolish to compare them to democracies. The inhabitants of countries such as Russia and Ukraine face immense difficulties, although they know that the old system is gone forever and few mourn its passing. The word "democracy" is often used there as a synonym for "market economy" or "Western civilization," but it is meaningless. That should remind both those who run these countries and those who analyze them of certain truths, stated at the beginning of this book: The removal of political and ideological controls on the economy is a first precondition for democracy, but it does not in itself constitute democracy. If we are to create a society that is at once democratic and developed and if endogenous development is to get under way, this negative precondition must be complemented by three positive preconditions: a state that can make decisions in accordance with democratic principles; economic leaders who want to invest and know how to conduct business; and political agents who can redistribute income and reduce inequalities. These three preconditions are equally important throughout the world, but the order in which they are created defines each particular country's situation.

Compared with the developing countries of the South, where the conspicuous consumption of the wealthy is blatant, the communist countries did establish a certain egalitarianism, at least in the cities. The long domination of the nomen-klatura, however, destroyed legal and administrative regulation. The first priority is therefore the construction of a state, especially in the former Soviet Union, where everything depends on a leader or a small group of leaders. Businessmen will not appear until a state has been built. In the absence of a state, it is easier to become wealthy by appropriating state privileges or speculating abroad than by investing in what is still a chaotic market; but this brutal modernization is already under threat because the economic initiatives that are being taken are so out of touch with social reality. A population whose most immediate interests are threatened tends to seek refuge in extreme populism and nationalism, to look for a providential savior, to take its revenge on a scapegoat, or to retreat into aggressive fundamentalism.

Only the reconstruction of a democratic political system can ward off these threats. Because the state was not destroyed and the formation of an entrepreneurial class was extraordinarily rapid in Poland and Hungary—the latter of which has benefited from the positive effects of the economic reforms introduced in 1968—these postcommunist countries of central Europe have found it relatively easy to introduce a political system capable of warding off the threat of social and political breakdown. Democracy was and is the central factor in the success of these countries. Hungary still faces acute national problems, for one-third of those who regard themselves as Hungarians live outside its borders, in Romania, Slovakia, and Vojvodina; but it has not yet been engulfed by nationalism. In 1992–93, Hungary even saw the formation of a powerful antiracist movement focused mainly on defending the Gypsies, and that movement put an end to the dangerous rise of the extreme right-wing leader Czupka. In Poland, the first postcommunist country to embark on a program of extreme economic liberalization, the population rapidly drifted away from the "left-wing" parties that had supported liberalization and retreated into a defensive, Catholic, and popular nationalism, which strengthened the strong anti-Solidarity tendencies within the Polish church. The country almost fragmented as a result. The political system, reinforced by the wisdom of President Walesa, did prove able to contain these tensions, however, and the Suchocka government marked the beginning of recovery. In 1993, however, popular discontent led to the electoral victory of the former communists. Still, there was no reason to fear that the old regime would be reestablished; such crises simply mirrored the abrupt changes taking place in the economic system. What proved more important was the stability of the political system, which enabled it to handle dramatic tensions without breaking up.

The contrast between these countries and the Soviet Union is obvious. The absence of a political system, exacerbated by the open conflict between President Yeltsin, who was elected by the new Russia, and the Supreme Soviet, a pseudoparliamentary body inherited from the old Soviet Union, has not only paralyzed Russian political life; it has also slowed economic recovery. If Russia does not succeed in organizing a political system and establishing a real debate between parties that are capable of representing different interests and projects, it will continue to be undermined by corruption, speculation, and violence. Memories of communist rule are all that protect the country from chaos and the subsequent emergence of an authoritarian regime. The virtues of the market economy alone will not reconstruct society, nor will the creative force of a social, political, or cultural movement. The people cannot create a new society, nor can economic recovery restore order to society. With its economy in ruins and its social and cultural forces destroyed, the new Russia will either stand or fall by its political institutions.

Two years after the failed conservative putsch that led to the abolition of the Communist Party of the Soviet Union and the adoption of Yegor Gaidar's free-market policy, a second violent clash between Yeltsin and his opponents clearly revealed that political restructuring had been a failure. Given the powerful upsurge in populist nationalism, it was by no means clear that the general elections and the ratification of a new constitution would allow Russia to escape chaos and to move toward democracy and development. It is quite possible that political restructuring will end in failure, and many fear the rise of a new authoritarianism in Russia, which cannot forget that it was once the Soviet Union and one of two superpowers that dominated the world.

In other postcommunist countries of the East, nothing could prevent the rise of fundamentalist nationalism. The result has been war and misery in both the Caucasus and the former Yugoslavia. Although Romania's situation is not so bleak, it has not succeeded in building a democratic political system, so powerful is the hold of the communist nationalism created by Ceaușescu. President Iliescu was both Ceaușescu's heir and the architect of a limited economic and political openness.

The breakup of Czechoslovakia, in contrast, was not brought about by a clash between two nations, but by an inability to control the social effects of the liberalization of the economy. Because Slovakia was worst affected, it has sought protection from the effects of liberalization by adopting Meciar's nationalist populism, while Klaus's Bohemia is taking a cautiously liberal line in the hope that German investment will hasten the country's integration into the West, now that it is rid of Slovakia.

Thanks to its highly developed national consciousness, Poland has succeeded in avoiding the rift between economic openness and populist reaction to which

Czechoslovakia has succumbed. Surely this demonstrates that democracy is an essential precondition for development and that the market economy in itself is no guarantee of either economic development or political democracy, even though it is a precondition for both. In other words, the concentration of economic decisionmaking, political power, and ideological authority in the hands of a leader or a party-state is an insurmountable obstacle to development and democracy alike. This truism should put an end to the widespread tendency to confuse economic liberalism with political liberalism. Postcommunist countries need both, but they are different aspects of social modernization and reconstruction. The Poles have made a courageous and historic choice that will have decisive effects for the whole region, opting for a complete overhaul of their economic system. However, this approach would soon have ended in chaos and disaster, had they not rapidly succeeded in creating parties, an outlet for the political expression of the populace's anxieties and demands.

Many observers have lamented the mediocrity of political life in the postcommunist countries of central Europe. While they may be right, their criticism in fact serves to highlight how successful democracy has been in some of these countries, which have succeeded in handling economic and political changes that seemed cataclysmic rather than liberating to most of the population. In both Poland and Hungary, despite the pressures that have been brought to bear, primarily by the Catholic church, democratization has been the decisive factor in the reconstruction of a society that had been destroyed twice: first by the communist regime, and then by its fall. Democracy is indeed a necessary precondition for economic development, but it is not reducible to the political aspects of the liberalization of the economy.

Latin America: Democracy Under Tutelage

Europeans are accustomed to political extremes. They think that democracy must mean full democracy and that authoritarian regimes in turn inevitably take paroxysmal forms. This conviction is the heritage of the age of revolutions: It is either the king who wields power or it is the nation. Political life is always a drama, and democracy is most active when it appears to be facing fundamental choices. Postcommunist Europe has yet to supply any alternative political model, as it is defined by its rejection of the party-state and is looking toward western Europe and its political institutions, economic system, and intellectual liberty.

The less extreme political situations that pertain in other parts of the world, however, should not be regarded as unstable transitional situations. In this category one could of course mention India, which remains a hierarchical and segmented society; but we will restrict our discussion to Latin America. The differences between Chile, Mexico, and Colombia are no greater than those between

France, Great Britain, and the United States; so what Gino Germani called the national-popular regime (Germani 1961) is therefore an ideal type that allows us to understand many national political situations.

When modernization is not endogenous—as is the case in Latin America, where for better or worse it obviously came from outside—democracy is restricted by the partial fusion of state, political society, and social actors. This fusion can be transformed into authoritarian dictatorship, but in most cases it has protected society against the modernizing authoritarian state. Mexico and particularly Brazil have had Bismarckian nation-states and have experienced authoritarian industrialization, but the continent's more common model is much weaker. The predominant model is a state that distributes resources derived from elsewhere. This state is supported by an urban middle class that is largely dependent on it; and the state controls either indirectly or directly all companies and banks as well as unions and associations. The weakness of this regime is obvious: The mix of actors is such that the spread of clientelism and corruption can weaken both the actors and the state.

These national-popular regimes began to degenerate in the 1960s. The regimes' impending collapse led to an irrational economic protectionism, a hypertrophic public sector managed in accordance with political criteria, and the incorporation of popular forces into a neocorporatist state apparatus. Yet it is all too often forgotten that these regimes coincided with a very long period of economic growth, urbanization, and improvements in education—and above all, following the era of the caudillos who dominated the poorly consolidated states after independence was won, they represented a space of liberty, sometimes limited but sometimes quite extensive. With the exception of Central America and the Caribbean, the continent was thus protected from real dictatorships and above all totalitarian regimes. With the exception of Trujillo's Dominican Republic and Stroessner's Paraguay, such regimes are almost completely unknown in Latin America. The military dictatorships that did recently exist in the south of the continent were primarily antipopulist reactions. Sometimes, as in the case of Pinochet's Chile, they successfully restored the power of export-oriented financial groups and stimulated growth by becoming part of the world market.

These national-popular regimes sometimes approached European-style democracy, as did Chile before 1973; in other times and places, they bordered on dictatorship. In Venezuela, Peru, Bolivia, and Ecuador, the state regimes began to build a political system; in contrast, in Colombia, even when it was pluralistic, oligarchic domination kept political life far away from the arenas of economic interests and social demands, which were often relegated to the margins. Periods of nationalist populism were the exception to the rule.

Thus, it would be unfair to condemn national-popular regimes like Argentina's Perónism by accusing them of verging on fascism. It would be fairer to view them as predemocratic regimes that extended political participation, as did the Mexican revolution and, to a lesser degree, Irigoyen's regime in Argentina, Arturo Alessandri's regime in Chile, and, at an earlier stage, Batlle y Ordóñez's pioneering government in Uruguay. These regimes fell because they were paralyzed by protectionism, clientelism, and corruption or swept away by a populism that became revolutionary and was in turn destroyed by military dictatorship. It must not, however, be forgotten that their existence and their achievements confirm the idea we are defending here—namely, that there is a close link between democracy and development. These regimes opened up the political system to a considerable extent and organized the modernization of the continent; but modernization did not provide them a remedy for social dualization.

Can we now argue that the fall of the authoritarian regimes that overthrew these national-popular states had a democratizing effect? Yes, but to a limited extent. The abolition of the military monopoly and the introduction of free elections do not in themselves justify talk of democracy. Social inequalities are growing and human rights are often violated. In most Latin American countries there is no consciousness of citizenship. Only Chile, Uruguay, and to a lesser extent Costa Rica fit the definition of democracy we have adopted. Latin America has of course been reintroduced into world markets, and net capital flows have been positive since the second half of 1990; but what Anibal Pinto calls "structural heterogeneity" is so great that the national unity of many of these countries is being weakened or has already been destroyed. Fortaleza is a long way from São Paulo, and the Bolivian government has little or no political or fiscal control over part of its territory. Peru has been torn apart by a so-called people's war. Northern and southern Mexico are growing further apart, and guerrillas and the drug trade pose a greater threat than ever to Colombia's national unity.

Given that our aim here is not to analyze Latin American situations but to define the preconditions for democracy in developing countries, we will use the same categories that we used to analyze postcommunist Europe. In both cases, the market economy cannot in itself guarantee either development or democracy. The major difference between the two regions is that in central and eastern Europe, the main task is the creation of a state and entrepreneurs. In Latin America, where it is less difficult to achieve those goals, the most important and most difficult task is to create social and political actors who can struggle against the inequalities that make democracy and development impossible. Most of the countries concerned have made the leap to an open market economy. Chile, Bolivia, Mexico, and Colombia were the first to do so. Argentina has adopted the same policy in dramatic circumstances and has broken completely with half a century of its own history. Peru, in contrast, initially attempted to prolong the populist experiment, and a civil war there has subordinated the economy to the military logic of the state. Venezuela has succumbed to domination by a state corrupted by oil profits. Brazil, where the Bismarckian model did at first produce good results, has long been reluctant to abandon its nationalism and paralyzed by the conservative populism of a state that has replaced the redistribution of good years with the corruption of bad years. The social cost of a change in economic policy is high, but it has in most cases led to a real recovery by stemming the decomposition of societies like those of Bolivia and Argentina, which were being destroyed by hyperinflation. If, however, the recovery is to result in endogenous development, the state must first acquire an adequate decision-making capacity. The great project of Mexico's presidents de la Madrid and Salinas de Gortari was to free the state from the PRI party-state to improve the administration's level of competence. Colombia also has done much to modernize its state, but the pressure exerted by narcotrafico makes this an endless task. In certain countries, the full reform of the state will require the formation of a world of businessmen capable of cultivating a spirit of resourcefulness rather than expecting state subsidies. That will be a difficult task for a country like Argentina. In the case of Brazil and Venezuela, in contrast, the entrepreneurial talent is already there, and the clear priority is to reduce the social inequalities that have provoked popular uprisings in Venezuela and reduced whole sectors of Brazilian society to poverty, chaos, and violence, especially in the Rio metropolitan area and northeast.

There will be no democracy and no development in Latin America without an active struggle against the inequalities that are being exacerbated by inflation as every day goes by. As I write, the struggle against social inequalities and for national integration has not begun in any Latin American country, with the exception of Chile, where the proportion of the population living below the poverty line fell from 40 percent to 32 percent under the Aylwin government. Although the situation of the affluent groups generally is improving, they are afraid of the violence of the marginal population. We cannot call "democratic" regimes that have such negative social consequences. This negative conclusion is a restatement of the conclusion we reached (albeit in much less pessimistic terms) with respect to the industrialized countries of the North. Powerful forces that might lead to the breakup of national societies are at work. In some cases, unemployment affects a sizable fraction of the population, and the political system is often in a state of serious crisis, especially in western Europe.

In developing countries, purely liberal policies will inevitably have antidemocratic effects. They offer part of the population—in fact, a greater part than economic statistics indicate—the lifestyle of rich countries; but they exclude or marginalize many categories that would like to play a part in social life as both consumers and citizens. If the invocation of democracy is an invitation to condemn authoritarian regimes whose primary rationale was to crush a demand for popular participation that could not be met by the economy and the state, so be it; but those authoritarian regimes no longer exist, and Latin American countries are now in a much more dangerous position than are the countries of the developed center. As dualization increases, there is a growing social rift between the mass of consumers and the excluded and marginal. Democratization therefore implies political intervention, a concerted attempt to manage social and economic changes, and above all a firm will to give a real priority to the struggle against the inequalities that are destroying national societies. This latter tendency will probably be most pronounced in Brazil, where social actors are sturdy now that the country is emerging from a political and financial crisis that had arisen because the state continued to some extent to play its old role. It is, however, quite likely that Uruguay and Chile will take the same path. In any event, we cannot agree that democracy simply means the disappearance of military dictatorships. Nondemocratic aspects of regimes born of free elections, such as Alberto Fujimori's regime in Peru, and the fall of Carlos Andrés Pérez in Venezuela and of Fernando Collor in Brazil, to say nothing of the corruption and electoral fraud that exist in many countries, are reminders of the serious inadequacies of a purely negative definition of democracy.

It has to be asserted that democracy is associated with endogenous development, but we also must be able to recognize the presence of democratic action even where poverty, dependency, or internal political crises have temporarily destroyed democratic institutions. We must seek out democratization in countries experiencing exogenous development and even in countries that have become caught up in the process of underdevelopment. No situation renders democracy completely impossible, and authoritarian regimes have less resilience in crises than do democracies. Latin America provides the unexpected spectacle of military dictatorships collapsing in the middle of a "lost decade," a period marked by economic retrenchment and rising foreign debt. In the 1990s, the world conjuncture improved for Latin America, and certain of its countries have taken the road to democratic development, sometimes with excessive caution, but also with a good chance of success.

Latin America is very similar to postcommunist Europe. In both cases, a region has split into two categories of countries. Thanks to the stability of their political systems, some countries are succeeding in managing the tensions and contradictions that arise when the outmoded statist model is abandoned. Others are succumbing to those tensions. They are decomposing, and sooner or later an authoritarian regime will be restored. Latin America is divided: Some countries are being taken over by violence, corruption, and the clandestine economy because their system of political representation is unable to manage relations between conflicting interests. In other countries, the political system has been reconstructed and has demonstrated its strength. In Latin America, as in postcommunist Europe, neither popular movements nor the logic of the economy will determine the success of postauthoritarian reconstruction; only the workings of the political system can do so.

The Limitations of Economic Liberalism

Authoritarian regimes collapse primarily as a result of their weakness; but once they have collapsed a democratic consciousness becomes a precondition for development. Democratic consciousness is at this moment weak, and the political system is either disorganized or unable to cope. In most countries, we are therefore seeing whole fractions of the population drifting out of "modern" life—minority groups in rich countries and majority groups in poor countries. Excessive state intervention and the crimes of totalitarian regimes have led to a rejection of politics and to an individualism that is destroying collective actors and leaving the field open to the logic of systems of production and management as they attempt to accumulate resources and to impose their interests on all who are involved, either as producers or consumers, in the system of production and exchange. Developing countries need an open political system even more urgently than other countries.

If a system of political integration is not reconstructed and the market economy is expected to solve the very problems it often exacerbates, then a large part of the world may be engulfed by civil wars, ethnic struggles, and conflicts between nationalities. Democracy is often fragile in developing countries, yet it is as indispensable there as it is in countries experiencing endogenous modernization; and in postcommunist countries, China included, as in postpopulist countries where military dictatorships have fallen, the creation of a democratic political system is even more urgent than the reestablishment, thanks to the market, of the autonomy of economic management, indispensable as it may be.

Economic policy alone cannot provide a long-term program for developing countries. If the goal is to struggle against poverty, inequality, and the fragmentation of national unity, then a political authority that can make democratic interventions is essential.

If we reduce democracy to the workings of political institutions, it is logical to conclude that democracy is an attribute of the most highly "developed" countries or of those countries that are best able to respond institutionally to social demands that have been partly satisfied by the success of the economy and personal mobility. This argument in fact confuses two things: the difficulty of the problems the political system has to solve and the latter's ability to solve them while still acting in the interests of the majority. A society besieged by poverty, invaded by foreign interests or lifestyles, or governed by an oligarchy or dictatorship cannot be expected to manage these transformations by adopting procedures established by wise men. Democratic action does, however, exist in such situations and does tend to replace arbitrary rule and the interests of the few with the interests of the majority, even if that implies the overthrow of an electorally organized power-sharing arrangement that has put two fractions of the oligarchy in power.

Conversely, societies that are not confronting serious problems are proving similarly incapable of reducing social inequalities. The phenomenon of social exclusion is spreading, and these societies are either governed by a restricted power elite or dominated by a transnational network of economic interests. In many cases, their extraterritorial actions are destroying the very liberties that they protect within their territory. Just as it is impossible to speak of democracy if free elections are not held at regular intervals, it would be absurd to claim that a political system is or is not democratic without investigating its motives and the social consequences of its actions.

We therefore should strive to temper the enthusiasm of those who view the fall of communist regimes, military dictatorships, and authoritarian nationalist regimes as signaling the triumph of democracy. The absence of an authoritarian regime is not democracy. The postcommunist countries in particular are still so busy destroying the communist system, which refuses to die in many of the republics that have emerged from the Soviet Union, that it is impossible to describe them all as having created new democracies. What is true of Poland and Hungary is obviously not true of Serbia, Croatia, or even Romania.

Conclusion

The starting point of this book was liberal in inspiration. We almost spontaneously adopted a modest conception of democracy as "negative" liberty, defined as a set of guarantees against political arbitrariness. After nearly a century of totalitarian regimes, how could we not begin by demanding political liberty, the limitation of state power and, therefore, respect for the specific criteria that organize and evaluate every domain of social life, from the economy to religion, the family, art, and so on? How could we not extend this mistrust to the entire Jacobin conception of democracy, which imposed the rule of society on the nation with a brutality that rivaled or exceeded that of the imposition of the religious or monarchical orders of old? For too long, the appeal to universal man was used to justify the repression of workers and colonized peoples, the confinement of women within private life, and the subordination of children to an authoritarian system of education designed to turn them into rational beings and citizens by preventing them from referring to any particular social or cultural loyalties. I react strongly to this because—being a French citizen—I have always been bothered by the constant French tendency to prioritize "democratic centralism," be it bureaucratic or revolutionary rather than the autonomous action of social and cultural actors. Given that my sympathies lie with the victims of communist regimes in Budapest and Poznan in 1956, in Prague in 1966, and in Poland in late 1981, and with the victims of Franco, General Pinochet, and the Greek colonels, I have learned that the road to democracy is equidistant from the road to revolution and the road to dictatorship.

Yet the more I thought about it, the more this position seemed unsatisfactory. Must we abandon all attempts to change the world, reduce inequality, or introduce more justice just because totalitarian and authoritarian regimes have used these ideas as ideologies? On the contrary, I believe we cannot do without a "positive" conception of liberty. If democracy were no more than a system of institutional guarantees, who would defend it when it is threatened? If society were nothing but a set of markets and procedures, who would risk their lives to defend political liberties? And how are we to reconcile the twin convictions that there can be no democracy unless power is limited and that there can be no democracy without the pursuit of the "good life"? The answer around which this book is organized and that defines what I have called democratic culture is that democracy is the regime that recognizes individuals and collectivities as subjects, or in other words protects them and encourages their will to live their own lives and to give their lived experience a unity and a meaning. Power, then, is limited not only by a set of procedural rules but also by a positive will to promote the liberty of all. Democracy is the subordination of social organization and political power to an objective that is ethical rather than social: the liberation of every individual. If this task could be fully accomplished, it would dissolve society. However, when it is undertaken in a democratic society, it means oppposing the forces of domination and social control and allowing every individual to take more initiative in their pursuit of happiness. It means that every social actor must recognize that the other has the right to form projects and preserve memories.

This conclusion does not bring us back to ancient conceptions of citizenship and the civic spirit, and therefore the liberty of the ancients. Like the liberals, we have abandoned that conception, and there is no going back. Nor is it a matter of abolishing social and cultural differences by appealing to a general will; on the contrary, it is a matter of doing everything possible to increase the internal diversity of society, of moving toward a recomposition whose goal is both the creation of a new world and the recovery of what has been forgotten and scorned. It is not a matter of abolishing the past in order to build a radiant future but of living in as many spaces and times as possible, of replacing the monologue of reason, history, or the nation with a dialogue among individuals and cultures. We have even abandonded the dream of self-management, that last avatar of the liberty of the ancients, because we know from experience that no matter how small it may be, a group can be dominated by a conservative corporatism, a petty tyrant, or a power apparatus, and that the constraints such domination brings to bear on individuals are all the more severe in that they are brought to bear in a small space. If everyone is to be free, an open public space and controlled democratic procedures are absolute necessities.

Critiques of the purely political conception of democracy are usually premised on the need to transform society; but our century forces us to recognize that the form of political power is even more important than the social organization of production, and that, if it is not based upon political liberty, an action designed to liberate the workers can trap the whole population, including the workers, into a new form of slavery. The way to escape from a purely political conception of democracy is, thus, to begin at the bottom and not the top. The primary goal of democracy is therefore not the creation of a politically fair society or the abolition of all forms of domination and exploitation; rather, it is to allow individuals, groups, and collectivities to become free subjects who produce their own history and whose actions can reconcile the universalism of reason with the particularism of a personal or collective identity. We can resist every form of what Alessandro Pizzorno called absolute politics (Pizzorno 1993) by prioritizing the right of every individual to assert his or her liberty through his or her experience and in the face of particular relations of domination.

The general principles of liberty were initially asserted by a fraction of the English, Dutch, American, and French bourgeoisies. The labor movements then made it clear that this liberty had to be defended in the context of concrete work relations. Colonized or dependent nations fought foreign domination to gain their freedom. Similarly, women asserted their identity in the face of the domination they suffered due to their gender. The history of liberty in the modern world is the history of the emergence of an increasingly close link between the universalism of human rights and the particularity of the social situations and relations within which those rights must be defended. Only actors can establish that link; the dream of an ideal society cannot do so. Utopias subordinate social reality to a single principle; usually, the triumph of reason. Democracy, in contrast, is by its very nature anti-utopian. It gives the last word to the majority, which is by definition constantly changing. It is the majority that decides how to reconcile conflicting demands or principles, such as liberty and equality or universals and particulars; and the way in which these conflicting principles are combined is always subject to modification. All democratic schools of thought attempt to defend the common man or woman rather than the dominant elites. The best way to implement this general principle is to recognize that the leading role in the building of democracy is played by the social actors themselves and not by vanguards or a *sanior pars*. We therefore have to define democracy as a culture as well as a set of institutions or procedures.

Pro-democratic thought and action were for a long time identified with the free construction of a political space that could serve as a base for attacks on a hierarchical and segmented society dominated by tradition, privilege, and injustice. The main strength of the democratic idea initially sprang from this will to destroy the traditional society of the ancien régime and to invent a new society. The basis for political action was therefore very different from the basis of civil society. Civil society was the domain of particular interests, whereas political action was the domain of the universal, and therefore of reason and of a future defined as the triumph of reason. That is why the democratic idea was so closely associated with the construction of absolute power. Witness the idea of the general will, as conceptualized by Jean-Jacques Rousseau and later by the enlightened revolutionary and nationalist regimes that were his heirs. In its most attenuated forms, this universalism resulted in a scientistic discourse. The "republicans" of the late nineteenth century and those who remain faithful to their ideas today still cling to that discourse. The goal of democracy, in their view, was not so much to open up the political system as to free it from tradition and the pressure of social interests. The goal was, so to speak, to desocialize the political system in order to make social life more "natural" and more rational. As a result, a great deal of energy went into education and the provision of information in an attempt to enforce the most enlightened solutions.

This model of political rationalization is now exhausted, primarily because we have come a long way from that hierarchical and segmented society. It has been destroyed by two hundred years of accelerated modernization. In many countries of the world, the twentieth century has seen the triumph of despotism, which be-

lieved itself enlightened and claimed to be democratic. It in fact forced what it saw
as rational solutions on a society that could not be the actor of its own transformation because it was, according to the despots, still suffering from exploitation
and alienation. These despotic regimes resulted in totalitarianism, which in turn
collapsed, exhausted and paralyzed by its own actions. Within the space of a few
years or decades, it became impossible to identify democracy with the modernizing revolution.

In the past, social movements and democratic action appealed to a higher principle, such as God, reason, or the meaning of history, in order to fight the social
order. Universal reason went against tradition and privilege. Historical necessity
and the totality of history would overcome the obstacles created by profit and arbitrary power. Being the highest expression of free political action, the revolution
would, in voluntaristic fashion, create a society that was transparent to both nature and history. Today, we no longer appeal to a meaning of history that supposedly dominates societies; in our struggle against the established order, we appeal
to the liberty and responsibility of the individual, the community, and the minority. That is why democracy takes a dim view of any reference to a totality. We
should never lose sight of this liberal principle, although we are acutely aware of
its inadequacy. The democracy of the moderns is not based on participation, representation, or even communication but on the creative liberty of the subject, on
the subject's ability to be a social actor and to modify the environment so as to
clear a territory where it can experience its free creativity.

This conception does not, however, justify the reduction of democracy to an
open political market where consumers can choose a candidate either of their
own volition or because they have been persuaded to do so by increasingly inva-
sive political marketing. Such extreme or libertarian liberalism shares an important characteristic with enlightened despotism: both believe in rational solutions
and distrust political debates and political ideologies. The reduction of liberalism
to the idea that society should be viewed as a set of markets has led, in this domain as in others, both to majority participation in all forms of consumption and
to increased marginality and exclusion. As a result, communitarian defenses are
being erected. There is a new obsession with identity and a return to tradition.
The world is now divided into the globalized uiverse of the market and the segmented territory of national, religious, and cultural identities: on the one hand,
the accelerated circulation of money and information; on the other, a radical
multiculturalism. These tendencies are as symbiotic as they are contradictory, because when there are no longer any universal criteria for the evaluation of forms
of social and political life, then the market alone can establish communications
between hermetically sealed units whose attitude toward other units constantly
oscillates between indifference and curiosity, tolerance and aggression.

At a time when so many voices are rejoicing at the triumph of democracy and
when so many believe that the whole world has adopted a single political

model—that of liberal democracy—we should, instead, be worrying about the impoverishment of the democratic idea and about its loss of meaning. It is no longer capable of acting against its own enemies, as we can see from the cowardly abstention of western European countries in the face of the violence that has been unleashed in Bosnia by the practitioners of ethnic cleansing. It is true that in a great number of countries, the impotence of authoritarian regimes is obvious; but is the failure of democracy's enemies its sole *raison d'être*? We once placed too much trust in politics; now we do not place enough trust in it. It is not democracy that is triumphant today, but the market economy. To some extent, the market economy is democracy's antithesis, as the market attempts to prevent political institutions from intervening in its activity, whereas democratic politics attempts to promote intervention so as to protect the weak from the domination of the strong.

Appealing to the great principles of equality and liberty is annoying to the majority, whose interest, on the contrary, is stimulated by consumption and whose demands are molded by supply-side categories. The most magnanimous and active individuals devote themselves to humanitarian causes, while political action increasingly resembles a profession, or at times, even a class attribute, and is rejected because it is alien to individuals' deepest needs.

How can democracy be strong when its three principles are rejected or inspire only indifference? The very term "citizenship" seems ambiguous, and the continued existence of the nation-state, which was once the classic framework for the exercise of citizenship, is, at least in Europe, by no means certain. Can we speak of the representation of the interests of the majority when the word now designates a vast middle class that has access to mass consumption and defends itself in conservative fashion against those it is only too willing to describe as marginal and whom it rejects, just as it rejected the "dangerous classes" in the nineteenth century? Finally, how can we speak of basic rights when political power is increasingly a matter of cultural identity and there is widespread distrust of universalism, which is suspected of being the ideology of dominant nations? When it is not rejected, the democratic idea is being replaced by a tolerant, laissez-faire attitude that feels no need to pass ethical or political judgments on anything.

Every country and every company defends its market share; accordingly, the obsession with identity can take either the form of a consumerist individualism or that of communitarianism. The intervening political space has been deserted, and the democratic idea is becoming a matter of indifference to the inhabitants of rich countries. In poor countries, it is being rejected by those who expect economic growth to provide a better future than political liberation, which has disappointed them.

We have yet to come to terms with many of the implications of the great historical transformation that from the 1970s on put an end to the civilization based on production of material goods and a belief in progress and destroyed the link between social struggles and democratic reforms. The period that began in the late eighteenth century was dominated by the ideas of progress and development. In the rich countries, it culminated in economic growth, rising living standards, and improved welfare and social services. In the Third World, it reached its apotheosis when the Bandung Conference established a link between struggles for independence and struggles for modernization and social justice. In less than a generation, elements that seemed strongly united have been divorced. Modernization has been replaced by the market. Societies are governed from outside rather than from within. To adopt Ostrogorski's terminology, political forms and forces are being separated, as are political institutions and social actors. We once defined ourselves as self-producing and self-organized societies that could generate social relations. We now see ourselves as living in consumer societies. We are either in or out, and we no longer have any image of social relations and conflicts, of intellectual debates and political choices, to help us choose a future. We speak of conjunctures much more often than we speak of structures. It is not only the democratic idea that has been weakened as a result; it is also the existence of social actors and the ability to think about society. The new *homo œconomicus* has forced the social sciences into retreat, and they must now appeal to philosophy for asylum.

Must we accept as inevitable a conjunctural reversal that means the loss of all hope for some and, for others, boundless faith in their ability to compete? Certainly not. Such regression is unacceptable. If we took that view, we would have to accept that an increasing proportion of the population will fall prey to violence and chaos. We must instead rediscover a political consciousness. We must again convince ourselves that we can be the actors of our own history and not simply winners or losers in battles that are waged on international markets.

We must find ways of giving democracy a new lease on life, a new force, and a new passion. The word "democracy" has turned soft, and it is used in official discourse and international organizations more often than in poor neighborhoods or nations. Democracy is not merely a set of institutions, indispensable as those institutions may be. It is primarily a demand and a hope. In the past, democracy struggled first for political freedom, and then for social justice. What struggle is it waging today?

This book offers an answer: democracy's *raison d'être* is the recognition of the other. Charles Taylor provides the most forceful definition of what this politics of recognition should mean (Taylor 1992). The expression does, however, require some clarification. Recognition of the other's difference cannot found democracy; at best it provides a foundation for tolerance, because if the other and I are defined solely in terms of our difference, we do not belong to the same social group. Conversely, the recognition that we both share in the universal nature of human beings does not help us to recognize our differences. It allows us all to define ourselves as beings endowed with reason or as the children of God, without making reference to our material situation and our social relations. Neither theories of absolute difference nor Enlightenment universalism can found a democratic social and political order. Democracy is necessary only if individuals and groups who are at once different and the same must live together, only if they belong to the same society but are at the same time mutually differentiated or even hostile.

The twofold nature of human relations corresponds to the twofold nature of social action. There can be no action and, to speak in more concrete terms, no modernization unless they are based on both instrumental rationality and personal or collective identity or, in other words, on both a universal objective and a personal mobilization involving body and soul, past and future. Rather than identifying democracy with a political liberty that destroys social and cultural loyalties, we should recognize that it is an institutional space where the particular nature of an experience, a culture, or a memory can be reconciled with the universalism of scientific or technical action and of juridical and administrative organization. Democracy is a place for dialogue and communication: The politics of recognition makes possible and organizes a recomposition of the world, which must bring together that which has been separated. For centuries, the arrogance of modern reason has rendered ever more tragic the rifts between social categories, especially those between modernity and tradition and between public and private life. This explains why even today it is in the political realm that the inferiority and marginality of women is so pronounced. Public life has been identified with a rationalization that was invented by men, and it was supposed to break with tradition and feeling—the inferior domains to which women were confined.

Communication is not merely a recognition of the other, or of the other's culture, moral values, and aesthetic experience; it is a dialogue with a man or woman who combines in a different way the elements whose interdependence defines the human condition and human action. It is a recognition that the other gives a *particular* and different response to the *same* questions. Democracy is the institutional organization of relations between subjects. It is in and through democracy that the other can be recognized as a subject, as an inventor of modernity who is trying, like any subject, to reconcile instrumentality and identity, or in a nonmodern society, to reconcile community and the experience of transcendence. The criterion by which a democratic society is to be gauged is not the form of consensus or participation it has attained but the quality of the differences it recognizes and manages. It is the intensity and the depth of the dialogue between different personal experiences and cultures, which are so many particular and limited responses to the same general questions.

Rather than looking solely to the future and becoming enslaved by its own power, as did triumphal rationalism, democratic society looks in all directions and tries to understand the meaning of experiences that are as far removed from one another as possible in both time and space.

This is why I have designated the immigrant as the emblematic figure of modern society. An immigrant is at once integrated into the society in which he or she lives and foreign to it. The host society must recognize his or her experience and language. It must experience his or her presence, not as a threat but as the return of a part of human experience that the host society has been denied or has lost. Anything that asserts or enforces the *one best way* of Taylorism or identifies one norm of conduct with the universalism of reason is a threat to democracy.

This search for diversity is not reducible to pluralism, much less to a taste for the exotic or a tourist's curiosity. Many societies are trying to incorporate into their cultures and ways of life techniques and forms of organization that were developed in the most modern and richest countries. For their part, the latter are trying to rediscover what they lost at the time of the urban-industrial revolution, when the burden of social rules was lightened. Yet in both cases, this combination may simply result in the creation of a dual society. In the Third World, an American- or European-style society is being created on top of decomposing communities. In the industrialized countries of the North, enclaves of marginality—whether poor or rich, marginalized or informed—are creating or defending "alternative" cultures; but at the same time, they are also drawn to the lights of the consumer society. Democracy is an essential defense against this dualization. Democracy organizes a dialogue between different cultures that might otherwise become increasingly blind to one another even though they coexist in the metropolis.

Recognition of the other is not merely an attitude; it necessitates forms of social organization that are, on the whole, quite different from those created by the liberty of the ancients. Membership in the collectivity, the civic spirit, and therefore participation in collective actions and symbols must give way to as direct an encounter as possible with the other. The ability to listen and debate must replace mobilization toward a common goal. Examples include the sit-ins organized by the Free Speech Movement in Berkeley in 1964 and recreated by Daniel Cohn-Bendit in Paris in May 1968. They represented a break with the more classical "repertoire" of mass demonstrations bequeathed by the nineteenth century and transformed by parties and unions into civic pilgrimages stewarded by a militant clergy. Democracy would be no more than an empty form if it did not translate into educational programs that accord great importance to an understanding of the other, if it did not recognize the origins and life stories of immigrants, if it did not train hospital staff to understand patients as well as to treat their illnesses, and if it did not recognize that men and women are both different and equal. Recognition of the other, which can trap us all inside our specificity, must be based on *equality*. Equality is the central and permanent theme of all democratic thought and politics. Rationalist modernity was nonegalitarian, even elitist. Radical theories of difference, for their part, emphasize distances in a way that necessarily implies inequality and even exclusion. Today's equality cannot be merely an equality of rights or opportunity or even a reduction of social distances and of the unequal distribution of material or symbolic resources. Equality must be based on an awareness that we all belong within a human space that belongs to no one in particular; neither the rich nor the poor, neither moderns nor ancients have any special claim on it.

Although the enemies democracy fights provide a clearer definition of it than do the principles it defends, democracy is in danger whenever a society rejects the other, requires its members to conform to beliefs and norms, or imposes the general will of the mobilized masses or of a manipulated public opinion—even in the name of fighting the enemy. Democrats must fight fanaticism and normalization of all kinds.

Modern Europe is afraid of the other, the barbarians camped outside the city gates. It is afraid of the poor South and of the East as it tries to come to terms with a traumatic crisis. That is why democracy is in danger in Europe today, just as it is threatened by the rise of "fundamentalist" movements in other parts of the world. Europe, the United States, and Japan have no grounds for claiming to be democratic in an attempt to resist threats from the East or the South. True, the richest regions enjoy the benefits of the market economy and cultural tolerance; but would they be willing to defend democracy if it were directly threatened? When the rights of minorities are infringed on, protests are muted. The protests against the massacres, deportations, and rapes taking place in Bosnia are equally muted. Can a democracy be alive when there is no outburst of indignation from it at such contempt for human rights?

No society is naturally democratic. A society becomes democratic if its laws and mores act as checks and balances that correct the inequality and concentration of resources and permit communication, whereas the market creates distances and imposes dominant models. In an industrial democracy, limits and constraints are imposed on dominant groups so as to allow wage earners to negotiate their working conditions collectively. This intervention is essential if dominated categories and individuals are to emerge from the shadows, if they are to cease being regarded as resources or as a mass, and if every individual is to be recognized in his or her particularity.

There is another reason for the weakness of democracy in Europe. Democracy developed within the framework of nation-states, especially in England and France, during the democratic revolutions of the seventeenth and eighteenth centuries and the period of social democracy. It is now possible to envisage the emergence of larger political units, although the absence or weakness of democratic institutions and mechanisms at the supranational level is worrying. The referenda held in certain countries to ratify the Maastricht Treaty—especially in Denmark—demonstrated that the population was actively hostile to what it saw as a bureaucratic institutional construction that was dominated by the interests of finance capital, which would, it was feared, undermine the democratic institutions and processes that already existed at the national level. The idea of a united Europe is in itself no more democratic than that of the United Nations. Although there is now a demand for democratization in European and world political institutions, there are no grounds for saying that the globalization of the economy will automatically produce a world democracy or even the mutual conviction that responsibility for the planet's affairs should be shared.

The democratic spirit increasingly diverges from the type of state that identified itself with reason and then became intertwined with the political system. Democracy's slow descent into civil society, which began with union action and industrial democracy, will continue. Democratic institutions will become increasingly porous, and representation will become increasingly direct. As we move from political democracy to social democracy and then cultural democracy, day-to-day practices are increasingly bound up with political debates and political decisionmaking. Rights and liberty are now being defended at the level of the business enterprise as well as in parliaments. In the future, they will be defended in hospitals, schools, and the media, as parliaments come to be more closely associated with state responsibilities. Legislative intervention is, however, still of vital importance, even when—as in the case of bioethics—it is influenced by debates and initiatives originating in civil society.

Whereas the Enlightenment state identified itself with reason and then acquired the rights of an enlightened despot, the democratic nation-state was the first great modern example of the recognition of the autonomy of the political system. The political system was recognized as being autonomous both from a state that was preoccupied with its own construction and with the internal and external struggles that ensued and from a society that was still dominated by local and community life. Great Britain, the United States, the Netherlands, France, and the countries that adopted their models built democratic states of this kind and sometimes even granted the political system such excessive autonomy and power that it became detrimental to state and civil society alike. The fragile balance between state, political society, and civil society has now been destroyed. The globalization of markets, the construction of Europe and the long Cold War period have taken away the political system's ability to make decisions, while the state has become the leader of an economic, scientific, military, and political force that defends national interests in an increasingly competitive and dangerous international theater.

Given these conditions, I see two potential pitfalls ahead. The first is that political society and civil society will disintegrate because both have been reduced to markets. It is possible that the population will shun the responsibilities of citizenship for the pleasures of mass consumption and will expect the state to be a benevolent policeman, distributing aid to those who have been left behind by economic change and protecting decent people. The second danger is very different: Civil society may become introverted, transformed into communitarianism, and demand the formation of a communitarian state, as in Afghanistan, Serbia, or Croatia. In both cases, democracy would cease to exist. In the first case, it would disappear quietly, as its passing would be masked by the fact that decisionmakers are sensitive to the way public opinion reacts. In the second case, its demise would be brutal, as the defining features of the communitarian state are the suppression of the political system and the quest for a cultural and political homogeneity that rejects minority rights and even the idea of citizenship. Just as we should support a national consciousness that demands the building of a democratic nation-state, so we should condemn communitarian states. One can readily accept that the Serbs and Croats have the right to self-determination, to secede from the decomposed Yugoslav federation and to build a nation-state, but that right is conditional on that state's recognition of the basic rights of citizens, especially of minorities.

It is essential to defend national societies against global free-tradism. There are no grounds for identifying democracy with the globalization of the economy and the geo-economic strategies of the great powers. It is, however, perverse to defend a national society if doing so involves the authoritarian creation of a national community. Political movements with ideas similar to the communitarian nationalism to be found in Serbia and Croatia also exist in western Europe, especially France, Belgian Flanders, and Austria; these movements are just as antidemocratic as their Serbian and Croatian counterparts, and the fact that they have developed within a framework of political liberties cannot alter that fact.

The map of actual threats to democracy is therefore very different from the map that is purported to show a conflict between a democratic West and a supposedly nondemocratic East and South. Democracy is threatened on the one hand by authoritarian regimes that are using economic liberalism to extend their own power and on the other by communitarian states, which exist in the West as well as the East, the North as well as the South. The reaction of democratic political societies to these threats has been muted, especially at the level of public opinion, as they are preoccupied with consumption and employment rather than politics, while their national institutions are absorbed in the task of economic management.

Democratic action, which seems to be occurring everywhere, is seeking refuge at the margins of official institutions—in voluntary associations, the initial goals of which were humanitarian but which have become the main defenders of the rights of oppressed or excluded minorities, nations, and social categories. One would like to see intellectuals play a more active part in the recognition and defense of democracy's new spaces and issues, but they are torn between a purely political liberalism and a dangerous communitarianism, which has, for example, led many former communists to become nationalists. Similarly, the countries of the South are torn between an absolute trust in the virtues of the world market, which ignores the need to defend political liberty, and a fundamentalist communitarianism that is hostile both to secularization and to the autonomy of the political system.

Threatened on all sides, democracy no longer has a clear image of itself. It is often content to be reduced to an open political market and cultural tolerance, especially now that the "popular classes" are no longer a majority. The majority now consists of a vast middle class of consumers who are defending themselves against the elitism of oligarchies and against the threat to law and order posed by the excluded and the marginal. Thus, study of democracy should not be purely descriptive but also prescriptive. If it is to be a living force, democracy must mean more than laissez-faire. Now that the fight for civil rights has been won and social justice has been defended, democracy must be an instrument for the recognition of the other and for cultural communication. If we fail to construct this well-tempered multiculturalism and to take an active part in the recomposition of a world that is being torn apart by globalized markets and introverted identities, we will contribute to the demise of democracy, which, after having brought about the triumph of popular sovereignty in the nineteenth century and having given political meaning to social justice from the late nineteenth century on, no longer has any objectives or convictions.

Although it may seem less threatening than authoritarian policies, the advanced decomposition of social life has eliminated all checks and balances on the social dominance of the central managerial forces and reduced actors to defending their threatened identities. In this situation, the fate of democracy will be decided not at the top, as is the case when free individuals risk their lives and liberty in a confrontation with authoritarian power, but at the base. Every individual who tries to integrate into his or her mode of behavior the shattered elements of social reality helps to reconstruct a democratic society. The teacher who transmits knowledge and tries to prepare his or her pupils for the world of work yet is also concerned about their personal problems and their successful integration is a supporter of democracy because he or she is attempting to reconcile forms of social organization with subjectivities. The same is true of the young immigrants who want to be part of the society in which they live and make a success of their personal lives yet at the same time preserve their original identity. Likewise, women who seek to do more than merely catch up with and emulate men, who endeavor to live a multifarious life in both personal and professional terms, are also helping to recompose a society that men have divided into the separate spheres of private space and public space.

Everything that establishes a link between difference and communication—all forms of discussion, understanding, and respect for the other—contributes to the building of a democratic culture. In contrast, democracy is threatened by the imposition of shared values, norms, and practices, extremist theories of difference, and the extreme individualism that leave social life to the mercy of managerial structures and market forces. Similarly, social movements degenerate into political pressure groups when they are not based on the responsible work of the many individuals who wish to become social actors and who in their personal lives establish links between the majority and the minority, public life and private life, universals and particulars, and openness and memory.

We must reject both our blind faith in markets and our communitarian fanaticism in order to defend political liberty and democracy and to make these latter the servants of a cultural and political pluralism that is reconciled to the unity of citizenship, the law, and rational action. Democracy has lost its capacity for self-understanding and self-defense. It must rediscover that capacity, if it is to stop the world from being engulfed by a planetary civil war between obsessive identities and the markets that are destroying both the diversity of cultures and the spaces where we can make political choices.

Democracy must be a new idea. It cannot exist without a respect for negative liberty or without the ability to resist authoritarian power; but it is not reducible to that defensive action. Democratic action is equidistant from aggressively communitarian theories of difference and from the apolitical liberalism that is indifferent to inequalities and exclusions. Democratic culture is a means toward the end of recomposing the world and individual personalities by encouraging different cultures to come together in such a way that we can all share as much as possible of the human experience.

Bibliography

Abensour, Miguel. 1993. Réflexions sur les deux interprétations du totalitarisme chez Claude Lefort. In *La Démocratie à l'Oeuvre: Autour de Claude Lefort*, eds. Claude Habib and Claude Mouchard. Paris: Seuil.

Ardigo, A., A. Giddens, R. Loewenthal, N. Luhmann, C. Mongardini, and G. E. Rusconi. 1983. *La Società liberal-democratica e le sue perspettive per il futuro*. Rome: Bulzoni.

Arendt, Hannah. 1954. *Between past and future: Six essays in political thought*. London: Faber.

———. 1962 (orig. ed. 1951). *The origins of totalitarianism*. London: George Allen and Unwin.

———. 1963. *On revolution*. London: Faber.

Aristotle. 1995. *The politics*. Tr. Ernest Barker, revised by R. F. Stalley. Oxford: The World's Classics.

Aron, Raymond. 1965. *Essai sur les libertés*. Paris: Calmann-Lévy.

———. 1970 (orig. ed. 1965). *Democracy and totalitarianism*. Tr. Valence Ionescu. London: Weidenfeld and Nicolson.

———. 1972. *Etudes politiques*. Paris: Gallimard.

Association Internationale de Sociologie. 1961. *Le Elite politiche*. Bari: Laterza.

Aubenque, Pierre, ed. 1993. *Aristote politique*. Paris: Presses Universitaires de France (PUF).

Baczko, Bronislaw. 1982. *Une Education pour la démocratie*. Paris: Garnier.

Bagehot, Walter. 1964 (orig. ed. 1867). *The English constitution*. Introduction by R.H.S. Crossman. London: Watts.

Beilharz, Peter, Gillian Robinson, and John Rundell, eds. 1992. *Between totalitarianism and postmodernity*. Cambridge, Mass.: MIT Press.

Bellah, Robert, et al. 1985. *Habits of the heart: Individualism and commitment in American life*. Berkeley: University of California Press.

Bergounioux, Alain and Bernard Manin. 1979. *La Social-démocratie ou le compromis*. Paris: PUF.

———. 1989. *Le Régime social-démocratique*. Paris: PUF.

Berlin, Isaiah. 1969. *Four essays on liberty*. Oxford: Oxford University Press.

———. 1991. *The crooked timber of humanity*. New York: Knopf.

Berlin, Isaiah, and A. K. Sen, V. Mathieu, G. Vattima, and S. Veca. 1990. *La Dimenzione etica nelle società contemporanea*. Turin: Fondazione Giovanni Agnelli.

Birnbaum, Pierre. 1982. *La Logique de l'Etat*. Paris: Fayard.

———, ed. 1994. *La France de l'affaire Dreyfus*. Paris: Gallimard.

Birnbaum, Pierre, and Jean Leca, eds. 1986. *Sur l'individualisme*. Paris: Presses de la Fondation Nationale des Sciences Politiques.

Bobbio, Norberto. 1988. *The future of democracy: A defense of the rules of the game*. Tr. Roger Griffith. Minneapolis: University of Minnesota Press.

———. 1990. *L'Età dei diritti*. Turin: Einaudi.

Bottomore, T. B. 1964. *Elites and society.* London: C. A. Watts.

Bouretz, Pierre, ed. 1991. *La Force du droit: Panorama des débats contemporains.* Paris: Seuil.

Bowles, Samuel, and Herbert Gintis. 1986. *Democracy and capitalism: Property, community, and the contradictions of modern social thought.* New York: Basic Books.

Bracher, Karl Dietrich. 1971 (orig. ed. 1969). *The German dictatorship: The origins, structure, and consequences of national socialism.* Tr. Jean Steinberg. London: George Weidenfeld and Nicolson.

Braud, Philippe. 1991. *Le Jardin des délices démocratiques.* Paris: Presses de la Fondation Nationale des Sciences Politiques.

Bredin, Jean-Denis. 1988. *Sieyès: La Clé de la révolution française.* Paris: De Fallois.

Bryce, Lord. 1893. *The American Commonwealth.* 2 vols. London: Macmillan.

Buamama, S., A. Cordeiro, and M. Roux. 1992. *La Citoyenneté dans tous ses états.* Paris: L'Harmattan.

Burdeau, Georges. 1971a. L'Etat libéral et les techniques politiques de la démocratie gouvernée. In *Traité de science politique,* t. 6, vol. 1. Paris: LGDI.

_____. 1971b. Le Fondement constitutionnel et les formules gouvernementales de la démocratie gouvernée. In *Traité de science politique* t. 6, vol. 2. Paris: LGDI.

_____. 1972. La Démocratie gouvernante: Son assise sociale et sa philosophie politique. In *Traité de science politique,* t. 7. Paris: LGDI.

_____. 1974. La Démocratie et les contraintes du nouvel âge. In *Traité de science politique* t. 8. Paris: LGDI.

_____. 1979. *Le libéralisme.* Paris: Seuil.

Burke, Edmund. 1955 (orig. ed. 1790). *Reflections on the revolution in France.* Chicago: Gateway.

Cohen, Jean, and Andrew Arato. 1992. *Civil society and political theory.* Cambridge, Mass.: MIT Press.

Cohen-Tanugi, Laurent. 1989. *La Métamorphose de la démocratie.* Paris: Odile Jacob.

Colletti, Lucio. 1976 (orig. ed. 1969). *From Rousseau to Lenin: Studies in ideology and society.* Tr. John Merrington and Judith White. London: New Left Books.

Constant, Benjamin. 1980 (orig. ed. 1819). De la liberte chez les modernes. In *Ecrits politiques.* Paris: UGE.

Copp, David, and Jean Hampton, eds. 1993. *The age of democracy.* Cambridge: Cambridge University Press.

Couffignal, Georges, ed. 1992. *Réinventer la démocratie: Le défi latino-américain.* Paris: Presses de la Fondation Nationale des Sciences Politiques.

Croce, Benedetto. 1986. *La Religione della libertà: Antologia degli scritti politici.* Milan: Sugarco Edizioni.

Crozier, Michel. 1979. *On ne change pas la société par décret.* Paris: Grasset.

_____. 1987. *Etat modeste, état moderne.* Paris: Fayard.

Dahl, Robert. 1956. *A preface to democratic theory.* Chicago: University of Chicago Press.

_____. 1989. *Democracy and its critics.* New Haven: Yale University Press.

Dahrendorf, Ralf. 1967. *Society and democracy in Germany.* New York: Doubleday.

_____. 1968. *Essays in the theory of society.* Stanford: Stanford University Press.

_____. 1990. *Reflections on the revolution in Europe.* London: Chatto and Windus.

Debray, Régis. 1983 (orig. ed. 1981). *Critique of political reason.* Tr. David Macey. London: Verso.

_____. 1989. *Que vive la République.* Paris: Odile Jacob.

Derathé, Robert. 1974. *Jean-Jacques Rousseau et la science politique de son temps.* Paris: Vrin.

Dubet, François. 1991. *Les Lycéens.* Paris: Seuil.

Duhamel, Alain. 1993. *Les Peurs françaises.* Paris: Flammarion.

Duhamel, Olivier. 1993. *Les Démocraties: Régimes, histoire, exigences.* Paris: Seuil.

Dumont, Louis. 1977. *Homo aequalis.* Paris: Gallimard.

_____. 1983. *Essais sur l'individualisme.* Paris: Seuil.

Dunn, John. 1979. *Western political theory in the face of the future.* Cambridge: Cambridge University Press.

_____. 1985. *Rethinking modern political theory.* Cambridge: Cambridge University Press.

_____. 1990. *Interpreting political responsibility.* Cambridge: Polity.

_____. 1992. *Democracy: The unfinished journey, 508 B.C. to A.D. 1993.* Oxford: Oxford University Press.

Dworkin, Ronald. 1977. *Taking rights seriously.* Cambridge, Mass.: Harvard University Press.

Feher, Ferenc. 1987. *The frozen revolution: An essay on Jacobinism.* Cambridge: Cambridge University Press.

Ferry, Luc. 1995. *The new ecological order.* Tr. Carol Volk. Chicago: University of Chicago Press.

Finley, Moses. 1973. *Democracy ancient and modern.* London: Chatto and Windus.

_____. 1983. *Politics in the ancient world.* Cambridge: Cambridge University Press.

Fourastié, Jean. 1950. *Le Grand Espoir du XXe siècle.* Paris: PUF.

Fukuyama, Francis. 1992. *The end of history and the last man.* London: Hamish Hamilton.

Furet, François. 1981 (orig. ed. 1978). *Interpreting the French revolution.* Tr. Elborg Forster. Cambridge and Paris: Cambridge University Press and Editions de la Maison de l'Homme.

Furet, François, Antoine Liniers, and Philippe Raynaud. 1985. *Terrorisme et démocratie.* Paris: Fayard.

Furet, François, Jacques Julliard, and Pierre Rosanvallon. 1988. *La République du centre: La fin de l'exception française.* Paris: Calmann-Lévy.

Gauchet, Marcel. 1989. *La Révolution et les droits de l'homme.* Paris: Gallimard.

Gellner, Ernest. 1992. *Post-modernism, reason and religion.* London: Routledge.

Genre humain. 1991 (special issue). Le Religieux dans la politique. Paris: Seuil.

Germani, Gino. 1962. *Politica y sociedad en una época de transición.* Buenos Aires: Editorial Paidos.

Goyard-Fabre, Simone. 1987. *Philosophie politique XVI-XX siècles: Modernité et humanisme.* Paris: PUF.

Habermas, Jürgen. 1989 (orig. ed. 1985, 1987). *The new conservatism: Cultural criticism and the historians' debate.* Ed., tr. Shierry Weber Nicholsen. Cambridge, Mass.: MIT Press.

_____. 1992 (orig. ed. 1962). *The structural transformation of the public sphere: An inquiry into a category of bourgeois society.* Tr. Thomas Burger and Frederick Lawrence. Cambridge: Polity.

Habib, Claude, and Claude Mouchard, eds. 1993. *La Démocratie à l'oeuvre: Autour de Claude Lefort.* Paris: Seuil.

Hansen, Morgens Herman. 1991. *The Athenian democracy in the age of Demosthenes: Structure, principle, and ideology.* Tr. J. A. Crook. Oxford: Blackwell.

Havel, Vaclav. 1989. *Power of the powerless: Citizens against the state in eastern Europe.* New York: M. E. Sharpe.

Horkheimer, Max. 1947. *The eclipse of reason.* New York: Seabury Press.

Jimenez de Parga, Manuel. 1993. *La Ilusión política: Hay que reinventar la democracia en España?* Madrid: Alianza.

John Paul II. 1994. Veritatis splendor. In *Understanding* Veritatis splendor: *The encyclical letter of Pope John Paul II on the church's moral teaching.* Ed. John Wilkins. London: SPCK.

Julliard, Jacques. 1985. *La Faute à Rousseau: Essai sur les conséquences historiques de l'idée de souveraineté populaire.* Paris: Seuil.

Kelsen, Hans. 1988 (orig. ed. 1920). *La Democratie: Sa nature, sa valeur.* Paris: Economica.

Kepel, Gilles. 1991. *La Revanche de Dieu.* Paris: Seuil.

Khosrowkhavar, Farhad. 1993. *L'Utopie sacrifiée: La révolution iranienne et ses acteurs.* Paris: Presses de la Fondation Nationale des Sciences Politiques.

Kolakowski, Leszek. 1978 (orig. ed. 1972). *L'Esprit révolutionnaire: Marxisme, utopie et anti-utopie.* Brussels: Complexe.

Lacorne, Denis. 1991. *L'Invention de la République: Le modèle américain.* Paris: Hachette.

Lamberti, Jean-Claude. 1983. *Tocqueville et les deux démocraties.* Paris: PUF.

Lapeyronnie, Didier. 1993. *L'Individu et les minorités: La France et la Grande-Bretagne face à leurs immigrés.* Paris: PUF.

Laski, Harold Joseph. 1943. *Reflections on the revolution of our time.* London: Allen and Unwin.

Lefort, Claude. 1981. *L'Invention démocratique: Les Limites de la domination totalitaire.* Paris: Fayard.

_____. 1988 (orig. ed. 1986). *Democracy and political theory.* Tr. David Macey. Cambridge: Polity.

Lenin, V. I. 1970 (orig. ed. 1917). The state and revolution. In *Selected works,* vol. 3. Moscow: Progress Publishers.

Linz, Juan, and Alfred Stefan, eds. 1978. *The breakdown of democratic regimes.* Baltimore: Johns Hopkins University Press.

Lipset, Seymour Martin. 1960. *Political man: The social bases of politics.* London: Heinemann.

Locke, John. 1960 (orig. ed. 1690). *Two treatises of government.* Cambridge: Cambridge University Press.

_____. 1968 (orig. ed. 1689). *A letter concerning toleration.* Oxford: Oxford University Press.

Lukács, Georg. 1971 (orig. ed. 1923). *History and class consciousness: Studies in Marxist dialectics.* Tr. Rodney Livingstone. London: Merlin Press.

MacIntyre, Alasdair. 1985. *After virtue: A study in moral theory.* (2d ed.). London: Duckworth.

Macpherson, C. B. 1962. *The political theory of possessive individualism: Hobbes to Locke.* Oxford: Clarendon Press.

_____. 1973. *Democratic theory: Essays in retrieval.* Oxford: Clarendon Press.

_____. 1977. *The life and times of liberal democracy.* Oxford: Oxford University Press.

Maffesoli, Michel. 1988. *Le Temps des tribus: Le déclin de l'individualisme dans les sociétés de masse.* Paris: Klincksieck.

Manent, Pierre. 1993. *Tocqueville et la nature de la démocratie.* Paris: Fayard.

Manin, Bernard. 1985. Volonté générale ou délibération? In *Le Débat* 33.

_____. 1992. *La Democrazia degli moderni.* Milan: Anabasi.

Marcuse, Herbert, Barrington Moore, and Robert Paul Wolf. 1969. *A critique of pure toler-ance.* London: Cape Editions.

Marshall, T. H. 1950. *Citizenship and social class, and other essays.* Cambridge: Cambridge University Press.

Martin, Dominique. 1994. *Démocratie industrielle: La participation directe dans les entre-prises.* Paris: PUF.

Marx, Karl. 1975a (orig. ed. 1843). Critique of Hegel's Doctrine of the State. In *Early writ-ings.* Tr. Rodney Livingstone and Gregor Benton. Harmondsworth: Penguin.

_____. 1975b (orig. ed. 1843). On the Jewish Question. In *Early writings.*

Mayorga, René Antonio, ed. 1992. *Democracia y gobernabilidad: América latina.* La Paz: Nueva Sociedad.

Melucci, Alberto. 1989. *Nomads of the present: Social movements and individual needs in contemporary society.* Eds. John Keane and Paul Mier. London: Hutchinson Radius.

Michels, Roberto. 1911. *Political parties: A sociological study of the oligarchic tendencies of modern democracy.* Tr. Eden and Cedar Paul. New York: The Free Press.

Michnik, Adam. 1985. *Letters from prison and other essays.* Berkeley: University of Califor-nia Press.

Mill, John Stuart. 1977a (orig. ed. 1835). De Tocqueville on democracy in America (I). In *Col-lected Works,* vol. 18 (*Essays on politics and society*). Toronto: University of Toronto press.

_____. 1977b (orig. ed. 1840). De Tocqueville on democracy in America (II). In *Collected works,* vol. 18. Toronto: University of Toronto Press.

_____. 1977c (orig. ed. 1861). Considerations of representative government. In *On liberty and other essays.* Oxford: World's Classics.

_____. 1991 (orig. ed. 1859). On liberty. In *On liberty and other essays.* Oxford: World's Classics.

Mongardini, Carlo. 1990. *Il Futuro della politica.* Milan: Franco Angeli.

Mongin, Olivier. 1991. *La Peur du vide: Essai sur les passions démocratiques.* Paris: Seuil.

Montesquieu, Baron de. 1989 (orig. ed. 1748). *The spirit of the laws.* Tr. and ed. Anne E. Cohler, Basia Carolyn Miller, and Harold Samuel Stone. Cambridge: Cambridge Univer-sity Press.

Morin, Edgar. 1965. *Introduction à une politique de l'homme.* Paris: Seuil.

Mosca, Gaetano. 1939 (orig. ed. 1896). *The ruling class.* Tr. Hanna D. Kahn. New York: Mc-Graw Hill.

Moscovici, Serge. 1979. *Psychologie des minorités actives.* Paris: PUF.

_____. 1981. *L'Age des foules.* Paris: Fayard.

Neumann, Franz L. 1944. *Behemoth: The structures and practice of national socialism, 1933–1944.* New York: Oxford University Press.

Nicolet, Claude. 1982. *L'Idée républicaine en France (1789–1924): Essai d'histoire critique.* Paris: Gallimard.

_____. 1992. *La République en France: Etat des lieux.* Paris: Seuil.

Nozick, Robert. 1974. *Anarchy, state and utopia.* Oxford: Basil Blackwell.

Ostrogorski, Moisei. 1993 (orig. ed. 1903). *La Démocratie et les partis politiques.* Paris: Fa-yard.

Pareto, Wilfredo. 1984 (orig. ed. 1921). *The transformation of democracy.* Tr. Renata Girola. New Brunswick and London: Transaction Books.

Paul, Jeffrey, ed. 1982. *Reading Nozik: Essays in anarchy, state and utopia.* Oxford: Basil Blackwell.

La Pensée politique. 1993. Situation politique de la démocratie. Paris: Gallimard and Seuil.

Pizzorno, Alessandro. 1993. *Le Radici della politica assoluta.* Milan: Feltrinelli.

Polin, Raymond. 1960. *La Politique morale de John Locke.* Paris: PUF.

Rawls, John. 1971. *A theory of justice.* Oxford: Oxford University Press.

_____. 1993. *Political liberalism.* New York: Columbia University Press.

Rémond, René. 1982. *Les droites en France.* Paris: Aubier-Montaine.

Rials, Stéphane. 1988. *La Déclaration des Droits de l'Homme et du Citoyen.* Paris: Hachette.

Rosanvallon, Pierre. 1981. *La Crise de l'Etat-providence.* Paris: Seuil.

_____. 1990. *L'Etat en France de 1789 à nos jours.* Paris: Seuil.

_____. 1992. *Le Sacre du citoyen: Histoire du suffrage universel.* Paris: Gallimard.

Rosselli, Carlo. 1987 (orig. ed. 1930). *Socialisme libèral.* Brussels: Ed. du Jeu de Paume.

Rousseau, Jean-Jacques. 1973 (orig. ed. 1762). The social contract. In *The social contract and discourses.* Tr. G.D.H. Cole. London: Everyman.

Sandel, Michael, ed. 1984. *Liberalism and its critics.* Oxford: Blackwell.

_____. 1987. *The theory of democracy revisited.* London: Chatham House.

Sartori, Giovanni. 1957. *Democrazia e definizioni.* Bologna: Il Mulino.

_____. 1993. *Democrazia cosa' è.* Milan: Rizzoli.

Schnapper, Dominique. 1991. *La France de l'intégration: Sociologie de la nation en 1990.* Paris: Gallimard.

Schumpeter, Joseph A. 1976 (orig. ed. 1943). *Capitalism, socialism, and democracy.* London: George Allen and Unwin.

Shklar, Judith. 1968. *Man and citizen: A study of Rousseau's political thought.* Cambridge: Cambridge University Press.

Skinner, Quentin. 1978. *The foundations of modern political thought.* Cambridge: Cambridge University Press.

Sociedad. May 1993 (special number). La Democracia Latinoamericano entre la ineficiencia y la pobreza. Buenos Aires.

Starobinski, Jean. 1957. *Jean-Jacques Rousseau: La transparence et l'obstacle.* Paris: Plon.

Strauss, Leo. 1950. *Natural right and history.* Chicago: University of Chicago Press.

Talmon, Jacob-Lais. 1970. *Les Origines de la démocratie totalitaire.* Paris: Calmann-Lévy.

Taylor, Charles. 1992. *Multiculturalism and the politics of recognition.* Princeton: Princeton University Press.

Terré, François, ed. 1988. *Individu et justice sociale: Autour de John Rawls.* Paris: Seuil.

Tocqueville, Alexis de. 1964 (orig. ed. 1856). L'Ancien régime et la révolution. In *Œuvres complètes.* Paris: Gallimard.

_____. 1994 (orig. ed. 1835–1840). *Democracy in America.* Tr. Phillips Bradley. London: Everyman's Library.

Totalitarian democracy and after: A colloquium in memory of Jacob Talmon in Israel. 1985. Jerusalem: Academy of Arts and Sciences.

Touraine, Alain. 1966. *La Conscience ouvrière.* Paris: Seuil.

_____. 1988. *La Parole et le sang.* Paris: Odile Jacob.

_____. 1995 (orig. ed. 1992). *Critique of modernity.* Tr. David Macey. Oxford: Blackwell Publishers.

Veca, Salvatore. 1982. *La Società giusta: Argomenti per il contratualismo.* Milan: Il Saggiatore.

_____. 1990. *Cittadinanza.* Milan: Feltrinelli.

Vellinga, Menno, ed. 1993. *Social democracy in Latin America: Prospects for change*. Boulder: Westview.

Walzer, Michael. 1983. *Spheres of justice: A defense of pluralism and equality*. New York: Basic Books.

Wieviorka, Michel. 1988. *Société et terrorisme*. Paris: Fayard.

_____. 1993. *La Démocratie à l'épreuve: Nationalisme, populisme, ethnicité*. Paris: La Découverte.

Wolton, Dominique. 1993. *La Dernière utopie: Naissance de l'Europe démocratique*. Paris: Flammarion.

About the Book and Author

In this sequel to *A Critique of Modernity*, Alain Touraine questions the social and cultural content of democracy today. At a time when state power is being increasingly eroded by the economic might of transnational capital, what possible value can we ascribe to a democratic idea that is defined merely as a set of guarantees against the totalitarian state?

If democracy is to survive in the postcommunist world, Touraine argues, it must accomplish two urgent goals: it must somehow protect the power of the nation-state at the same time as it limits that power (for only the state has sufficient means to counterbalance the global corporate wielders of money and information); and it must reconcile social diversity with social unity and individual liberty with integration.

This is not merely a philosophical problem but a dilemma whose resolution will dramatically affect the immediate future of people everywhere. If we want a resolution in democracy's favor, then it is time, in Touraine's view, for us to redefine democracy in terms of active intervention rather than mere defensive institutions. To preserve the power and effectiveness of our states and societies, we must make visible strides—and soon—away from a politics of particularity toward the integration and balancing of women and minorities, of immigrants, of rich and poor. If our states become too weakened, too debased by the politics of competing identities and interest groups, we will one day find ourselves without the means to protect the very values we believe we are fighting to uphold.

Alain Touraine is a sociologist. He created the Centre d'Analyse et d'Intervention Sociologiques (CADIS) at the École des Hautes Études en Sciences Sociales and is the author of *Self-Production of Society*, *The Voice and the Eye*, *The Return of the Actor*, and *Critique of Modernity*.

Index

Absolutism, 37, 91, 98, 186
Access, 22, 157
  controlled, 82–83, 109
  equal, 135
Advertising, 135, 149, 150
Alessandri, Arturo, 180
Ancients, 23–24
  liberty of, 24, 25, 67, 81, 84, 118, 120, 129, 186
Anomie, 86, 133
Anti–Corn Law League, 95
Antimodernism, 103, 125
Antiracist movement, 176
Antirevolutionary regimes, 14
Arendt, Hannah, 25
  on totalitarianism, 102, 104
Aristocracy, 23, 104
Aristotle
  political animal of, 8, 24
  on political regimes, 23–24
Aron, Raymond, totalitarianism and, 98, 104
Assembly, freedom of, 10, 115, 149
Authoritarianism, 8, 14, 47, 57, 89, 98, 142, 177
  antidemocratic actions of, 145
  collapse of, 7, 157
  corruption and, 156
  crisis and, 161–164
  democracy and, 17, 42, 59, 70, 110, 172, 178, 184, 189
  development and, 62, 160
  liberalism and, 48
  liberation struggle and, 18
  market economy and, 154, 157
  resisting, 170, 197
  social actors and, 62, 110
  threat of, 16, 72, 132

Authority, distrust of, 45

Bandung Conference, 174, 190
Basic rights, 23, 26, 38, 90, 123, 164, 189, 195
  majority rule and, 140
  power and, 28, 40, 109
  recognition of, 27, 28, 32, 34, 70, 72, 107
Bellah, Robert, 169
Bentham, Jeremy, 90
  individual happiness and, 86
Berlin, Isaiah, 103
  cultural pluralism and, 49
  liberty and, 48
  on subject, 45
  universalist rationalism and, 49
Bill of Rights, 79, 108
Bobbio, Norberto, 9, 47
  on democracy, 8
  on political cultures, 50
Bodin, 77
  individuation/socialization and, 80
Bonapartism, 79, 84
Borsellino, Judge, 162
Bracher, Karl Dietrich, 103
Bredin, Jean-Denis, 80
Bryce, Lord, 84
Burdeau, Georges
  consensual democracy and, 117
  on social democracy, 116–117
  on social thought, 117
Burke, Edmund, 127
  authoritarian totalitarianism and, 14
  on voluntarism, 88
Bush, George, 43

Castro, Fidel, 89, 102

209